WITHDRAWN

Leisure, gender and
poverty

THEMES IN THE TWENTIETH CENTURY

Series Editor: Pat Thane, Reader in History,
Goldsmiths' College, University of London

Current titles
Andrew Davies: *Leisure, gender and poverty*
Junichi Hasegawa: *Replanning the blitzed city centre*

Forthcoming titles
Steven Fielding: *Class and ethnicity*
Bernard Harris: *The health of the children*

Leisure, gender and poverty

Working-class culture in Salford and Manchester, 1900–1939

Andrew Davies

Open University Press
Buckingham • Philadelphia

To my family, and to Charlie and Elsie,
who started me off

Open University Press
Celtic Court
22 Ballmoor
Buckingham
MK18 1XW

and
1900 Frost Road, Suite 101
Bristol, PA 19007, USA

First Published 1992

British Library Cataloguing in Publication Data

Davies, Andrew
　　Leisure, gender and poverty: Working-class culture in Salford and Manchester,
　　1900–1939. – (Themes in the twentieth century)
　　I. Title　II. Series
　　942.7082

　　ISBN 0-335-15638-X
　　ISBN 0-335-15637-1 pbk

Library of Congress Cataloging-in-Publication Data

Davies, Andrew, 1962–
　　　Leisure, gender, and poverty: working-class culture in Salford and Manchester,
　　1900–1939/Andrew Davies.　　p.　　cm. – (Themes in the twentieth century)
　　Includes bibliographical references and index.
　　　ISBN 0-335-15638-X (cased) – ISBN 0-335-15637-1 (pbk.)
　　　1. Working class – England – Manchester – History – 20th century.　2.
　　Popular culture – England – Manchester – History – 20th century.　3. Working
　　class – England – Salford (Greater Manchester) – History – 20th century.　4.
　　Popular culture – England – Salford (Greater Manchester) – History – 20th
　　century.　I. Title.　II. Series.
　　HD8400.M32D38　1992
　　305.5′62′094242732–dc20　　　　　　　　　　　　　　91-31689 CIP

Typeset by Graphicraft Typesetters Limited, Hong Kong
Printed in Great Britain by Biddles Ltd, Guildford and King's Lynn

Contents

Series editor's introduction		vii
Acknowledgements		x
Note on oral evidence		xii
Map of central Salford		xiii
	Introduction	1
one	Poverty	14
	Poverty before the First World War	15
	Poverty and unemployment between the wars	20
	Poverty and 'human needs'	26
two	Men: Poverty, unemployment and the family	30
	Poverty and the denial of leisure	31
	Unemployment and the denial of leisure	43
	Leisure as a 'cause' of poverty	48
three	Women: Housekeeping, leisure and independence	55
	Time and money	56
	Drink and respectability	61
	Cinemas	73
	Fortune-tellers and spiritualists	79

four   Young workers: Parents, police and freedom   82
    Family economy and family relationships   83
    Dance halls   89
    Cinemas   94
    Corner gangs   96
    Monkey parades   102

five   Streets, markets and parks   109
    Street life and neighbourhood relationships   110
    Street entertainers and working-class charity   116
    Street customs   124
    Saturday night markets   130
    Parks   138

six   Gambling   142
    Back entry bookmakers and the police   144
    Bookmakers and neighbourhood life   152
    Gambling schools and working-class sports   155
    Gambling and working-class culture   163

Conclusion   168
Appendix 1: Occupational structure of Manchester and
              Salford, 1923–37   174
Appendix 2: Respondents' biographical details   175

Notes   182
Select bibliography   202
Index   208

Series editor's introduction

A great deal both of everyday conversation, and of academic analysis of contemporary society, embodies assumptions about the past, including the quite recent past, for which actual evidence is slight. Indeed, the history of Britain in the first half of the twentieth century seems sometimes to have taken on an almost mythic character. This is largely because until very recently social historians have been reluctant to explore history beyond the First World War. Since British empirical sociology did not take off on a large scale until the 1950s, there has been an important gap in our knowledge of the twentieth century, which has distorted interpretation of the whole time-span and limited our understanding of post-war Britain by deracinating it.

Recent work has begun to dispel some widely held convictions about this period, though most of it has yet to be absorbed either into everyday consciousness or academic social science. It is now clear, to take just a few examples, that there was not a significant movement of women into 'male' occupations during the First World War;[1] that such a shift is not the main explanation for the partial concession of votes to women in 1918;[2] that feminism did not die away after women obtained the vote but was especially vibrant in the 1920s;[3] that the 1930s was not a time of overwhelming Slump, but of contrasting prosperity and recession in different regions;[4] that women were not peremptorily ejected from the paid labour market after the Second World War, but rather exhorted to stay on.[5]

The aim of this series of books is to take the demythologizing further by subjectinng previously unexplored areas of recent British history to empirical scrutiny in order to deepen our understanding of major themes in twentieth-century experience. The history and sociology of the British working class is notably encumbered with historical mythology. A vivid set of images has been created of a 'traditional' working class, peopled by cloth-capped, fish and chip eating, pub-going, football watching working men, taking holidays in Blackpool. The females of the class are more shadowy, presumably because they are assumed to have been incarcerated in domesticity in their back street terraces, except when gossiping over the clothes lines; and young people even more so, until they burst onto the stage as teenage consumers in the 1950s.

This image of a 'traditional' working class was conjured up in the 1950s and 1960s by those who thought they detected, and regretted, its demise.[6] Its life was assumed to have been relatively brief. E.J. Hobsbawm, supported by Gareth Stedman Jones, described a pattern of working-class life and culture which became increasingly standardized from the 1870s, providing solid cultural foundations for a strong, united, if unimaginative, labour movement.[7] The most vivid representations of this image have emerged from Salford: Lowry's paintings and drawings, the novels of Walter Greenwood, the memoirs of Robert Roberts, *Coronation Street*, and so it is especially suitable that Andrew Davies sets his critique of this image and the assumptions associated with it in the city of Salford.

Hobsbawm saw the development of mass commercialized leisure, including association football and the seaside holiday, as crucial to the 'making' of this working class. Davies similarly focuses upon leisure, seeing it, as others have, as an apt medium through which to assess a variety of important aspects of social life: in particular, living standards, relations within families and relations of power more generally. Most such studies, however, have focused upon organized, commercial leisure: music hall, cinema, association football, dance halls – in which working people spent a relatively small amount of their time, and some none at all. Davies, rather, emphasizes how the poverty that continued in Salford, and elsewhere, through the inter-war years limited the leisure activities of working people, in particular their involvement in its commercialized forms. The most usual leisure activities were cost-free or very inexpensive (walking in the park or, for adolescents, the 'monkey parade', watching street entertainers, or the variety of activities around weekend street markets, illicit low stake gambling, street football), activities as characteristic of the mid-nineteenth as of the mid-twentieth century, and whose survival sheds doubt on the notion of a late nineteenth-century wholesale remaking of working-class culture.

It also calls in question assumptions about the effectiveness of nineteenth-century 'social control'. Uncommercial and sometimes illegal leisure pursuits were clearly less successfully tamed in the nineteenth century than some have thought. Davies' entertaining account of illicit gambling in the Salford backstreets shows the failure of the police to define and enforce acceptable patterns of behaviour, tireless working-class ingenuity in evading police control, and a degree of collusion between police and people which suggests, if we still need it, the inadequacy of simple top-down models of the exercise of authority and the need to build at least an element of negotiation into analysis of such processes.

Davies' evidence indeed suggests not increasing standardization of working-class culture from the later nineteenth century, but its growing diversity as new commercialized pursuits were added to old and were more readily accessible to the more affluent workers of more prosperous expanding towns, such as Coventry, but just occasional treats for many in Salford. They were more likely to be accessible to employed adolescents than to older people with family responsibilities and Davies vividly explores other sources of cultural diversity than income, particularly age and gender.

Women were shadows in conventional academic (though not visual or literary) representations of the working class, partly because they are less prominent in documentary sources than the men. Davies demonstrates, as others have,[8] the value of – indeed the necessity for – oral history for the reconstruction of crucial elements of past experience which were too mundane, undramatic and taken for granted to be recorded. Though young people had certain freedoms, the degree to which many of them were constrained by parental authority emerges strikingly from the oral evidence. Though females had more restricted leisure opportunities than males, the numbers who squeezed pennies and time from the household resources for a trip to the cinema (even if the children had to come too) or to a spiritualist or fortune teller or for a drink or two come to life in Davies' pages. His evidence also suggests how unhelpful are other supposed forms of division within the working class, which have been too readily taken for granted, in particular that between 'rough' and 'respectable', and between a 'labour aristocracy' and lower strata of workers. Such conceptions of strict stratification within the working class have come to look increasingly implausible[9] and Davies shows how cultural patterns cut across boundaries of occupation and skill, and how the drunkenness of a parent could have a more decisive affect on a household's living standards than the level of his or her earnings.

Davies describes and brings to life the diversity of working-class experience, even within one city, but in a manner which does not degenerate into random empiricism but constantly relates the data to larger issues, and which generates questions and insights applicable not just to Salford but to some of the major themes in the history of the twentieth century.

Pat Thane

Acknowledgements

Many people have helped during the course of my research, but my first debt is to Alastair Reid, of Girton College, Cambridge, who supervised the doctoral dissertation upon which this book is based. I have benefited enormously from his advice, criticism and encouragement. I would also like to express my gratitude to all the people who took part in my oral history interviews between 1985 and 1987, for their assistance and the warmth of their hospitality, and for taking so much interest in my progress. For their help in arranging interviews, I am most grateful to Pauline Day, Nicki Elfman, Don Rainger, Pauline Reid, Ann Robinson and Tommy Rourke. Alison Dickens arranged a number of interviews, and also allowed me to draw upon her own research in Ordsall. For their expertise and endless patience, I would like to thank the staff of the Manchester and Salford Local History libraries, especially Tim Ashworth, Allan Barlow, Margaret de Motte, Justine Norbury and David Taylor; Audrey Linkman of the Documentary Photography Archive, and Duncan Broady of the Greater Manchester Police Museum.

I would like to thank Ian Qualtrough for his care in preparing the illustrations and, for permission to reproduce them, I am grateful to Mrs Atkin, Mr Gill, the British Film Institute, the Documentary Photography Archive, Manchester Central Library, The Right Image, Salford Local History Library and the Lowry Centre at the Salford Museum and Art Gallery. My thanks are also due to Sandra Mather, for drawing the map of central Salford. For their invaluable financial support, I am deeply grateful to King's College, Cambridge; the Ellen McArthur Fund, administered by the Faculty of History, University of Cambridge; and the Twenty-Seven Foundation at the University of London.

I would like to thank my colleagues at the University of Liverpool for their support over the last two years, especially Mike Tadman and Sheila Blackburn, Val Dodd, Henry Finch, Pat Hudson, Helen Jones, Tony Lane, Robert Lee, Rory Miller, Mike Power, Alan Johnson and Eric Taplin. I am also indebted to all the students who registered for my course on culture and community in 1990, for keeping me on my toes. On a personal note, I am grateful to my parents and my brother Simon for their sustained encouragement, and to Will Jacques, Mick Stevens, Joanna Midgley, Jane Elliott, Noj McLeod, Wendy Holden, Trevor Parsons, Mark Gallop, Lawrence Grasty, Peter Compton, Gill Darby, David Hay, Marian Hay, and especially Ann-Marie Barnes. Thanks also go to Norman Whiteside, Mark Hughes and all the revellers in the Three Legs of Man in Greengate on cup final day, 1990.

A number of people read earlier versions of chapters presented here, and I would like to thank Michelle Abendstern, Judith Ayling, Anna Davin, Jennifer Davis, Miriam Glucksmann, Dermot Healy, Paul Johnson, Nev Kirk, Elizabeth Roberts, Gareth Stedman Jones, Jerry White and Terry Wyke. I found their comments and criticisms very useful. My examiners, V.A.C. Gatrell and Michael Rose provided much encouragement, along with suggestions for improvements which I have done my best to incorporate. Through many enjoyable hours of discussion, Steve Fielding, David Fowler, Jon Lawrence and John Shaw have all helped me to sharpen my arguments considerably. Finally, I owe a huge debt to Fiona Devine and Pat Ayers for taking time out from their own work to comment so perceptively on mine, to Naomi Williams for help in preparing the manuscript, and to Pat Thane for her invaluable support from an early stage in the project to its completion. It goes without saying, however, that no-one can take any responsibility for the views expressed here except myself.

Note on oral evidence

References to interviews conducted as part of my own research project give a set of initials only. Brief biographical information for each of the respondents is given in Appendix 2. Pseudonyms are used throughout the text, in order to preserve the anonymity of the people who took part in the interviews. Copies of the transcripts will eventually be held in Salford Local History Library.

Supplementary oral evidence is drawn from the Manchester Studies Tape Collection, held at Manchester Polytechnic. References to the Manchester Studies interviews give the initials M.S.T.C., followed by the serial number of the interview cited. Extracts from oral testimony used in the text have been edited where necessary to avoid repetition.

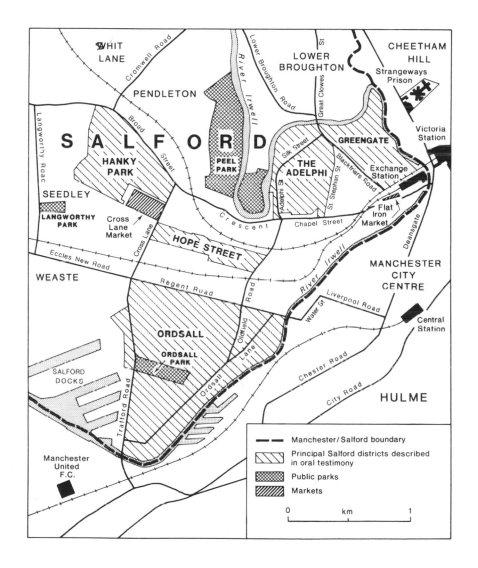

Central Salford in 1930

Introduction

When older working-class residents of Salford and Manchester discuss the nature of leisure in the early twentieth century, whether in autobiographies or in interviews with oral historians, they repeatedly insist that leisure activities must be understood within the context of the poverty which governed family and neighbourhood life. Financial constraints are portrayed as the main factor shaping working-class social life, although glimpses of improvements in living standards, especially during the 1920s and 1930s, are also provided. However, in this collective portrayal of the two cities, the relation between poverty and leisure is paradoxical. Poverty restricted the social lives of working people, yet indulgence in leisure is also recognized as a cause of domestic poverty: heavy drinking or gambling could lead to families 'going without', to lower standards of diet and dress. This study attempts to explore this paradox, by examining leisure as part of everyday life in working-class districts of Salford and Manchester, with direct reference to poverty and the family economy.

Leisure activities were also firmly structured by gender, and through a comparative survey of leisure patterns among married men and women, it is possible to examine a fundamental element of working-class lifestyles in terms of gender difference. Women enjoyed substantially fewer opportunities for leisure, and this surely indicates that women's living standards were significantly lower than those of their husbands. Moreover, disputes over male spending on leisure were the most common source of conflict within working-class households. Many men spent only modest portions of their income upon leisure, but those who drank or gambled heavily risked plunging their families into destitution, so the need to establish a balance between the desire for recreation and the needs of the household economy was of central importance in working-class marriages. Any examination of male leisure patterns, therefore, has important implications for our understanding of power relations within the family.

The division of leisure according to gender and poverty underpins the analysis presented here. In contrast, historical approaches to working-class culture have sometimes tended to emphasize the uniformity of working-class experience, stressing the importance of class rather than gender divisions.[1] In part, this reflects an attempt to use the analysis of working-class culture to explain shifts in class consciousness and politics, seen in the highly influential contributions of Eric Hobsbawm and Gareth Stedman Jones.[2] For both Hobsbawm and Stedman Jones, leisure activities are central to the analysis of working-class culture. However, this tendency to focus upon the political repercussions of developments in leisure has meant that the diversity of working-class experience has sometimes been obscured.

When historians have examined divisions within the working class, attention has traditionally centred upon the notion of a 'labour aristocracy', originally devised in studies of Victorian society. The labour aristocracy model hinges upon divisions of skill within the male workforce, and draws connections between occupational status and styles of behaviour, including leisure patterns and religious and political beliefs.[3] However, retrospective evidence concerning working-class life in the early twentieth century offers only limited support to the notion of a separate stratum of better-paid skilled manual workers, with a distinct, and highly respectable, lifestyle.[4] Perhaps surprisingly, it is by no means uncommon for oral testimony to provide examples of skilled workers who conformed to patterns of behaviour which contemporaries and social historians alike have labelled 'rough', indulging, for example, in heavy drinking.[5] Oral evidence confirms that differences in levels of income were profoundly important, but suggests that skilled workers and labourers alike faced pressures to limit their spending on leisure for the sake of the family budget. Divisions between adult women and men, and those between youths and adults, appear to have been more fundamental to the organization of working-class leisure than observable differences according to levels of skill.

Whereas the experience of leisure in the weekly rhythm of working-class life is the principal concern of the present study, specialist studies of leisure in Britain have been largely concerned either with middle-class attempts to reform popular amusements, or with the commercialization of leisure following the growth of the leisure industries from the 1880s. Most of the published work in this field, including the important surveys by Helen Meller, Peter Bailey and Hugh Cunningham, deals with the nineteenth century, and the focus of studies of the Victorian period has been partly determined by the nature of the most accessible sources. The commentaries of middle-class social reformers and business records relating to commercial ventures such as the music hall underpin much of the historical writing on this period. Moreover, in the most authoritative study of inter-war recreation, Stephen Jones was mainly concerned with the expansion of commercial leisure after 1918, and the politics of leisure, including the responses of the organized labour movement to developments in recreation.[6]

Following the trend established in studies of working-class culture, historians of leisure have generally paid much less attention to the role of poverty and household budgeting in determining patterns of working-class social life. By contrast, feminist historians, including Ellen Ross, Elizabeth Roberts, Pat Ayers and Jan Lambertz, have examined the family economy in considerable depth, drawing attention to the importance of the allocation of resources within the family and disputes over male spending on leisure.[7] These insights have important implications for historical approaches to working-class leisure. Hugh Cunningham, in a perceptive overview of leisure at the turn of the century, pointed to the poverty cycle as an important factor in determining access to leisure, and the present study develops this perspective, examining the impact of the life-cycle alongside gender differences and household budgeting arrangements.[8]

I have followed a definition of 'working class' set out by Elizabeth Roberts, which relates to the holding of manual occupations, and to limited economic standing. As she has argued:

> Men and women believed themselves to be working class because they worked with their hands, were employees and not employers, and, in comparison with the latter, were poor and lacked material goods: even the better-paid workers had comparatively few consumer goods and little surplus income.[9]

My own research focuses on districts which were largely populated by the families of manual workers. In interviews, they are often described as 'poor' areas. Although some residents – usually corner shopkeepers or clerks – cannot be classified as working class, patterns of neighbourhood life were dominated by working-class customs and attitudes.

The central districts of Salford and Manchester were populated by the families of both skilled and unskilled manual workers.[10] In contrast, more prosperous districts on the outskirts of the two cities, like Seedley and Weaste in Salford, contained higher concentrations of skilled workers and families who could be classified as lower middle class. My own study focuses on the central districts. Had I focused specifically on Seedley or Weaste, or on Openshaw in Manchester with its high concentration of skilled engineers, the findings might have been very different. However, the present survey should not be seen as restricted to the 'lower' working class. Even the most notorious districts of Salford, such as Greengate, the Adelphi and Ordsall, housed the families of many skilled workers.

The underlying concerns of poverty and gender are apparent in the structure of the book. Chapter 1 examines contemporary surveys of the nature and extent of poverty from the late nineteenth century in order to provide a documentary basis for subsequent discussions of the impact of poverty upon everyday life. Perhaps surprisingly, there were relatively few surveys of poverty in Manchester and Salford, so the fragmentary local sources are set alongside evidence from other English towns and cities in order to provide an assessment of working-class living standards in a national context.

In Chapter 2, a contrast is drawn between those men who spent heavily on leisure, and those who restricted their personal spending in order to make a fuller contribution to the home. As feminist historians have rightly stressed, women were most acutely affected by poverty as they bore responsibility for managing the family budget. However, men's social lives were clearly affected by poverty and unemployment, and this chapter examines the various responses to poverty among men in their daily lives. Contemporary claims that drink and gambling were among the most common 'causes' of poverty in the early twentieth century are re-examined in the light of oral testimony concerning districts in Salford and Manchester.

Leisure among married women is discussed in Chapter 3. Women held responsibility for feeding, clothing and housing their families, and because they took responsibility for making ends meet, it was harder for women to find money (or time) for recreation. None the less, in the early decades of the twentieth century, leisure was by no means an exclusively male sphere. This chapter examines a series of women's leisure activities. Some, such as going to the cinema, are well known, but others have been largely hidden from history, and oral and documentary sources are used to uncover networks of fortune tellers and spiritualists who rarely feature in the existing social histories of leisure. Leisure patterns varied widely among working-class women, and through an investigation of attitudes towards activities like drinking, competing notions of feminine respectability are examined in some depth.

Chapter 4 questions the notion that distinct forms of 'youth culture' first emerged in Britain during the 1950s. As David Fowler forcefully argues, many of the principal forms of commercial entertainment during the 1920s and 1930s, including cinemas and dance halls, were heavily patronized by the young and single.[11] In Salford and Manchester, these trends can be clearly traced back to the turn of the century and beyond, and the expansion of the leisure industries in the two cities was partly dependent upon the relative affluence of youths within working-class families. Oral testimony shows that leisure among young workers took communal as well as commercial forms. Hanging around in street gangs, and taking part in the 'monkey parades' (whereby young people promenaded through the principal thoroughfares of the two cities with the aim of picking up members of the opposite sex) provided additional activities which brought young workers together. Within this separate sphere of leisure among youths, new identities were forged and maintained.

The role and pervasiveness of communal forms of leisure are discussed in Chapters 5 and 6. Jerry White's survey of Campbell Bunk in North London provides by far the strongest historical account of the communal cultures of working-class streets, but his emphasis upon the 'lumpen' character of Campbell Road raises the question of how far his findings are representative of working-class culture in a wider sense.[12] The standard accounts of popular recreation provide a thorough analysis of many aspects of commercial leisure, but often fail to examine, in any significant depth, the more informal street-based activities which were also central to the social life of working-class districts. In contrast to commercial enterprises such as the music hall and the cinema, informal amusements left no business records and this partly explains the bias towards institutionalized forms of leisure in the existing literature. Chapters 5 and 6 examine the use of streets, markets and parks in Salford and Manchester as arenas of leisure, while developing the analysis of the relation between poverty and the use of free time. For example, the custom of touring the main Manchester market at Shudehill or Salford's Flat Iron market on Saturday nights was immensely popular throughout this period. These Saturday night markets were highly valued among the inhabitants of the poorer districts of the two cities, as free alternatives to commercial attractions such as the cinema.

As Jerry White pointed out, gambling was one of the most important street activities. Working-class forms of gambling were illegal before 1960. Measures such as the 1906 Street Betting Act were prompted, to a considerable extent, by the desire to stamp out heavy spending on gambling, which was widely seen as a cause of poverty, and thus to prevent working people spending their money foolishly. Historians who have examined the enforcement of Victorian legislation designed to regulate popular leisure (including gambling), have argued that the police succeeded in enforcing considerable changes in popular patterns of behaviour. Policing has attracted the attention of an increasing number of social historians, but as in the history of leisure, most of the literature has focused upon the nineteenth century. Few scholars have examined policing beyond the turn of the century.[13] In Chapter 6, which examines the policing of gambling after 1900, this view of the transformative role of the state is challenged, through an analysis of the persistence of mass forms of illicit gambling. Of course, by no means all of the leisure activities found in Salford and Manchester during the early-twentieth century are examined in depth here. I have focused upon the activities, and the opportunities and constraints, which appear to have featured most prominently in the lives of the working people of the two cities.

Throughout the present study, in the surveys of patterns of leisure among different groups in working-class society and in the analysis of communal forms of leisure, wide use is made of oral evidence. The arguments presented here draw upon sixty sets of oral history interviews concerned primarily with Salford life in the early twentieth century. Through the use of interview techniques, it is possible to relate information concerning leisure patterns to household budgeting strategies within specific families. Moreover, women's leisure as well as men's can be traced during interviews, providing an important balance to the male-orientated nature of many contemporary sources. Whereas contemporary social observers frequently resorted to stereotyping in their attempts to characterize the 'typical' leisure pursuits of the urban poor, portraying the inhabitants of working-class districts as heavy drinkers and ardent gamblers to a man, oral testimony continually illustrates the diversity of working-class behaviour. This is of some importance in the social history of leisure, as taped evidence provides a means of examining the role of personal choice in determining the use of free time, thus establishing a more sophisticated and realistic assessment of the role of leisure in working-class life.

Oral testimony is useful in the analysis of both commercial and communal leisure forms. Retrospective accounts supply background information about the participants in different activities, sometimes allowing the historian to form a more precise assessment of the social composition of crowds at public events. Commercial locations such as cinemas and dance halls varied widely, from super-cinemas and elaborate ballrooms to 'bug-huts' and low dancing rooms. Oral evidence uncovers hierarchies of cinemas, dance halls and pubs, and the reputations of individual establishments – whether rough or respectable – can reveal much about their functions within working-class neighbourhoods. Communal forms of leisure which left few written records can often only be studied in detail using a combination of written and oral sources, and interviews can alert the historian to activities which have been previously neglected. For example, the study of Saturday night markets in Chapter 5 was prompted by references to markets in interviews. This led to the discovery of a wealth of information in the local press, which both confirmed the impression obtained from retrospective evidence, and showed that markets had provided an important leisure haunt for the people of Manchester and Salford since the 1840s at least.

Despite the value of oral evidence in signalling new areas of historical inquiry, interviews do not allow the social historian to form a statistically precise assessment of forms of behaviour. Historians can attempt to discern patterns from a series of interviews, but must exercise caution in selecting the representative, and setting the unusual in context. At no stage of the inquiry are the arguments here based exclusively upon oral testimony. I have attempted to test written and spoken evidence against each other throughout the survey, and each type of source material suggested new ways of looking at the issues raised. My own interviews were conducted without the use of a rigid questionnaire, and although I aimed to cover a range of topics in each discussion, the interviews were free-flowing and I attempted to follow points initially raised by the participants.

It is perhaps more difficult to use oral evidence in studies of working-class politics. Retrospective testimony is most valuable when respondents describe aspects of their everyday lives, whereas shifts in political allegiance or belief are difficult to gauge, especially when interviews focus on the period of childhood, or youth. Moreover, while historians have paid much attention to attempts by the labour movement to establish alternative leisure forms, only a minority of working people were ever drawn into this distinct, socialist culture.[14] Among the politically active, any available free time could be devoted to party or trade union affairs, but activists were to a degree atypical within working-class districts. In my own interviews, socialist cultural organizations in Manchester and Salford, such as the Workers' Film Society, were rarely mentioned and although political meetings feature in the account of street activities in Chapter 5, I have chosen to focus in greater depth upon activities which occupy a more central place in accounts of life in the two cities.

Historians are divided in their assessments of the role of religion in working-class communities during the early twentieth century.[15] A substantial minority of working people did go to church, but it is difficult to provide a precise assessment of the scale of religious attendance in Salford and Manchester prior to 1939. A survey of Ancoats undertaken by the Manchester University Settlement during 1937–38 found that in a sample of just over a 1000 adults, 39 per cent stated that they had a regular connection with a church, but it is not clear how many attended services from week to week.[16] Among my own sample, a few respondents grew up in staunchly religious households, where leisure revolved around mission or church, but they form a small minority. In other households, the parents attended weekly services while leading a largely secular social life, but in many families, the most active participants in church activities were the children, who attended Sunday schools and took part in the annual Whit walks, where religious identities were displayed and reaffirmed. Whit walks were an important expression of faith, even for parents who were not themselves regular church-goers. They are examined in Chapter 5.

Manchester is divided from her immediate neighbour, Salford, by the River Irwell. The two cities possess separate identities, although Manchester enjoys by far the greater reputation, as the cradle of the industrial revolution. Asa Briggs christened Manchester the 'shock city' of the mid-nineteenth century, pointing out that Engels based much of his account of *The condition of the working class in England* upon his observation of conditions in the city, where the social effects of capitalism were to be seen in a particularly severe form during the 1840s. Moreover, Engels' case study provided one of the principal empirical foundations for Marx's analysis of class relations, which prompted Briggs to suggest that if Engels had conducted his research in Birmingham instead of Manchester, *The Communist Manifesto* might never have been written.[17] Nineteenth-century Manchester has attracted the attention of a number of historians concerned to examine social relationships during urbanization and industrialization.[18] However, the city's development since 1900 has received scant attention from social historians. This is surprising, in view of Manchester's prominence as an early industrial centre and the city's continuing status as a provincial capital. During the inter-war period, the Manchester conurbation was the largest in Britain after Greater London, and by 1931, Manchester and Salford had a combined population of almost 1 million: Salford had over 220000 inhabitants, Manchester over 760000.[19]

Engels' knowledge of industrial conditions was gained in Salford as well as Manchester. He was employed in the offices of his family's firm, Ermen and Engels, off Deansgate in Manchester, but he also spent time at the firm's Victoria Mill, which was situated in the Weaste district of Salford. Moreover, in *The condition of the working class*, Engels described in some detail a dispute at the Salford brickmakers firm of Pauling and Henfrey in 1843. Strikers clashed with armed guards employed by the firm, and Engels used the incident to illustrate the courage of English working men during industrial conflicts. He also described housing conditions in Salford, which he found as appalling as in the worst parts of Manchester. Engels classified Salford as:

> ... one large working-men's quarter, penetrated by a single wide avenue ... an old and therefore very unwholesome, dirty, and ruinous locality is to be found here, lying opposite the Old Church of Manchester, and in as bad a condition as the Old Town on the other side of the Irwell ... All Salford is built in courts or narrow lanes, so narrow, that they remind me of the narrowest I have ever seen, the little lanes of Genoa. The average construction of Salford is in this respect much worse than that of Manchester, and so, too, in respect of cleanliness. If, in Manchester, the police, from time to time, every six or ten years, makes a raid upon the working-people's districts, closes the worst dwellings, and causes the filthiest spots in these Augean stables to be cleansed, in Salford it seems to have done absolutely nothing. The narrow side lanes and courts of Chapel Street, Greengate, and Gravel Lane have certainly never been cleansed since they were built ... Exactly the same state of affairs is found in the more distant regions of Salford, in Islington, along Regent Road, and back of the Bolton railway. The working-men's dwellings between Oldfield Road and Cross Lane, where a mass of courts and alleys are to be found in the worst possible state, vie with the districts of the Old Town in filth and overcrowding.[20]

Salford is well known to social historians through Robert Roberts' portrayal of the Hope Street district of the city, *The classic slum*, which has become a staple text for scholars of working-class life in the early decades of the twentieth century.[21] Roberts provided a wide-ranging and detailed account of the culture of the urban working classes, drawing attention to the many layers of social distinction within working-class society, while offering a unique series of insights into popular customs and lifestyles. Basing the phrase 'the classic slum' upon Engels' description of the Hope Street area (the district between Oldfield Road and Cross Lane), Roberts combined personal reminiscences with the techniques of the oral historian, drawing upon the memories of an older generation of Salfordians to provide a picture of urban life from below. Published in 1971, before oral history was widely adopted as a method of historical inquiry, *The classic slum* has been highly influential within the subsequent growth of English social history. Roberts has been widely consulted by historians who make little further use of retrospective sources, and almost all studies of the working class in the early twentieth century refer to his work.[22]

The symbolic importance of Salford does not rest entirely upon the success of *The classic slum*, for the city has also figured prominently in fictional representations of working-class life. Walter Greenwood's novel *Love on the dole*, first published in 1933, was set in the Salford district of Hanky Park. His depiction of the local impact of unemployment provided one of the leading accounts of the social consequences of economic depression, offering a rare fictional portrayal of a working-class community from within. *Love on the dole* is now widely cited in studies of British society between the wars, and the novel has consolidated Salford's status among historians as an archetypal industrial quarter.[23] Like Greenwood, the post-war Salford playwright Shelagh Delaney set her most famous work, *A taste of honey*, locally. *A taste of honey* was adapted as a film, shot in the Salford district of Brindleheath.

Salford also provides the backdrop to the two most influential visual representations of northern working-class society. L.S. Lowry's paintings and drawings of street scenes and industrial landscapes provide some of the most popular images of city life in the early twentieth century. Lowry studied at the Salford School of Art, and the city provided the scene for some of his best-known works, including views from the school's windows, looking out towards the Hope Street area, or over Peel Park and the districts of the Adelphi and Lower Broughton. He produced a number of works set in Salford districts such as Ordsall, Greengate and the Adelphi.[24] Moreover, in post-war televised drama, *Coronation Street*, originally set in Salford, has become the staple modern portrayal of 'the north'. The series was devised by Tony Warren, who based *Coronation Street* upon the area around his aunt's home in Ordsall. The terraced street, with its pub and corner shop, offers an enduring glimpse of a traditional working-class way of life, although the Ordsall streets which Tony Warren knew were demolished during the 1970s.

Salford, therefore, has a significant emblematic status for historians concerned with the 'traditional' working class in Britain, so when I started my own research, in 1985, I based my work in the city. The bulk of the oral history interviews conducted as part of my research cover the central working-class districts of Salford, areas known, prior to 1939, as the Hope Street district, Hanky Park, Ordsall (the dock area), the Adelphi and Greengate. Further interviews describe the outer Salford districts of Weaste, Seedley, Lower Broughton and Whit Lane. Meetings were arranged partly through a network of personal contacts, and partly with the help of the staff of old people's homes. Often one meeting would lead to a further interview, with a friend, neighbour or relative. The sample covers people living in quite diverse circumstances today. Some of the respondents still live in Salford, whether on new council estates or in old people's homes, whereas other meetings took place on overspill estates, principally in Irlam and Little Hulton. Another group of interviews were conducted with people now living on private estates, in areas such as Swinton and Boothstown. A small batch of interviews were conducted, at an early stage of the research, with people who were born in Manchester rather than Salford, and most of these meetings were prompted by an appeal in the *Manchester Evening News*.

The interviews were divided evenly between men and women, and approximately 85 per cent of the participants come from the families of manual workers. This sample covers a wide range of working-class occupations. Around 25 per cent of the respondents were drawn from families headed by skilled workers, whereas nearly 60 per cent were drawn from the families of the semi- or unskilled, and the unemployed. Most of the remaining respondents, around 15 per cent, come from the families of corner shopkeepers and clerks who lived in predominantly working-class districts. Details of the occupational and geographical spread of the sample are given in Appendix 2. Supplementary oral evidence is drawn from the Manchester Studies Tape Collection, held at Manchester Polytechnic. The Manchester Studies interviews were conducted nearly a decade before my own oral history project, and therefore provide information relating to various districts in Manchester and Salford from an older group of respondents.

In my own interviews, I found that some families moved house frequently, sometimes moving between the two cities as well as between different working-class districts. These respondents could therefore give evidence relating to neighbourhoods in both Salford and Manchester. Other respondents lived in one city and found work in the other. The engineering works on Trafford Park industrial estate in Manchester provided employment for thousands of Salford people, while the docks and factories of Salford attracted workers from neighbouring Manchester districts like Hulme. Although a majority of the respondents' parents lived and worked in Salford, in broad terms, the two cities constituted a single labour and housing market. For the people of both cities, a night 'in town' meant a night in the centre of Manchester. Shudehill market, and the city-centre cinemas and dance halls attracted many Salford people, so civic boundaries were easily obscured in the pursuit of leisure.

Although my oral history inquiry was weighted towards districts in Salford, the interviews therefore also provided a good deal of information about Manchester. This overlap was even more marked in the wider range of documentary sources used. Municipal records and social surveys relating specifically to Salford have been consulted, in addition to the weekly *Salford City Reporter*. However, there is a much greater body of social surveys dealing with Manchester, while the Manchester press provides a rich source for the study of working-class life throughout the two cities. Journalists employed by the Manchester newspapers often felt no need to distinguish between Manchester and Salford, or between the working-class districts within them. It was therefore necessary to broaden the scope of the study beyond Salford in order to make fuller use of an impressive and varied contemporary literature.

Most of the people interviewed grew up in terraced houses, with a living room and a kitchen-scullery downstairs, and two bedrooms upstairs. These 'two up, two downs' were by far the most common form of working-class housing in the two cities. A minority of the respondents lived in more substantial 'three up, three down' dwellings. Few lived in flats or tenements, which were rare in Manchester and Salford. In 1900, the landscapes of the central districts were dominated by factories and mills, which overshadowed the terraced streets of working-class housing. In Salford districts such as Hope Street, Greengate and the Adelphi, and in areas such as Ancoats and Hulme in Manchester, much of the housing had been built in the first half of the nineteenth century, and the problems of slum housing were exposed in a series of local surveys from the 1900s to the 1930s. The lower side of the Adelphi was described in 1931 as:

> ... a district of large works and factories with high chimneys and overshadowing walls, under which are huddled congested slum houses, mean streets, running at odd angles, designed only from the point of view of the most rigid economy of ground. Here and there is a narrow overhung passage, twisting into a confined croft or court, or an ill-paved, badly drained, narrow alley, in which rubbish collects ... many of the streets are very narrow ... the houses in these streets are airless and the sun seldom reaches them.[25]

Districts like Ordsall, where most of the housing was built in the late nineteenth century, were more uniform, but were still drab in the eyes of social observers. In 1948, Ordsall was described as an 'unrelieved mass of streets of terraced cottages'.[26] By the 1930s, the face of the two cities was slowly changing, as slum clearance programmes began to tackle districts such as Ancoats and Greengate. However, in Salford especially, the scale of redevelopment was limited prior to the Second World War.

The industries of the two cities were diverse. Despite her nineteenth-century label 'Cottonopolis', Manchester was also an important centre for engineering, which matched textiles in terms of numbers employed by the turn of the century and provided comparatively high wages, for skilled workers at least. The city was equally important as a centre for distribution and the service trades: transport and construction were major areas of employment, both contributing to Manchester's sizeable casual labour market, which Alan Kidd has described as 'more akin to ports like Liverpool and Hull than other inland cities like Birmingham or Leeds' by the late nineteenth century. In some of the central districts of Ancoats and Hulme, around 50 per cent of the workforce were casually employed during the 1900s.[27] The growth of the Trafford Park industrial estate, on the border of Salford, attracted further investment in heavy industry from the turn of the century, as firms such as Metropolitan-Vickers and Ford's set up new engineering and motor works. This may have led to a relative decline in the size of the casual labour market, although the Trafford Park estate was badly hit during the inter-war depression.

Salford's industries were just as varied (a more detailed account of the occupational structure of the two cities is given in Appendix 1). Cotton and engineering were the most important sectors of the Salford economy, with transport, chemicals, dyes, coal, paper-making, rubber goods and water-proof garment-making all prominent local industries. In 1924, there were an estimated 1000 factories and workshops in Salford, and the diversity of the city's industries was celebrated in the local saying, 'If a thing's not made in Salford, it's not worth making.'[28] The opening of the Salford docks following the completion of the Manchester Ship Canal during the 1890s enhanced the city's status as a distribution centre, while ensuring that the Ordsall district of South Salford, rather than the neighbouring area of Hulme in Manchester, assumed some of the characteristics of a port (including a significant local increase in casual employment).

Some of the leading cotton mills in South East Lancashire were located in Salford. For example, Richard Haworth's, situated in Ordsall, employed over 4000 people in various spinning and weaving mills. Haworth's dealt in each aspect of the industry, from the importation of raw cotton to the dispatch of finished goods. Industries associated with the cotton trade, such as dyeing, were equally well established in Salford. Worrall's dyeworks, the country's principal cotton velvet dyers, was situated next to Haworth's mills in Ordsall Lane.[29] Heavy engineering works, such as Farmer Norton's Adelphi Ironworks, which specialized in the manufacture of textile machinery and general factory equipment, were also prominent in Salford. By the 1920s, there were approximately 50 Salford firms engaged in different processes associated with the rubber industry. Seventy-five per cent of the national rubber textile industry was based in the city, with leading firms, such as the Greengate and Irwell Rubber Company and Mandleberg's, producing a range of waterproof rubber garments, and rubber goods for mechanical purposes, including hoses and engine packings.

The diversity of the Salford economy was mirrored within the specific districts of the city. For example, Ordsall was renowned locally as 'the dock area'. However, typically of Salford's industrial districts, the area also contained a mixture of textile and engineering works, including prominent local firms such as Haworth's. The docks gave Ordsall a distinct reputation, with Trafford Road, the main dock road known locally as the 'Barbary Coast', famous for cafes, lodging houses, rough pubs and prostitution. Yet Ordsall was never simply Salford's dockland. Similarly, Greengate contained a variety of rubber, engineering, textile, glass and furniture works. It is therefore difficult to characterize Salford districts according to occupations. Moreover, the Trafford Park industrial estate drew workers from all over Salford, including Greengate, not just the adjacent areas of Ordsall and Weaste.

The case study presented here is, in a sense, a broad survey, covering many of the central districts of two cities. It does not focus on a single community, but specific districts and venues are discussed in some depth and I hope that the book provides sufficient local detail to convey something of a sense of place to the reader. Throughout the study, I have used supplementary material from surveys of other English towns and cities, sometimes to confirm points made in interviews describing life in Salford, and occasionally as a means of adding statistical weight to passages which would otherwise have hinged upon purely qualitative data. The book addresses debates in social history through a local, rather than a national, study but many of the themes raised here relate to the findings of historians working on other urban areas.[30] Moreover, given that during the first half of the twentieth century, over 40 per cent of the British population lived in the seven largest conurbations, any case study of one of the major provincial centres must have broader implications for our understanding of British society. Further local studies may confirm or contradict the survey presented here, but in view of the central place of Salford and Manchester in our understanding of the 'traditional' working class, the two cities provide, in Robert Roberts' term, a 'classic' setting for a study of working-class leisure.

one

Poverty

Oral testimony suggests that poverty had a profound impact upon working-class life throughout the period from the 1900s to the 1930s. As Colin Bundy and Dermot Healy remarked, in an analysis of interviews covering districts in Manchester and Salford from the turn of the century, poverty 'provided the backdrop' to life in working-class neighbourhoods.[1] Retrospective sources indicate that the need to 'make ends meet' dominated the domestic lives of many working-class families, not just the families of the unskilled, setting limits to standards of home comfort, diet and dress, as well as leisure. However, retrospective evidence also suggests that the scale of urban poverty was less severe after 1920. Robert Roberts declared that:

> In spite of the massive unemployment of 1921 and of the slump years later, poverty was never again of the same depth and magnitude that we knew in Edwardian Britain. Repeatedly our old neighbours remarked, 'Times are bad now, but nothing like before the war'.[2]

None the less, accounts of working-class life during the inter-war decades are still laced with references to poverty, and the visual symbols of poverty, so familiar in accounts of the Edwardian years, such as jam-jars used as cups and raggedly dressed children, still appear frequently in descriptions of the 1930s.[3]

In attempting to measure the impact of poverty on the use of free time, historians are immediately confronted by methodological difficulties. Oral testimony does not provide a basis for a quantitative assessment of spending patterns. Moreover, the statistical investigations into poverty and working-class household budgeting conducted from the late nineteenth century, usually regarded as the standard sources for the study of poverty, conspicuously failed to provide an account of spending on leisure. As Eleanor Rathbone acknowledged in her survey of dockland families in Liverpool, this was the one area where reliable information was impossible to obtain. Spending on amusement was frequently concealed, while families who spent heavily on recreation were those least likely to cooperate with surveys like her own.[4] In Rowntree's *Poverty: A study of town life*, researched during 1899, the analysis of households in York where either parent drank heavily was based upon second-hand information, gathered from neighbours or other members of the family, and this is clearly an unreliable method of obtaining data relating to domestic budgeting.[5]

During the 1920s and 1930s, social investigators were likewise frustrated in their attempts to obtain accurate accounts of personal spending. According to an analysis of the weekly budgets of 9000 working-class households collected by the Ministry of Labour and National Service during 1937 and 1938, working-class families spent an average of only 9*d*. per week on drink. As the ministry's report conceded, this figure was unrealistic: 'There seems to be little doubt ... that the personal expenditure of many of the wage-earners on beer, spirits, etc. was not fully reflected in the budgets'.[6] However, although these statistical surveys are disappointing for historians of leisure, they do provide a means of testing the representations of poverty in oral testimony. This chapter seeks to address the question, to what extent do contemporary surveys confirm or undermine the assertion that poverty provided the backdrop to working-class life prior to 1939? The main sections of the chapter examine the scale of poverty before and after the First World War. Evidence is drawn from a range of English towns and cities, to supplement surveys conducted in Manchester and Salford. Definitions of poverty have, of course, been fiercely contested, and the chapter concludes with a contrast between the academic categories employed by social investigators and alternative, working-class interpretations of the term.

Poverty before the First World War

In his pioneering research into the nature and extent of urban poverty, Charles Booth estimated that 30.7 per cent of the population of late Victorian London were living in 'actual poverty'.[7] His assessment was influential in drawing attention to the scale of poverty as an urban social problem, but there were no surveys of poverty in Manchester or Salford conducted on a comparable scale. However, Booth's early research in East London prompted an investigation by Fred Scott into conditions in the Ancoats district of Manchester and the Salford district known as the Adelphi. His findings were published in 1889, in a paper entitled 'The condition and occupations of the people of Manchester and Salford.'[8]

Table 1.1 The standard of living in the Adelphi, Salford, 1889

Occupation	Number classified	Very poor (%)	Poor (%)	Comfortable (%)
Unemployed	—	—	—	—
Unskilled labour	716	79.6	15.9	4.5
Unskilled labour, superior	31	64.5	19.3	16.1
Artisans	303	55.4	20.1	24.4
Shopmen, warehousemen	37	56.7	29.7	13.5
Cotton operatives	48	56.2	27.1	16.7
Manufacturers, small merchants, dealers, shopkeepers	106	2.8	—	97.2
Street vendors, hawkers	15	73.0	20.0	6.7
Miscellaneous	76	68.4	14.5	17.1
Total	1332	65.5	16.4	18.1

Source: Calculated from data provided by F. Scott, 'The condition and occupations of the people of Manchester and Salford', *Transactions of the Manchester Statistical Society* (1888–89), p. 10.[9]

Scott's survey showed that chronic poverty was also to be found in the two cities. Indeed, the Ancoats and Adelphi districts contained much higher concentrations of poverty than suggested by the overall estimate for the capital put forward by Booth.

Scott divided the populations of the two districts into categories suggested by Booth's work, as follows:

- *Very Poor* (those who are always face to face with want): incomes of less than 4*s.* per adult per week.
- *Poor* (those who have a hand-to-mouth existence): incomes of less than 6*s.* 3*d.* per adult per week.
- *Comfortable* (all those who are in a position to save).[10]

Two children were taken as the equivalent of one adult. In Salford's Adelphi district, 65.5 per cent of those classified were 'very poor', with incomes below the level of 4*s.* per adult per week, and 16.4 per cent were 'poor', with incomes which provided no margin for recreation. In Ancoats, the respective figures were 50.2 and 23.0 per cent. Of the households classified in Scott's survey, therefore, only 18.1 per cent of the Adelphi sample and 26.8 per cent of the Ancoats sample enjoyed levels of income which provided for saving, or recreation, in addition to the 'bare necessaries' of life.[11] Scott's assessment of the standard of living in the Adelphi district is shown in Table 1.1. His study showed that poverty was not confined to households where the main wage-earner was a semi- or unskilled worker. Among the households headed by 'artisans' in the Adelphi sample, of those classified according to Scott's three categories,

55.4 per cent were 'very poor', 20.1 per cent 'poor' and only 24.4 per cent 'comfortable'. Only a quarter of the artisans living in the Adelphi could afford to participate in commercialized leisure activities without jeopardizing the family housekeeping budget. By comparison, among the families of the unskilled, 79.6 per cent were 'very poor', 15.9 per cent 'poor', while only 4.5 per cent enjoyed a standard of living which could be described as 'comfortable'.[12]

Scott pointed out that the survey was undertaken during a period of 'exceptionally full employment. How aggravated [poverty] must be when trade is bad and employment scarce!'[13] In both Ancoats and the Adelphi, irregular employment was a fundamental threat to the security of working-class living standards, even when trade was 'good'. A total of 21.2 per cent of the workers in the Ancoats sample were irregularly employed, along with 40.8 per cent of those in the Adelphi. In the Salford district, as many as 48 per cent of those classified as 'artisans' were irregularly employed.[14] Although Scott claimed that the two districts were representative of the 'densely-populated parts of Manchester and Salford', Alan Kidd has suggested that in Manchester at least, the central working-class districts of the city, including Ancoats, were 'more clearly characterised by casual labour than manufacturing districts like Gorton and Openshaw'.[15] If there were more prosperous working-class areas in the two cities, there were also others less affluent. Angel Meadow in Manchester and Greengate in Salford were the most notorious slum quarters at the turn of the century.[16] However, while Scott's survey was more limited in geographical scope than the broader investigations in London and York undertaken by Booth and Rowntree, his research highlighted the existence of areas with extremely high concentrations of poverty.

In his study of York, published in 1901, Rowntree followed Booth in measuring the extent of poverty in impressionistic terms. As E.P. Hennock has noted, 'Poverty for [Rowntree] as for Booth was what informed observers recognized as such.'[17] Judging by a survey of the appearances of households in the town, Rowntree estimated that 43.4 per cent of the working-class population of York were living in poverty. As a proportion of the population of York as a whole, the figure was 27.8 per cent, almost matching Booth's figure of 30.7 per cent for London: both these estimates were based on impressions of degrees of poverty.[18]

However, Rowntree also attempted to collect information concerning the income and expenditure of working-class families, and devised a 'poverty line', which he used to demonstrate that some of those in visible poverty were living on incomes which did not even cover the bare necessaries of life. Rowntree set out to measure the level of income required by families of different sizes 'to provide the minimum of food, clothing and shelter needful for the maintenance of merely physical health'. A family whose total income was theoretically sufficient to provide this basic standard were classed as living above the poverty line. As Rowntree stressed, this was a stringent standard:

... let us clearly understand what 'merely physical efficiency' means. A family living upon the scale allowed for in this estimate must never spend a penny on railway fare or omnibus. They must never go into the country unless they walk. They must never purchase a halfpenny newspaper or spend a penny to buy a ticket for a popular concert. They must write no letters to absent children, for they cannot afford to pay the postage. They must never contribute anything to their church or chapel, or give any help to a neighbour which costs them money. They cannot save, nor can they join the sick club or Trade Union, because they cannot pay the necessary subscriptions. The children must have no pocket money for dolls, marbles or sweets. The father must smoke no tobacco, and must drink no beer. The mother must never buy any pretty clothes for herself or for her children, the character of the family wardrobe, as for the family diet being governed by the regulation, 'Nothing must be bought but that which is absolutely necessary for the maintenance of physical health, and what is bought must be of the plainest and most economical description.' Should a child fall ill, it must be attended by the parish doctor; should it die, it must be buried by the parish. Finally, the wage earner must never be absent from his work for a single day.

If any of these conditions are broken, the extra expenditure involved is met, *and can only be met*, by limiting the diet; or, in other words, by sacrificing physical efficiency.[19]

Rowntree found that 15.4 per cent of the working-class population were living on incomes which fell below this poverty line. He classed these families as living in 'primary' poverty. He also identified a poverty cycle, pointing out that different families were living in primary poverty at different times. Labourers, for example, were most likely to experience poverty at three points during their lives: as children, as the parents of young children, and in old age.[20]

Rowntree therefore produced two estimates of the extent of poverty among working-class families in York: 43.4 per cent were found to be living in visible poverty, and 15.4 per cent were defined as living in primary poverty. Subtracting the second figure from the first, Rowntree categorized the remaining 28.0 per cent as living in 'secondary' poverty, a bracket used to classify families with incomes above the poverty line who were none the less living in visible poverty. The concept of secondary poverty was to become one of the most controversial features of Rowntree's work. He was quick to point out that had the poverty line not been set at such a minimal level, many more families would have been recorded as living in primary poverty. However, as Veit-Wilson has remarked, a stringent poverty line was necessary to prove that low income was a significant cause of poverty. If Rowntree had set a more generous poverty line, his critics could easily have argued that his figures for primary poverty simply overestimated the scale of urban deprivation.[21]

Rowntree acknowledged that the stringency of his poverty line bore little relation to existing patterns of household expenditure. Few families spent nothing over a minimum theoretical requirement on clothing and furniture, and few spent nothing on amusement or drink. Most made some allowance for such 'luxuries', even if they were required to cut the amount of money they had available for food as a result. However, as Rowntree remarked, the secondary poverty category also included families who spent heavily on drink or gambling. Rowntree was involved in campaigns against both these popular 'vices', and his construction of the secondary poverty bracket to account for the majority of cases of poverty in York appeared to give support to the view that some among the poor brought poverty upon themselves. He went so far as to claim that there was little doubt that drink was the principal cause of secondary poverty, even though he had been unable to collect weekly budgets from families where either spouse drank heavily.[22]

Rowntree's study did not inspire a latter-day Fred Scott to conduct a comparable survey in Manchester and Salford. Manchester's outstanding contributions to the 1900s debate concerning the 'physical deterioration' of the English nation were T.R. Marr's *Housing conditions in Manchester and Salford*, published in 1904, and C.E.B. Russell's *Manchester boys*, published a year later.[23] Evidence concerning the nature of poverty in Manchester and Salford during the 1900s is diverse, but unemployment was a serious problem locally during the decade prior to the First World War, with severe cyclical unemployment during the years 1903–05 and 1908–09. In these periods, skilled workers as well as the unskilled were widely threatened by poverty. In 1903, the Manchester and Salford Trades Council reported that:

> ... the scarcity of employment has been keenly felt by many during the past winter ... Many of the destitute unemployed are unskilled labourers, but we have reason to believe that distress has been felt among many who come under the heading of skilled workers.[24]

A census conducted by Manchester City Council during March 1909 revealed that nearly 16 100 men in the city were out of work: an unemployment rate of around 9 per cent. Like the city's endemic poverty, unemployment was concentrated in certain areas. Unemployment among adult males in Ancoats was three times higher than in Lancashire as a whole.[25]

From the autumn of 1908, a depression in local trade, exacerbated by a dispute in the cotton industry, prompted the establishment of the 'Lord Mayor's Fund for the Relief of Distress in Manchester', whereby relief was distributed in the form of food tickets, in allowances of up to 1*s.* per person per week.[26] In a study of cases dealt with by the fund, Charles Wyatt revealed that the majority of families receiving aid were headed by unskilled labourers, workers who were unemployed through sickness, or widows or deserted wives. However, he also found that a large number of skilled workmen were out of work. Wyatt provided information concerning

100 cases, 'a fair sample of the whole', in a paper published by the Manchester Statistical Society. Thirty-five of the heads of households belonged to skilled trades, although many had drifted into casual employment.[27] Details of 15 cases are given in Table 1.2 (I have selected the families of five skilled workers, five labourers, four other unskilled workers and one widow, in order to illustrate the range of households revealed to be living in poverty).

Wyatt's survey showed that during the winter of 1908–09, 'primary' poverty affected a variety of Manchester's working-class households, including the families of skilled workers such as turners, moulders and even fitters. General labourers and a variety of other semi- and unskilled manual workers were also living on incomes below the poverty line. Moreover, among families living in 'primary' poverty, the ages of the main wage-earners varied greatly, and were by no means confined to those living in one of the three stages of the poverty cycle identified by Rowntree. Some of the families included in Wyatt's survey contained juvenile wage-earners, whose wages, in working-class families, usually represented the best prospect of raising the housekeeping budget to a comfortable level.

In Manchester, therefore, poverty was not restricted to workers at the bottom of the occupational scale. According to Wyatt, the relief fund was aimed at 'persons not of the class usually relieved by poor-law agencies', to save those who would normally maintain their independence from the stigma of pauperism. Moreover, the degree of the poverty revealed by Wyatt's study was extremely severe. Many families were receiving incomes far below the poverty line, sometimes receiving weekly incomes which did not even cover the cost of rent. Among the 70 families whose level of income was given in Wyatt's sample, the average weekly income per person, once rent was deducted, was only 7*d*.[28]

Poverty and unemployment between the wars

Social historians have recently highlighted the improvement in working-class living standards after 1918.[29] Rising real wages, a narrowing of the gap between the wage rates of skilled and unskilled manual workers, the extension of state welfare and a decline in family size appeared to transform the material conditions of working-class life. The growth of the mass leisure industries, such as the cinema, is widely interpreted as an index of post-war prosperity, and working-class ownership of wirelesses, gramophones and even motor-cycles suggests that for some families at least, proletarian affluence had indeed reached levels unimaginable a generation earlier. There has been less attention paid to poverty in the 1920s and 1930s.

Whereas poverty was the subject of widespread concern during the 1900s, by the inter-war period, as John Stevenson has remarked, the dominant social issue was unemployment. The loss of employment was some-

Table 1.2 The circumstances of 15 households receiving aid from the Lord Mayor's Fund for the Relief of Distress in Manchester, 1908–09

Rent	No. of inmates	Age of applicant	Total income	Amount per head less rent	Occupation of head of family	Supplementary earners		Remarks
						Age	Sex	
5s.6d.	3	39	6s.	2d.	Turner	28	Wife	Deserving case
5s.	4	49	3s.	—	Fitter	—		Pawning to buy food
4s.3d.	3	27	8s.	1s.3d.	Moulder	24	Wife	Sober and respectable assisted by friends
4s.3d.	5	46	8s.	9d.	Moulder	17	F	Very poor people
5s.	5	28	4d.	1s.1d.	Cabinet maker	28	Wife	Work wanted
5s.	6	47	5s.	—	Labourer	28	F	
4s.9d.	5	30	7s.6d.	6½d.	Labourer	27	Wife	Selling goods out of house for food
4s.	3	54	7s.	5d.	Labourer	17	M	Respectable family
4s.9d.	5	25	15s.	2s.	Labourer	20	F	Very poor
5s.10d.	4	36	6s.	½d.	Labourer	33	Wife	Husband rheumatic
5s.3d.	7	34	20s.3d.	2s.6d.	Dock labourer	33	Wife	Respectable family
4s.6d.	7	34	15s.3d.	1s.9½d.	Carter	35	Wife	Husband very steady
5s.	8	38	6s.	1½d.	Waiter	14	M	Good home, food required
2s.	4	44	6s.	1s.	None	17	F	Careless, dirty family, widow
3s.3d.	4	30	6s.	7½d.	Hawker	—		Appear poor

Source: C. Wyatt, 'The Lord Mayor's Fund for the Relief of Distress in Manchester – winter of 1908–09', Transactions of the Manchester Statistical Society (1909–10), pp. 144–9.

times viewed primarily as a problem affecting adult male workers, and many inter-war surveys focused upon the psychological distress suffered by men who lost the weekly routines and personal satisfactions associated with work.[30] In contrast, poverty was seen as a domestic problem, affecting women and children as directly as men, if not more so. Of course, surveys of unemployment did sometimes examine its impact upon family life. Nevertheless, the initial focus upon the adult male worker may sometimes have deflected attention away from the domestic poverty wrought by unemployment. Historians tend to reflect the contemporary preoccupation with unemployment rather than poverty, by contrasting the mass unemployment in the traditional industrial areas of Northern England and South Wales with the overall improvement in living standards for the majority of the population to highlight the 'paradoxical' nature of the inter-war economy.[31]

Did poverty still affect large numbers of working people during the inter-war decades? Although real wages rose after 1918, inter-war surveys of working-class incomes revealed that much poverty still remained. During the inter-war period, a series of surveys was conducted using poverty lines based upon the concept of bare subsistence, or 'merely physical efficiency' employed by Rowntree in 1899. These updated poverty lines still made no allowance for leisure. For example, in their 1925 study *Has poverty diminished?*, Bowley and Hogg pointed out that: 'The minimum standard [adopted] allows nothing for trade union or society subscriptions, tram fares, amusement, beer, tobacco, newspapers or betting.'[32] Similarly, R.F. George, who made an influential attempt to calculate a contemporary poverty line during the mid-1930s, worked around the concept of a minimum needs standard taken directly from Rowntree's *Poverty: A study of town life*.[33] The 'George standard' was used in a number of surveys of urban poverty undertaken in 1937–38, including Tout's study of *The standard of living in Bristol*. Tout's account of the low level of the poverty line echoes the equivalent passage from Rowntree's earlier study:

> It will be observed that the minimum standard makes no allowance whatever for sickness, savings, for old age or burial expenses, holidays, recreation, furniture, household equipment, tobacco, drink, newspapers or postage. In practice families whose income is below the standard do not forego all expenditure on these items, but everything that they spend on them is at the expense of the meagre allowances made for the basic necessities.[34]

The new survey of London life and labour found that 10.7 per cent of the population of East London were living in primary poverty in 1929–30, although there were pockets of more widespread poverty, including Poplar (19.2 per cent), Stepney (16.3 per cent) and Bethnal Green (13.8 per cent).[35] This survey showed the extent of primary poverty only. Other surveys conducted during the 1920s and 1930s attempted to measure primary and secondary poverty, although Rowntree's controversial secondary poverty

Table 1.3 Poverty in two Manchester districts, 1933–38

Date of survey	Area	Primary poverty (%)	Secondary poverty/ insufficiency (%)	Total (%)
1933	Miles Platting	18.0	26.0	44.0
1937–38	Ancoats	30.7	33.0	63.7

Source: J. Inman, *Poverty and housing conditions in a Manchester ward* (Manchester, 1934), p. 18; Manchester University Settlement, *Ancoats: A study of a clearance area. Report of a survey made in 1937–1938* (Manchester, 1945), p. 20.

bracket was adapted, and sometimes relabelled 'insufficiency'.[36] 'Insufficiency' was defined as a level of income between 0 and 50 per cent above the poverty line. Significantly, the extent of insufficiency could be measured from a survey of weekly income levels: the focus on patterns of expenditure (whether useful or wasteful) which made Rowntree's concept of secondary poverty so controversial was no longer necessary. However, as a survey of Ancoats in Manchester conducted in 1937–38 pointed out, families with total incomes of less than 50 per cent above the poverty line were *likely* to fall into secondary poverty as conceived by Rowntree.[37]

It is impossible to draw direct comparisons between the results of the various inter-war social surveys because the investigations were not conducted on a uniform basis. However, despite differences in the nature of the samples chosen, and the varying estimates of the contemporary poverty line, a range of statistical inquiries revealed that poverty was an intractable feature of urban life. For example, *The social survey of Merseyside*, conducted in 1934, and Tout's study of *The standard of living in Bristol*, conducted in 1938, both suggested that at least 30 per cent of the working-class population was living in poverty (whether primary poverty or insufficiency). The Bristol inquiry covered the more prosperous of the two cities during the late-1930s trade boom, yet still testified to the survival of poverty. These surveys employed updated poverty lines based upon the concept of 'merely physical efficiency' used by Rowntree in *Poverty: A study of town life*.[38]

Surveys of two Manchester districts during the 1930s echoed Fred Scott's findings almost half a century earlier, by revealing that there were much denser pockets of poverty in Manchester than suggested by the general conclusions of city-wide studies elsewhere. Both studies used a poverty line based upon the notion of bare subsistence, making no provision for leisure. Their findings are shown in Table 1.3. As the level of primary poverty in the area shows, Ancoats was by far the poorer of the two districts. However, whereas in the Ancoats survey households with incomes between 0 and 50 per cent above the poverty line were classed in the 'insufficiency' category, in Inman's study of Miles Platting, only those with incomes less than 10*s*. over the poverty line were included. If Inman had adopted the same methods as those used 4 years later in Ancoats, the percentage of households found to have been living on 'insufficient' incomes in Miles Platting would have been significantly higher. It is easier to make direct comparisons between the Ancoats figures and Tout's findings in Bristol. Tout's study employed a larger sample, but the two surveys were conducted at around the same time (1937–38 and 1938) and both used a poverty line which approximated to the 'George standard'. Moreover, both used categories of primary poverty, and an 'insufficiency' category of those with incomes less than 50 per cent above the poverty line. In Bristol, 30 per cent of the working and lower middle class sample were in poverty or 'insufficiency'. In Ancoats, the proportion was 63.7 per cent. There were more affluent working-class areas of Manchester and Salford during the 1930s, which would have provided a different picture of the extent of poverty in the two cities, but the Ancoats study is useful because it illustrates the survival of immense poverty in central districts even in the more prosperous late 1930s.

The causes of poverty in the 1920s and 1930s were diverse, and as well as unemployment, included low pay, irregular employment, the sickness or death of the principal wage-earner and old age. Elizabeth Roberts has pointed out that wage levels for labourers and male textile workers fell below Rowntree's revised poverty line during the 1930s, and John Stevenson asserted that traditions of low pay among unskilled workers in the building trade, transport and municipal employment continued to make it difficult for these workers to support their families, even during periods of full employment.[39] As John Benson has remarked, the rapid rises in real wages enjoyed by workers in heavy industry were denied to large sections of the workforce.[40] In Manchester and Salford, low pay was still widely associated with casual labour. In Ordsall, irregular earnings were a serious cause of poverty among the families of dock labourers, whose economic position showed little improvement during the inter-war decades. In 1922, when the daily rate of pay was 11*s*., it was estimated that 75 per cent of the 4000 Salford dockers earned 33*s*. per week or less, with 50 per cent earning 22*s*. per week or less.[41] In January 1936, when the daily rate was increased to 12*s*., the majority were still working only 2–3 days a week.[42] Skilled workers' rates of pay were well above Rowntree's poverty line, but they remained vulnerable to short time and unemployment, and oral testimony provides numerous examples of skilled workers who were forced to seek alternative employment as they were unable to earn a living at their trade.[43] Family circumstances were still important. Even skilled workers enjoyed a lower standard of living when their children were young, while families without a male wage-earner were often among those living in poverty. Interviews concerning life in Salford suggest that families headed by widows were among the poorest in the city.[44]

Unemployment in Manchester and Salford did not reach the scale of the

Table 1.4 Percentage of insured population in Salford and Manchester registered as unemployed, 1927–37

Insured population	Salford 81 000–90 000	Manchester 332 000–367 000
1927	11.5	7.3
1928	13.6	7.6
1929	14.8	8.4
1930	24.1	17.8
1931	31.2	18.7
1932	25.7	16.3
1933	26.1	15.9
1934	18.8	13.9
1935	17.7	13.4
1936	14.8	11.3
1937	12.1	9.7

Source: Calculated from Ministry of Labour, *Local Unemployment Index*, monthly returns.[45]

most depressed areas in England and Wales, like Jarrow, where 68 per cent of the insured labour force were without work during 1934. None the less, unemployment in Salford in particular was a serious problem during the inter-war period, as Table 1.4 shows. The high rate of unemployment in Salford is partly explained by the location of the docks and the vast majority of the dock labour force in Ordsall, and by the decline of heavy engineering and electrical engineering in Salford during the 1930s.[46]

The domestic consequences of unemployment were severe. J. Andrew found that poverty was rife among the families of the unemployed in Manchester in 1922:

> Clothing and bedding are in very many cases in a very lamentable state ... Much bedding has been pawned, and few in working-class districts have been able to renew blankets which have worn out. There is little doubt that many adults are actually getting less food than they have been accustomed to, the men ... frequently missing the midday meal ... there is much distress in the poorer parts of the city ...[47]

In October 1932, Alf Purcell, Secretary of the Manchester and Salford Trades Council, declared:

> Winter is upon us. Want and hunger are rife in our midst. Hundreds of thousands of men, women and children in Manchester and Salford are going short of many things they need: are in desperate want: are going hungry: are suffering numerable privations.[48]

Families who relied upon unemployment assistance as their sole source of income were living in primary poverty according to estimates of the 'poverty line' during the inter-war period. The Manchester University Settlement Study conducted in Ancoats during 1937–38 found such families among the 30.7 per cent of households in their sample of 254 who were living in primary poverty. The survey contained details of a 'representative' weekly budget for a family of five including three children under 14 years. Their total income was 35s. a week, from the Unemployment Assistance Board, which left them 34 per cent below the poverty line. A total of 59 per cent of the family's income was spent on food, with a further 29 per cent spent on rent. This left only 14 per cent, or less than 5s. per week to provide clothing, fuel, furnishings and all additional household expenses for a family of five, before the 'need' for amusement could even be considered. The Ancoats survey showed that it was common for local families to spend 40–50 per cent of their income on food, a figure matched in the national survey by the Ministry of Labour and National Service.[49]

Poverty and 'human needs'

The Merseyside and Bristol surveys, although less startling than the Manchester studies, suggested that even in terms of poverty as measured by minimum needs, nearly a third of the working-class population were living in or on the margin of poverty during the 1930s. However, there are alternative conceptions of poverty which lead to the conclusion that a higher proportion of working people could have been classified as poor during the inter-war decades. As R.F. George argued in his own assessment of the poverty line in 1936:

> It should be emphasized at the very outset that under no circumstances can the 'Poverty Line' be regarded as a desirable level. It seeks to assess the cost of a standard of living so low, that while persons below it are living in extreme poverty, those just above it would commonly be regarded as very poor.[50]

It was left to Rowntree to move away from the principle of 'merely physical efficiency' towards a 'human needs' standard. In *Poverty and progress: A second social survey of York*, Rowntree measured the survival of poverty in 1936 both against the standard employed in his own survey of 1899, and against a new, alternative level outlined in his book *The human needs of labour*.[51] For an urban family of five (man, wife and three dependent children), Rowntree estimated that a weekly income of 43s. 6d., after rent, was needed to secure 'the necessaries of a healthy life'. In this new level, Rowntree incorporated an allowance to cover 'personal sundries', allotting 9s. per week to cover unemployment and sickness insurance, contributions to sick and burial clubs and trade unions, travel to and from work, stationery and recreation. This included 7d. per week for newspapers, 6d. towards a wireless, and 3s. 4d. for 'beer, tobacco, presents, holidays, books, travelling, etc'. Rowntree insisted that even this improved standard tended to 'err on the side of stringency rather than of extravagance'. None the less, his revised poverty line was unusually generous. As George pointed out, other investigators were still using the concept of 'merely physical efficiency' which Rowntree had set out over 30 years previously.[52]

When measured against the poverty line employed in his 1899 survey, Rowntree found that the proportion of working-class households living in primary poverty had declined from 15.4 per cent in 1899 to 6.8 per cent in 1936. As Rowntree pointed out, this represented a striking improvement in 'the standard of life of the people'. However, measured against his revised poverty line using the 'human needs' standard, Rowntree estimated that 31.1 per cent of the working-class population of York were living in poverty in 1936.[53]

Despite Rowntree's attempt to establish a 'human needs' standard, the debate over the level of the poverty line was dominated by the notion of minimum subsistence throughout the inter-war period. Even Rowntree made only marginal adjustments to his estimate of the poverty line to estimate the 'human needs' standard, allowing just 4s. 5d. per week for recreation for a family of five. If the poverty lines used in the series of social surveys conducted during the 1930s had been set to compensate for the level of 'spends' or pocket money commonly expected by working-class men or youths, the percentage of families recorded as living in poverty would have been much higher.

While statisticians isolated families living below a nominal poverty line as those in poverty, in wider debates on social issues among journalists and social reformers the term 'the poor' had a much broader meaning. Some commentators argued that the working classes could be classified in general terms as 'the poor'. In a study of 'Poor people's music halls in Lancashire' published in 1900, the Manchester Christian economists C.E.B. Russell and E.T. Campagnac explained:

We are to speak of one of the chief amusements of 'the poor', and we shall include among 'the poor' not only the unemployed and those who are on the verge of destitution, but also those who are in a somewhat better position. We know no satisfactory definition of 'the poor'. It might be urged that those are poor who are without adequate food and clothing; but such a definition would be fruitless, for there are comparatively few people who are always in such a state of destitution. Or again, it might be held that a test of poverty was provided by the amount of the balance left when the necessaries of life were furnished. This is also useless; for ... the necessaries of life vary in different grades of society ...

Instead of attempting a strict definition of poverty, Russell and Campagnac concluded that they understood by 'the poor ... those who are below the lowest rank of what are called the middle class'. They excluded clerks, shopkeepers or shop assistants: 'Labourers, artisans, porters, navvies, street-sellers of all kinds, are the people of whom we are thinking ...'.[54] Significantly, skilled workers were included in their assessment.

This broader conception of 'the poor' is shared by many of the older residents of working-class districts in Manchester and Salford. In interviews with oral historians, most elderly working people declare that they grew up in poor districts. Even those who, like Robert Roberts, are conscious that their own families were relatively well-off, point out that their lives were still constrained by their financial circumstances and recall many signs of poverty in the lives of neighbours and acquaintances. Working-class areas prior to 1939 are described as poor because, in the opinion of many respondents, local families were living on inadequate incomes. Considerable emphasis is placed upon the achievements of working-class mothers in making ends meet during this period.[55]

Despite the prevalence of poverty, money for entertainment was found in the working-class districts of the two cities, all of which supported a network of leisure facilities centred upon pubs, cinemas and bookmakers. For example, despite the depth of local poverty revealed in Fred Scott's survey, the Adelphi, in common with other working-class districts in Salford, contained an impressive array of pubs.[56] Throughout the late nineteenth and early twentieth centuries, the presence of so many pubs in Salford attracted the derision of middle-class moral entrepreneurs. As the authors of a survey of a district near the Adelphi noted, with some cynicism, in 1930: 'As found in other poor districts, the shops catering for wants rather than needs are surprisingly numerous ... six public houses, five supper bars, and five shops selling sweets and tobacco.'[57] But participation in leisure was often modest, and these aspects of social life were maintained despite the survival of poverty.

Heavy spending on leisure, especially on drink and betting, is frequently condemned in interviews by those respondents who recall the domestic tensions caused by such spending in their own or neighbouring homes. However, more restrained spending on amusements is rarely criticized, even in cases where weekly budgets were so tight that a single evening in the pub for a married couple could push their level of housekeeping below a theoretical poverty line. In working-class terms, modest spending on leisure was a reasonable expectation, and those who could rarely afford to spend money on amusement, or for whom such spending caused problems in making ends meet, could still be termed poor. By this standard, Rowntree's original poverty line, which provided nothing for recreation, was far too low.

Throughout the early decades of the twentieth century, the need to balance the desire for leisure with the demands of the family housekeeping was acutely important for working-class families. Few could afford to regard spending on leisure casually. Manchester University Settlement claimed that, in the late 1930s, a level of income 200 per cent above the poverty line was necessary to provide a 'reasonable margin for holidays, luxuries and saving'. In their own survey of Ancoats, only 4 per cent of local families were classified in this bracket, whereas in Tout's wider study of working- and lower middle-class families in Bristol, the equivalent figure was 19.3 per cent. Tout also argued that families with incomes 200 per cent above the poverty line could be classed as 'comfortable'.[58] Both surveys therefore effectively employed a 'prosperity line' as well as a poverty line, but found that the vast majority of working-class households were excluded from the more affluent category.[59]

In the absence of comparable social surveys, it is impossible to provide a quantitative assessment of poverty in inter-war Salford. However, the surveys of Ancoats and Miles Platting in North Manchester, and the range of investigations conducted in other cities during the 1920s and 1930s, appear to offer some support to the view that poverty was a dominant feature of working-class culture. In terms of minimum subsistence, or 'merely physical efficiency', a substantial minority of working-class families were living below the poverty line throughout the period from 1900 to 1939. If we adopt Rowntree's 'human needs' standard, the proportion of households which could be characterized as poor is much greater. In the light of these documentary sources, the centrality of poverty in oral testimony is perhaps unsurprising.[60]

two

Men: Poverty, unemployment and the family

Leisure was central to the formation of masculine identities in working-class neighbourhoods. Drinking, gambling and sport, three of the cornerstones of 'traditional' working-class culture, were all heavily male-dominated, and men were identified by their hobbies or by the pubs where they drank as 'regulars', as well as by their occupations and political or religious allegiances. Pub life was especially important to men's networks, as relations between neighbours, kin and workmates could be maintained through a night's drinking. Moreover, men used pubs to carve out a terrain which was exclusively male. By convention, women were barred from the vault, usually the biggest room in any pub, which effectively formed a masculine republic.[1] However, even among men, participation in leisure was widely regulated by financial constraints, and the first concern of this chapter is to examine the extent to which men's social lives were affected by poverty and unemployment. Pub culture is discussed in some depth alongside sport, holidays and the cinema.

Attitudes towards leisure among men varied widely, despite the centrality of gender divisions in working-class culture. Indeed, although poverty surveys failed to provide a comprehensive account of participation in leisure prior to 1939, it is possible, using the fragmentary evidence contained in contemporary surveys and the more detailed insights into individual leisure patterns which emerge from oral evidence, to discern two distinct patterns of behaviour among working-class men. Some strictly regulated their personal spending. Others spent heavily on leisure at the expense of the family budget, even if this meant that their wives and children were left short of money for food and clothing. A further concern of this chapter will be to explore these contrasting styles of male behaviour: such contrasts were frequently drawn by women within working-class neighbourhoods, in order to distinguish between 'good' and 'bad' husbands.

These two very different patterns of behaviour were found at each income level within the working class. It is difficult to reconcile evidence relating to specific individuals and families with the labour aristocracy model, which links levels of income to styles of behaviour among distinct occupational groups, such as skilled manual workers. Male leisure patterns do not appear to have corresponded with occupational status. Leisure activities were much more firmly structured by gender, and by the poverty cycle. Among men, access to leisure was frequently curtailed by poverty and unemployment, and financial constraints emerge alongside gender divisions as the key structural factors in shaping leisure patterns. Within this framework, however, personal choice remained significant, and there is evidence of considerable diversity in working-class behaviour.[2]

Poverty and the denial of leisure

In working-class autobiographies, some men take great pride in describing their role as breadwinners, recalling how they limited their own spending in order to provide more money for the home. Jack Lanigan, for example, was born into an extremely poor family in Salford in 1890. His mother was a widow, and he started work as an errand boy when he was 10 years old in order to supplement her income. She died shortly afterwards. In Lanigan's words, 'She was taken ill and paid the price of death by worry and starvation.' He spent a very poor youth living with relatives, before moving to Moston in North Manchester in 1912, once he was married. Lanigan portrayed himself as an archetypal good husband: 'I gave my wife every penny of my wages and walked to work every morning, which was a distance of four miles from Moston to the Town Hall, but she gave me the tram fare to come home.'[3]

Similar examples of men who proved to be good providers are provided by oral testimony. Mrs Grady's husband had served an apprenticeship as a packing case maker, but often worked short time during the inter-war period. He became a bus cleaner when he could no longer earn a living at his trade. However, in her view, 'there wasn't a better man walked'. He could be depended upon to 'tip up' his wages:

He'd give it me if he had nothing for himself. That's what kind of a man he was.
So did you used to give him his spends back?
He'd never ask me for anything. If he had anything, it was what he got if he'd done anything for anybody and they'd treat him ... everybody knew that over my husband.[4]

After the Second World War, he rose to the rank of inspector on the buses in Salford. He was then able to spend more money on himself, and travelled 'all over the place' to watch Manchester United, but his relative affluence by the 1950s contrasted sharply with the poverty of his early married life.

A pattern of limited spending on leisure was also adopted by many more affluent manual workers, including skilled workers in regular employment, who devoted a large proportion of their disposable incomes to maintaining higher standards of home comfort than could be afforded by families living closer to the poverty line. Miss Garton's father, for example, was head of the lamp-lighting department on the Salford docks. He sometimes drank in his local pub in Ordsall: 'But he was a man who would never be treated by anybody to a drink, and he wouldn't treat anybody. He had what he wanted and he paid for it. And that was that.' He believed in strict financial independence, refusing to allow any member of the family to buy goods on hire purchase, but his self-discipline was rewarded by his subsequent ability to pay cash for household items, like a Singer sewing machine.[5]

Although the pub remained a hub of neighbourhood life throughout the early decades of the twentieth century, drinking was further regulated by fluctuations in individual economic fortunes, both long and short term. In the short term, working people took part in pub life when they could afford to do so. Oral evidence confirms that many Salford men were occasional drinkers. Mr Lawton described how his father, who worked as a labourer on the Salford docks, set off for the pub at eight o'clock on a Saturday night, to be followed by his mother an hour later:

> More or less Saturday night was the main night them days, for going for a drink.
> *During the week would your father go out?*
> Very rare because he never had the money to go out. When I was a kid, when things were pretty good on the docks he did go out during the week at times, [but] I wouldn't say regularly.[6]

Mass Observation uncovered a similar situation in their survey of Bolton pubs undertaken in 1939. A publican made a direct connection between the trade cycle and the state of business in pubs, declaring that 'he would tell the state of trade of the works opposite by his takings, and a bad week's work for the men made a difference of £10 to his takings in no time'. In Bolton as in Salford, many men confined their drinking to Friday and Saturday nights. Moreover, as another landlord pointed out to Mass Observation: 'the most customers only come in on the last hour, unless they are carrying extra cash':

> Landlord says to observer 'The drinking is all weekend now'. He 'thinks' that if the pubs were shut at the beginning of the week everyone would be satisfied; doesn't think lunch-time opening is worth the trouble.

Barmaid: 'They just wait for the last hour; never mind what time you open or what time you close. It's all they've got the money for.'[7]

In their attempts to measure expenditure on alcohol, Mass Observation encountered many of the problems experienced by social investigators since the turn of the century: 'The question of drink is so inhibited by teetotal antagonisms and tradition that direct personal data are exceptionally difficult to obtain.'[8]

None the less, the Bolton survey did provide a good deal of impressionistic evidence which highlighted the impact of poverty on working-class social life. For example, most landlords were forced to offer their 'regulars' credit, through the fear that they would otherwise lose custom. As Mass Observation recognized, 'putting it on the slate' was 'vital in pub economy'. Among the clientele of a small pub in Bolton were:

A man who is so trustworthy that the landlord does not trouble to put down what he owes, as the man puts it down himself, in a small book that he carries with him. This has been going on for twelve years ...

A carter, who runs up exactly ten shillings credit every week. He doesn't like to let the other customers know about this and gets the landlord to give him the money in odd half-crowns. He always settled up, has been doing this for ten years.

A few customers disappeared as their 'slates' grew, but in Bolton as in Salford, credit was essential if landlords were to see their regulars through a bad week. The problem, for publicans as for corner shopkeepers, was gauging the reliability of new customers.[9]

In the longer term, leisure was also shaped by the poverty cycle identified by Rowntree. For married couples, the period before their children were old enough to contribute to the family budget allowed the lowest margin for spending on leisure, and both oral and documentary sources testify to the impact of the poverty cycle during the inter-war decades. Mr Prescott's mother was a mill worker, and his father worked as a park keeper for Salford Corporation, although he suffered bouts of unemployment during the inter-war period. During his childhood, they rarely went out:

He was never one for beer. Somebody'd come in and say, 'Come on Charlie, just have one'. But that'd be it, it'd just be one. My mother didn't drink either ... she was just content to be in the house ...
Do you know what your mother and father did in their leisure time, was there anywhere they used to go out?
No, not really, there was this pub, just up by us, but they used to nearly always go over to Alan's, that was their friends over the road. Even when we lived in the Oldfield Road dwellings, they very seldom went out. And when they were in Liverpool Street, we had the Duke of York two doors away, never used to go in there. No, I can't remember them going in there at all. There was loads of pubs. Well they couldn't afford it, to tell you the truth. Couldn't afford it at all.[10]

A number of respondents described how the early years of married life saw few opportunities for leisure. Yet prospects improved over time. As Mass Observation noted in Bolton during the late 1930s: 'A spinner with two sons and two daughters can afford to drink a lot more when they become old enough to go out to work, but not old enough to leave home.'[11]

For those with little to spend on leisure, free time could almost become a burden. In a striking passage in *The classic slum*, Robert Roberts remarked that:

> On the light evenings after a day's work many men, even if they had the desire, possessed no means of occupying body or mind. Ignorance and poverty combined to breed, for the most part, tedium, a dumb accidie of the back streets to which only brawling brought relief. Summer evening leisure for men without the few coppers to go into a tavern meant long, empty hours lounging between kitchen chair and threshold. How familiar one grew in childhood with those silent figures leaning against door jambs, staring into vacancy waiting for bedtime.[12]

Thus Roberts reversed the accusation levelled by temperance workers, who portrayed drink as the cause of poverty. To Roberts, poverty kept men out of the pubs, and provided the backdrop to life in the 'classic slum', where leisure activities like all others were shaped by financial hardship. Fragmentary contemporary evidence confirms Roberts' claim that the scarcity of financial resources was a common problem among working men. A journalist from the *Manchester City News* interviewed a Salford carter on a break from picket duty during the 1911 transport workers strike. He was married with four children, and declared:

> At the best we carters have a hard time of it. My weekly wage is not twenty-four shillings a week, out of which I pay sixpence to our trade union, sixpence goes to my nipper who helps me, and 5s. 9d. has to be paid in house rent. Not much remains for our keep, nor can I afford many luxuries with the few pence that falls to my own share ...[13]

The impact of poverty upon leisure is frequently discussed in working-class autobiographies. Richard Heaton was born in the Hope Street district of Salford, Roberts' own district, in 1901. At a number of points in his autobiography, *Salford my home town*, Heaton comments on the fragile balance between the management of poverty and the pursuit of leisure which he observed during his childhood and youth. His father, a carter, suffered a spell of unemployment prior to the First World War, so the family depended for a while on public assistance. His father was a skilful darts player:

> The landlord of the local pub put up prizes on Saturday nights – legs of mutton, beef or rabbits – and for a copper anybody could compete for them. The highest scorer with three darts was the winner and more than one prize was brought home to Boundary Street. That

would mean a feast of a meal for our Sunday dinner, with some for tea and leftovers on Monday. For the rest of the week there was very little, except for the threepenny's of meat from Markendale's [abattoir shop] each day.

I remember my father bringing home one Friday night a china clock set. It consisted of a clock and two vases, all carved in lovely patterns. They were put on the mantelpiece and I saw my mother eyeing them lovingly. I knew she would have liked to have kept them and my father told her they were hers. She kept them for a day or two, but eventually they went the same way as the other things. She said we had to eat, so that was that. My father was the captain of the local pub team, so you can see why the Sunday dinners came home so regularly.[14]

The clock, like the medals his father won, went from the publican to the pawnbroker. Landlords recognized the domestic tensions that drink could arouse, and responded by offering material rewards which men could use in turn to justify their 'right' to leisure. Significantly, these competitions, staged in the vault of the pub from which women were barred, were held for prizes designed to appeal to women as household managers.

Elsie Oman, who was born in Ordsall in 1904, made another series of connections between pub life and poverty in her autobiography *Salford stepping stones*. Her father, a seaman, frequented the Britannia Inn prior to the First World War:

Nothing fancy and people were having hard times and small wages, but everybody seemed to be enjoying themselves. At weekends the men dressed up by adding a $6\frac{1}{2}d$. dicky in front of their old shirt. This consisted of a stiff shirt with a collar attached and they looked fine, but dared not take their coats off anywhere. It was a muffler through the week ...[15]

The majority of the Britannia regulars were dock labourers, and although living on low and irregular wages, they placed great emphasis upon respectability.[16] 'Keeping up appearances', by whatever means, was important among all occupational groups, not just skilled artisans. Respectability, however makeshift, was ubiquitous in the face of poverty. Moreover, Oman's initial comment, that people seemed to be enjoying themselves despite the 'hard times', is widely echoed in retrospective accounts of pub life in Salford. Despite the depth of poverty in the city, Salford, with its high concentration of pubs, maintained a reputation as a good place for a night out, attracting drinkers from Manchester as well as locals.[17]

Confronted by demands to curb their spending, some men justified drinking by claiming that information concerning job vacancies was informally circulated in pub vaults. Mr Aston described the inter-war years:

... at that period things were bad, money was tight, everybody was looking for a job, and I think there were more good deeds, as regards

Pub outing, Prince of Wales Feathers, Windsor Street, Salford, 1920.

getting a man a job, in the vault than ever came from the rectory or from the labour exchange ... 'Hey Bill! I think somebody wants something, you get down there quick'. You'd get that in the vault.[18]

In Salford as in other ports, the daily allocation of casual work on the docks was widely associated with bribery. Among my own respondents, a number of former Salford dock labourers were scathing in their accounts of the role of foremen on the docks. The foremen were responsible for picking out the men needed each day from the pool of casual labourers. Dockers regularly fought each other for the 'tallies' they needed to begin work, as Mr Saunders recalled:

I started there in 1936, and it was only casualization. It wasn't regular, permanent work. You had to show up every morning for tallies at quarter to eight, and if you were lucky enough to get one, you could work while twelve o'clock, and then they could sack you at twelve o'clock. Then you'd have to come down again at quarter to one, and fight again to try and get another tally. If you didn't, you came back again at quarter to four to try and fight for 'half a night'. I mean fighting, before the war, it was dog eat dog. I've seen fellers there with cracked ribs and broken arms fighting for a tally ... The foremen in them days, they were all, you'll excuse the word, they were pure bastards ... The match box. In the Salisbury. Every Saturday afternoon, you used to finish, that's where you used to all go, in the Salisbury. And the foreman'd ask a certain man, 'Give us a match'. He gave him the match box, there might be two half crowns in it. All those little tricks went on ... They did pay for the work. And these foremen accepted. I told you what they were in the first place.[19]

However, the conflict between dockers and foremen could be paralleled in disputes between dockers and their wives, over the allocation of money for drink at the expense of the housekeeping.

In *The classic slum*, Robert Roberts offered support to the labour aristocracy thesis by stressing the role of divisions of skill in determining segregation within pubs: 'These divisions could be marked in many public houses, where workers other than craftsmen would be frozen or flatly ordered out of those rooms in which journeymen foregathered.'[20] In contrast, however, retrospective testimony reveals a more complex set of arrangements. Mr Aston told how the Trafford Park Hotel was divided into a series of rooms, including a vault and a lounge, or 'best room'. Men who usually frequented the vault would drink in the best room if they went out with their wives:

> ... that was more of a plush seat for them there, and you just sat there, they were the elite, if you were to take your wife with you sometimes, well you'd go in the best side, where you wouldn't normally. Everybody wanted to go in the vault, [where the men] were good company.[21]

This suggests that gender divisions were perhaps more significant than occupational status. Moreover, a number of respondents, including Mr Deighton, suggested that kinship was of paramount importance in shaping male leisure networks. His father, a tradesman glass-blower, did his drinking with his brothers in a pub on Cross Lane, Salford:

> *Where did he do his drinking?*
> Well, my father used to have his regular pub on Cross Lane. He had a big family, he'd seven or eight brothers and two sisters ... they were a very close family, they'd all meet, and when my father was in with his brothers, the vault was full ...
> *What was the pub called?*
> He'd go in the Church on Cross Lane, which was only a very small pub. He was never a feller who went in the 'room', like the lounge, he was always in the vault with his brothers ...[22]

Oral evidence suggests that family networks were of more importance than divisions of skill in shaping leisure patterns.

Of course, drinking was only one of a series of leisure activities which were regulated by poverty. For example, although betting was commonplace in working-class districts, a visit to the racecourse in Salford was beyond the means of many local residents. Mr Perry described the race-course in Ordsall at the turn of the century:

> ... there used to be a plot of land over the race course on Trafford Road ... and people who couldn't afford to go into the race used to stand there and watch the races. They used to call that 'skinner's hill'. And the lads used to go round selling pencils to them, to mark their race cards.[23]

Oral evidence confirms that football was a major focus of interest, but perhaps surprisingly, when the sport is recalled, it is often without reference to Manchester United or City. Mr Johnstone described Harpurhey in North Manchester in the inter-war years:

> *Did many people go to watch football?*
> I don't recollect anybody in my acquaintance going to watch first-class football, but an awful lot of people watched the local clubs. There was one well-known club called Miles Platting Swifts, and another one called Manchester North End. But there was a lot more interest in local sports.

His father was a keen footballer who had played briefly as an amateur for Crewe Alexandra: 'He never went to the City, or Manchester [United]. Quite honestly I don't think a lot of people could afford it, even in those days it was a shilling, or one and six to get in.'[24]

Documentary sources confirm that many people were unable to afford to go to professional matches,[25] so despite the growth of football as a mass spectator sport, watching United or City was never a universal pastime. A survey of Manchester council estates in 1937 found that on the estates on the outskirts of the city, particularly the Wythenshawe estate over 6 miles from the centre, many men were unable to afford the extra transport costs incurred in attending Manchester United or City matches. Although the corporation estates housed some of the better-paid manual workers in the city, the higher municipal rents and the cost of journeys to work meant that men who moved to the estates had to accept lower disposable incomes in return for a cleaner environment.[26] Although as Hobsbawm suggested, professional football was central to the national pattern of working-class culture by 1900, the sport still excluded women and many men despite its capacity to draw massive crowds.[27]

In contrast to the emphasis upon professional football among social historians, retrospective accounts show that the sport retained a local base, and suggest that neighbourhood rather than civic loyalties were aroused. Matches between teams drawn from Salford pubs were played on patches of waste ground in the poorest areas of the city, with communal wagers of 6*d*. or 1*s*. per player at stake, and these contests aroused passions as strong as any professional encounter. Mr Lomas described contests between pub teams in the Adelphi:

Duncan Villa, Ordsall, 1900.

They used to play football on the [Adelphi] croft for a shilling a man, which was quite a good sum of money. And they used to play different pubs. The Adelphi pub would play the Rob Roy or the Olive Branch.
Would anybody watch those games?
Oh yes, it was quite a Sunday afternoon entertainment. The teams had followers, gangs, and chaps that went in the pub that didn't play football. They'd come down, twenty or thirty strong ... And they'd all be round the croft and they used to shout the team on. They'd nothing else to do.
Did they wear a kit in those pub games?
No kit, no studs, they just turned out in the ordinary day clothes.
What would they have on their feet?
Ordinary boots or shoes.[28]

At this level, football was informally organized, and provided a free spectacle.

Family-centred activities were similarly regulated by poverty. Some men chose to spend much of their free time at home, and for sections of the working-class population, the quality of domestic life was enriched by the spread of gramophones and then wirelesses during the early twentieth century. Mrs Jackman was born in Ordsall in 1895, one of the youngest of 13 children. Her father worked as a tradesman dyer in the Adelphi. He could be relied upon to tip up his wages, and his elder children were of working age as Mrs Jackman grew up, so she enjoyed a more comfortable upbringing than many other respondents. Her family owned a piano, a sure sign of prosperity in a working-class street, and her father also possessed an accordion, a gramophone and a magic lantern. Much of the family's entertainment was therefore home-centred. It should be stressed, however, that this standard of home comfort was unusual in Ordsall, and that here, as in other predominantly working-class areas, the contrasts between neighbouring families can only have been sharpened by the advent of the wireless during the inter-war period.

Although in national terms, the expansion of radio broadcasting was perhaps the outstanding innovation in leisure between 1918 and 1939, oral evidence suggests that in many districts of Salford, possession of a wireless set was a symbol of relative affluence, especially before the late 1930s. In the words of one respondent, in the 'late 20s and early 30s, you *were somebody* if you had a wireless'.[29] Walter Greenwood claimed in 1936 that often working men did not possess wirelesses even if they were in continuous employment, and in many districts this was the case.[30] In Liverpool, according to *The social survey of Merseyside* published in 1934:

> In the slum areas and among the poorer classes generally, the wireless is almost unknown. A clergyman working in one of the poorest parishes in the city declares that there is hardly a set in his district.[31]

During the 1930s, the means test enforced the sale of household items, including pianos, gramophones and wirelesses, by families seeking to qualify for assistance, so unemployment, which in Salford peaked at over 30 per cent in 1931, exacerbated the uneven spread of indoor entertainment. One of the major processes of change in inter-war recreation was therefore only piecemeal. Mr Pearson's family was means tested: 'If you had a piano or anything like that you had to flog it. And a gramophone, you had to flog it before you'd get (anything) ...'.[32] According to people who worked in pawnshops in Salford after 1918, household goods such as gramophones were frequently pledged. Gramophones and musical instruments, including accordions, were among the forfeited pledges regularly put up for sale by pawnbrokers, along with the more commonly pawned bundles of clothing and bedding.[33] For many families, improvements in living standards during the inter-war years were clearly precarious.

Seaside holidays were also accessible to sections of the working-class population only. John Walton, the leading historian of the English holiday industry, has claimed that the annual trip to the seaside became the 'norm' in the textile towns of Lancashire by the end of the nineteenth century.[34] More recently, however, Stephen Jones provided a more pessimistic assessment, remarking that in the cotton districts during the 1930s, there was 'a considerable section of the working-class who could not afford a holiday'.[35] In 1936, among the cotton workers in Manchester and Salford:

> ... the term 'holiday' was a misnomer for a vast number of people. The reality of the situation according to some union officials was that

holidays without pay amounted to lock-outs, or in the words of the secretary of the Manchester and Salford Weavers' Association, 'enforced collective unemployment'.[36]

There is widespread evidence confirming that in many working-class areas of Manchester and Salford, family holidays were unattainable luxuries throughout the period from 1900 to 1939. The Manchester University Settlement survey of household budgets in Ancoats in 1937–38 revealed that trips to the seaside were far from the norm. Some local residents were able to travel, but the majority of families spent their holidays in Ancoats:

> Saving up for holidays was mentioned by certain families – but not many. A few of these went as far away as Skegness and Brighton. One family owned a wooden hut on the shore at Blackpool, letting it when it was not wanted for their own use, and here the whole family spent their holidays every year. Fishing at Marple provided the occasion for frequent picnics at the week-end for a father, mother and small boy, and possibly for other men without families. But on the whole, the impression is gained that holidays were more often spent at home, though cycling and, more rarely, walks into the country appeared sometimes as the week-end and Bank Holiday recreation of wage-earning sons and daughters.[37]

Retrospective evidence confirms that seaside holidays were beyond the means of many Salford families, indicating that the poverty cycle was particularly important in determining whether families could afford to 'go away'. Older married couples, whose children were contributing to the family economy, were often those best placed to afford holidays. Moreover, teenagers often travelled independently, taking holidays with workmates rather than their families.[38] Without children of their own to provide for, it was easier for young workers to save for the coveted week at Blackpool.

In contrast, parents with young children frequently found that they lacked the resources needed for a week or even a day at the seaside. Oral testimony provides many examples of families in this category. Mr Pearson's family never joined the exodus to the coast. However, his uncle, who was a bachelor, and in regular work, went to the Isle of Man for a holiday every year:

> *Did you ever have any holidays when you were young?*
> No. The first time I saw the seaside was after I left school. It was Blackpool.
> *Were there not many families who would go away for a holiday?*
> No, nobody, there was no such a thing ... my uncle, he had a regular job, he was with the Metrovicks, and he always went away, always ... [to] Cunningham's Camp.
> *That's the Isle of Man?*
> Isle of Man, aye, he loved the Isle of Man.[39]

Mrs Daly's account suggests that in Greengate, the rise of the seaside holiday by the 1930s may have sharpened feelings of deprivation among families who were left out. In her own street, the people who went on day trips tended to stand aloof from the neighbourhood. Even a day out of Salford was beyond the reach of families like her own:

> *You were saying that you didn't go away on holidays when you were young?*
> Oh no, never. The only time I went away was when my brother took me. I put my money in a little money box, and when I'd saved it up he'd take me away for a day to Southport. He was married then ...
> *Did many of the people round where you lived go away for day trips or anything like that?*
> Well a few of them did, the snobby ones did, yes. They used to go away for a day, if it was a day it was something out of this world, but they'd never give you any rock or anything, they wouldn't bring you anything back.
> *What were they like?*
> They were nice enough, they had lovely homes, but they wouldn't talk to you. If you used to say 'Hello', or 'Nice day', they'd just look at you as if you were silly.[40]

Oral testimony suggests that in cases where parents did take their younger children to the seaside, day trips were often the norm. A full week away from home was more unusual. Mrs Hill was born in Hanky Park in 1901. Her father was a colour mixer at a dyeworks, and she was one of 13 children: 'They used to take us so many each year, they used to go to either Southport or Blackpool, just for the day.'[41]

Among men, perhaps the most popular trips were pub outings, which were organized annually from pubs throughout Salford and Manchester. Such trips, like pub vaults, were for men only. Even so, philanthropic initiatives ensured that children were more likely to 'go away' than their parents. For instance, Mr Prescott attended the holiday camp for poor Salford children at Prestatyn in North Wales during the 1920s. Holidays were provided as charity, although the children's parents were expected to provide them with money as spends:

> ... they used to have what you call a 'Poor Children's Camp', it's still there now at Prestatyn, and we used to go there once a year. If you were lucky, if your name was called out, you went to this place. Your mother saved up, and your aunts dished in, and you got two and sixpence [spends].
> *What about your parents getting to the seaside?*
> Well, your parents, it was very seldom, my parents anyway, and people round about that I knew, it was very seldom that they went to places like that.[42]

Seaside holidays, like gramophones and wirelesses, were status symbols which appear to have sharpened feelings of relative deprivation in working-class neighbourhoods during the inter-war decades. Some families were enjoying new levels of affluence, but those trapped by the poverty cycle or unemployment were often acutely aware that they were missing out.[43]

Unemployment and the denial of leisure

Historians have recently suggested that unemployment did not lead to exclusion from the world of commercial leisure. Stephen Jones, for example, argued that men without work 'were not far removed from the products and services of the leisure industry', claiming that gambling and the cinema, at least, provided important means of escapism for the unemployed.[44] Ross McKibbin, in a sensitive account of inter-war unemployment, provided a more cautious assessment, pointing out that men without work attended the cinema less frequently, and were likely to desert their regular pubs. However, he maintained, 'the dole was a kind of wage and it permitted a good deal of social continuity', ensuring that the unemployed 'were not wrenched from their class and community'.[45] Detailed local evidence drawn from Salford and Manchester suggests that a more pessimistic assessment of the social impact of unemployment could perhaps be developed. The loss of work did lead to widespread exclusion from a series of commercial leisure activities, and although men without work turned to the established street life of working-class districts for ways of killing time, unemployment still bred a form of social segregation in the two cities during the 1920s and 1930s.

Unemployment was one of the major causes of primary poverty during the inter-war period, and the Manchester University Settlement survey of Ancoats, undertaken during the late 1930s, showed that for those dependent on unemployment assistance, it was not possible to provide a full diet if even a moderate budget was set aside for leisure. Significantly, the poorest diet in the sample belonged to a family of eight where the head of the household 'unlike others on unemployment assistance did not give the whole allowance to his wife for housekeeping but retained 5s. a week for himself'.[46] In Ancoats, as in Salford, some unemployed men deprived their families of housekeeping resources, even when their initial income fell below the poverty line. However, the Settlement survey suggested that this style of personal spending was only indulged in by a minority. The majority of unemployed husbands in Ancoats contributed their full allowance to the housekeeping and, as a consequence, their participation in commercial leisure must have been minimal.

Drinking was probably the activity which was most severely curtailed in the wake of unemployment. Rowntree and Lasker described the family of an unemployed man in York during 1911:

> Beer, which is popularly supposed to be 'feeding', is tabooed by them, though not because of any conscientious scruples. As Mrs Nevinson says, 'When he was in regular work he liked his glass of beer as well

as any one, but now we can't get bread, let alone beer, and you don't find a man who goes out many a morning at five fasting, because he wants to leave what crust there is for the children and me, dropping into the public with the first shilling he earns – nor me neither.'[47]

Social investigators working on the *New survey of London life and labour* during the inter-war period encountered a similar state of affairs:

> Men who are obviously poverty-stricken, or those known to be unem-
> ployed, are very rarely seen even in the lower-class public-houses. The
> unemployed regard the public-houses as closed to them, and in
> conversation will admit to be being afraid someone will stand them
> a drink they can't return. The activities discussed in the bar will be
> in any case mainly closed to them, and the feeling of most of them
> appears to be that they would be both embarrassed and a source of
> embarrassment even if they could raise the price of a drink.[48]

Retrospective evidence confirms that in Salford as in London, men's networks, which often hinged upon pub culture, were severely disrupted by unemployment. Men without work were thus denied access to the principal arena of masculine leisure, and in areas where pubs did operate as channels of labour market information, this further circumscribed an unemployed man's chances of finding work.

Professional sport, another of the staple elements of 'traditional' working-class culture, was similarly undermined by unemployment. During the inter-war period, there was some recognition of the impact of trade slumps upon attendances at football and rugby league matches: at Old Trafford, Manchester United's ground, and at the Willows, Salford's rugby league ground in Weaste, prices for those out of work were reduced, to enable more unemployed men to attend.[49] However, the willingness by the clubs to cut their prices indicates that they were aware that unemployment had an adverse effect upon crowds. In Liverpool, the Pilgrim Trust found that during the 1930s:

> On a Saturday afternoon, when an important League match is on, the
> unemployed men in Liverpool turn out and gather along the streets
> where the crowds go up by foot, tram, bus or motor car to watch it.
> To watch a match is in itself a second-hand experience … and the
> unemployed man … has to make do with this substitute for it.[50]

Unemployment also led to a serious decline in sports such as pigeon fancy-ing, which required a consistent commitment of resources. Mass Obser-vation's survey of Bolton showed that the sport was in decline by the late 1930s. Colliers, who in Bolton as in Salford were among the keenest fanciers, told observers that short time and unemployment in the local mining industry had undermined the basis of the sport. Too many men without work were unable to enter birds for races.[51]

Unemployment could therefore lead to the erosion of established social networks. Historians who have argued the opposite case, pointing to the integration of the unemployed within the mainstream of working-class social life, have usually based their assertions upon records of cinema attendance. A study of male youths in Glasgow, Cardiff and Liverpool between 1936 and 1939 found that despite high levels of youth unemployment, 80 per cent went to the pictures once a week, and historians have used this figure to demonstrate that cinema attendances were not seriously threatened by the inter-war depression.[52] However, surveys focusing on unemployed youths failed to reveal the extent of the financial pressures facing adults without work. Significantly, other studies conducted during the 1930s suggested that cinema audiences, in Liverpool for example, were directly reduced by unemployment.[53]

The Manchester University Settlement study of Ancoats showed that even in 1937–38, a trip to the pictures was a luxury beyond the means of many local people.[54] Some men rejected the cinema in favour of the pub, but others, especially those living in primary poverty, had little access to any form of commercial entertainment. Moreover, when unemployed men did go to the cinema, they often attended matinee performances, which meant that they were segregated from those who were still working. In Manchester in 1933, local cinemas and theatres provided 23 000 free matinee tickets to be distributed at centres for the unemployed, but retrospective testimony suggests that the atmosphere at matinees was very different from the celebratory feel of a Saturday night at the pictures for more affluent families.[55]

If the denial of commercial leisure was one of the common experiences of the unemployed, how did they actually spend their time? Unemployment did not result in a simple increase in 'free' time. On weekdays, the most active occupation of those without work was the search for a job, conducted on foot. As Mrs Phelan declared, her unemployed father 'traipsed his feet off' looking for work in the industrial districts of Salford and Trafford Park.[56] Mr Rowlings, who was himself unemployed during the 1920s, described the search for work as a daily ritual:

> I was lucky because I was never out of [work] very long, but my lady [mother] wouldn't tolerate any of this lying in bed business. Seven o'clock, no matter what weather it was, you were out ... Bear in mind my father died when I was ten years of age and [we had] a big family. But I had to come in at the same time each day, because if I came home early and told her that I hadn't got a job, she said I hadn't looked for it. If I came home too late, I'd disappoint her because she thought I'd started work ... If you were out at seven o'clock in the morning and got home about half past ten, that seemed reasonable. But we used to stand at one particular place in Trafford Park, Friedland's ... they used to burn all the scrap wood at the back, and we used to stand around the fire until it was time that you could venture home, because there was no work knocking about.[57]

In his autobiography, *There was a time*, Walter Greenwood described how men without work spent their days hanging around outside the motor works in Trafford Park, waiting to replace any worker who was sacked. In Hanky Park, these crowds were christened the 'Band of Hope'.[58] Others found alternative ways of passing the time, and in Greenwood's novel *Love on the dole*, there is an ironic account of unemployed Salford men watching work taking place on the new road between Manchester and Liverpool:

> A brand new thirty-odd-mile road, magnet for unemployed men of all trades who lined the cutting, lounging in the grass. Not in the expectation of work, it was merely an interesting way of killing time. Men of all trades, joiners, painters, bricklayers, engineers, dockers, miners and navvies; all watching a handful of men working.[59]

As Greenwood's various accounts confirmed, the unemployed faced two problems: the search for work and the need to 'kill' time. Lacking the money to frequent pubs, Hanky Park's unemployed spent much of their time standing in 'groups of scarecrow spectres at street corners'.[60] The image of men without work 'lounging' at street corners was widely used to symbolize the despair of the unemployed during the 1920s and 1930s. For example, in an address on unemployment given in 1925, the Medical Officer for Hulme in Manchester declared that: 'I know these men as few know them, they do not want to waste the intellect that God has given them – to lie half a day in bed and hang about on street corners.'[61] Greenwood used the same image in *Love on the dole* to describe a young unemployed worker killing time by 'lounging at the street corner with the rest of the dole birds', and the same spectre is constantly raised in retrospective accounts of working-class life in Manchester and Salford.[62] However, our familiarity with this image should not lead us to dismiss it as a cliché. As Bundy and Healy pointed out, such images may be instantly recognizable precisely because of the ubiquity of the experiences they recall.[63] Indeed, 'lounging' was a central form of urban leisure during the nineteenth and early twentieth centuries. Working men had traditionally spent much of their free time in street-corner gatherings, and while in the 1900s the term 'street loafing' was widely used in hostile accounts of working-class street life, by the 1920s, as public concern for the unemployed mounted, street corner cliques were more sympathetically reviewed.[64]

Street gambling was another established means of killing time adapted by those without work during the inter-war period:

> ... there was a lot of out of work, and you'd congregate in back entries. Now, the game then, you'd be watching them, you'd be young lads, eight, nine and ten, and you'd be watching the older ones, the out o'works. And they'd have a dart board hung up on somebody's back door, and you used to watch for hours.[65]

Established street gambling pitches became known as daytime haunts of the unemployed. 'The hollow', an area of open land near the dock gates in

Ordsall, and the Ellor Street pitches in Hanky Park both attracted 'out o'works', although men without work were likely to attend as spectators as they lacked the money to take part in gaming.[66] These activities drew upon another traditional feature of life in the streets of working-class districts. The street was the last remaining resort of those with little to spend on recreation.

Walter Greenwood reflected upon the social impact of unemployment at length in both *Love on the dole* and *There was a time*, and there is a striking convergence between the two works. The autobiography repeats detailed points made in *Love on the dole*, as though Greenwood sought to confirm that his fictional portrayal was based upon the reality of life in Hanky Park during the 1920s. For example, the exclusion from leisure suffered by the central characters in the novel matches the experiences of his own acquaintances, as depicted in *There was a time*.[67]

In his autobiography, Greenwood claimed that even young men, usually among the most privileged working-class consumers, were severely affected by the loss of work:

> Segregation asserted itself in subtle ways. Those who were out of work tended to avoid their luckier counterparts and the embarrassment was mutual. Pay day brought a constrained uneasiness. 'Where are we going tonight?' The customary question of a week-end among friends was avoided if, standing by in the group, were any whose pockets were known to be empty. For those who had a job, the sight of friends to whom all doors of entertainment and conviviality were closed could bring sharp, apprehensive shivers, aware as they were that this fate could be anybody's in these uncertain times.[68]

This echoes the findings of the *New survey of London life and labour*, which reported that older unemployed men avoided pubs through the same fear of mutual embarrassment. Clearly, the collective masculine world of pub vaults and football terraces could be only partially reproduced during periods of high unemployment.

Greenwood's most graphic description of the plight of the unemployed had been set out over 30 years previously, in *Love on the dole*. The central character in the novel was portrayed as having no sign of work after completing his apprenticeship:

> Nothing to do with time; nothing to spend ... he would slink around the by-streets to the billiard hall, glad to be somewhere out of the public gaze, any place where there were no girls to see him in his threadbare jacket and patched overalls. Stealing into the place to watch the prosperous young men who had jobs and could afford billiards, cigarettes and good clothes.

Lacking the price of two seats at the cinema, he was 'a prisoner at large':

> The walls of the shops, houses and places of amusement were his prison walls; lacking money to buy his way into them the doors were

all closed against him. That was the function of doors and walls; they were there to keep out those who hadn't any money.[69]

Greenwood suggested that those without work were frequently left with no money for leisure whatsoever. As a result, a form of informal apartheid undermined the collective life of working-class neighbourhoods.[70] Unemployed men could only resist this subtle segregation by keeping money for themselves out of their unemployment allowances. Some chose to do so, although they ran the immediate risk of leaving their families in very severe domestic poverty.

Leisure as a 'cause' of poverty

In Victorian and Edwardian social commentaries, drink and gambling were widely portrayed as two of the principal causes of poverty. Rowntree, who was prominent in the anti-gambling lobby as well as the temperance movement, appeared to offer some statistical support to this moral critique of working-class leisure with his assertion that 'secondary' poverty accounted for the bulk of the visible poverty in York at the turn of the century. While recognizing that his notional poverty line was impossibly low, Rowntree none the less described the causes of secondary poverty as follows:

> Drink, betting and gambling. Ignorant or careless housekeeping, and other improvident expenditure, the latter often induced by irregularity of income ... There can be but little doubt, however, that the predominant factor is drink.[71]

His investigation therefore appeared to confirm the traditional accusation of the temperance lobby: drink, it seemed, was indeed a grave national evil. Rowntree's own position was relatively sophisticated. He sought to establish a series of causes of poverty, and effectively highlighted a range of problems, from low wages to the penalties of the poverty cycle. However, his use of the secondary poverty bracket tended to conflate economic categories and moral judgements.

The majority of social observers showed much less subtlety than Rowntree. In 1906, the *Manchester City News* published a feature by H.J. Oldham entitled 'A voice from the slums: The seamy side of life in Salford', which provides a classic illustration of a traditional strand of social criticism. He claimed to have been an observer of Salford life for over half a century. However, the moral tone of the city's slums still frightened him, and according to Oldham's account, the 'week-end in slum life' comprised a festival of drink and violence lasting from four o'clock on Saturday afternoon until the early hours of Monday morning. He described events he claimed to have observed in Salford during a recent weekend. On the Saturday afternoon, he saw a man attack his wife on the balcony of a block of flats or 'dwellings', trying first to throw her over, then beating her until the cries of the crowd persuaded him to stop. The woman committed suicide: her body was recovered from the canal on the Sunday. The same Sunday night, Oldham witnessed a concert after pub closing-time, at which beer and spirits flowed freely among local men and women. During the sing-song, another woman was attacked by her husband on the same balcony, and left sobbing outside.[72]

Oldham displayed a Victorian tendency to stereotype the inhabitants of poor districts as uniformly degraded. However, contrary to the more lurid claims of moral entrepreneurs, many men in working-class families spent little on drink or gambling. Leisure activities were curtailed due to the need to balance the family budget. Moreover, Oldham's account gave no indication of the distinct moral code which existed within working-class areas. 'Good' husbands were usually considered to have the right to a limited amount of pocket money, even if the task of making ends meet was more difficult as a result. 'Bad' husbands, who withheld the majority or even all of their earnings for drink or gambling could plunge their families much deeper into poverty. Working-class wives were only too aware of this contrast, although Oldham drew no such distinctions between families. Similarly, Rowntree's category of secondary poverty failed to distinguish between 'good' and 'bad' husbands.

Men exercised considerable financial power simply because they received their wages in cash, and gave a portion to their wives as they chose. Although the level of money handed over was frequently a source of dispute, men were in a stronger position, as they could sometimes conceal the real extent of their earnings from their wives.[73] However, the authors of the Manchester University Settlement survey of Ancoats in 1937–38 were deeply struck by the profound differences between the arrangements found within working-class households:

> A good many wives do not know what their husbands' wages are ... In other families the procedure is almost the reverse. The men hand over their wages-packet intact to their wives, who buy their clothes and often their tobacco for them, handing back a small sum for pocket money, commonly known as 'spends'.[74]

These differences can be partly explained by the competing notions of masculinity which prevailed within working-class districts. Among women, a good husband was a man who put the needs of his family first. Some men shared this conception of their role as breadwinners. Others, however, took pride in asserting their financial independence, and for such men, to hand over an unopened wage packet was a sign of weakness.

Mr Pearson made a series of points about leisure and poverty, and attitudes towards money among men. Power relations within marriage hinged, to a large extent, upon arrangements over money and drink:

> *Was there much pressure from people, in families or neighbours, against men drinking, or did everyone just accept that?*
> Oh it was accepted, drinking. I'm not talking to the extent that you hear now, alcoholics, never heard of alcoholism them days. Mind you,

they didn't get the money. There was more rolling home drunk. I
don't know how they did it, when I come to think, the wages they
were getting ... of course a lot of homes went without. And sometimes a woman would more often have a black eye than she had her
wages in them days ... I was a young lad working, I had to hand my
wages over, but if a man handed his wages over in them days, he
wasn't a man. There was a few did it, but it was recognised, if he took
his whole packet home not opened. It leaked out, because the women
talk like they do now, and it came out, it would leak out somehow.
That say, Jim, he handed his wage packet over. Quite a lot of rowing
in houses over wages, you got a feller worked a bit of overtime, I
suppose he expected to keep it, they'd be rowing over money. Money
would be the most [common] thing they were rowing about.[75]

His account captures many of the ambiguities in the relation between
poverty and leisure. In his view, during the 1920s, wages were low, yet
drunkenness was common. This can only be explained with reference to
the family economy: families 'went without', disputes over money were the
main source of friction between husbands and wives, and some marriages
were characterized by male violence.

Oral evidence suggests that this was only one of the patterns of behaviour common among working-class men, although further detailed local
research is needed before we can attempt to measure the proportion of
men who took their spends out before handing their wages over to their
wives. Significantly, however, oral testimony shows that men from a wide
range of occupations conformed to this notion of the 'real man'. Skilled
workers were among those who left their families in dire poverty. Mrs
Sugden was born in Ordsall in 1915, and her father worked as a moulder,
but:

When we were all kids he worked at the Westinghouse. He used to
come home, throw ha'penny on the table for the remainder of his
wages.
How did your mother manage?
Well she had to work, go out and clean, didn't she? She brought us all
up.
What would the money be going on if he wasn't bringing it home?
Drink.[76]

Mr Brookman's father worked as a boilerman at the Broughton Copper
Company in the Adelphi, but his contributions to the family budget were
extremely unreliable:

The old feller would never tip nothing up to my mother.
Not at all?
No.
Where did it go then?
On booze.[77]

His mother worked as a cleaner to raise her housekeeping, but the family diet was supplemented by scavenging: as a child, Mr Brookman took part in the weekly scramble for faded fruit discarded by the traders at Smithfield Market in Manchester. Oldham's account of Salford in 1906 made a similar observation concerning leisure patterns among skilled workers:

> A percentage of the tenants of the slums are skilled artizans, getting what is termed 'good money', but who prefer to live in these miserable dwellings in order that they may have the more to spend on drink, betting, and other forms of gambling. The women who are the wives or 'companions in arms' of such creatures are by their circumstances dragged down to the rock bottom of a degraded social life.[78]

Of course, such behaviour was by no means confined to skilled workers. In fact, as Russell and Campagnac observed in Manchester in 1900, even families in 'primary' poverty, who appeared to 'stand on the margin of destitution' sometimes adopted the pattern of spending which Rowntree considered characteristic of 'secondary' poverty, by spending money on leisure to the detriment of the weekly housekeeping budget:

> ... it is often the case that those who have least money, and appear to stand on the margin of destitution, have a larger proportion of their actual means to spend for *extras*, for amusements of various kinds than those who have a better income.[79]

Oral testimony provides cases of excessive spending on leisure among men on low incomes, and even among the unemployed who were living in primary poverty during the inter-war decades. Mrs Phelan's father was out of work up to 1939. Although he was a teetotaller, he did not always tip up his unemployment allowance:

> He never drank, my father, he gambled ... He always looked down on pubs.
> *What did he bet on?*
> Favourites on the horses. I used to take him a thri'penny bet.
> *Could he still have a bet when he was out of work?*
> Yes, he had a bet. He used to gamble a lot sometimes. Gamble too much really. He used to gamble a lot of the dole money. In fact, he used to gamble it all sometimes.
> *How would your mother manage if he did that?*
> Well we used to have to borrow a shilling ... we'd go over the road to Mrs Hopkins and borrow a shilling off her.[80]

The consequence of his failure to provide housekeeping was that the family were poorly clothed. Mrs Phelan remarked: 'I never knew what a new dress was.' This was most keenly felt during Whit week, when families who could afford to do so bought new clothes for their children to wear on the annual

Whit walks. Mrs Phelan and her sister were kept indoors. Moreover, their home was barely furnished. As a child, she scrubbed bare boards in the bedrooms and on the stairs.

Press reports also provide evidence of this pattern of behaviour among some unemployed men during the 1930s. John Williamson was sentenced to two months imprisonment in 1938 for neglecting his four children. Despite a warning six months earlier by an officer from the National Society for the Prevention of Cruelty to Children (NSPCC), on two occasions in September he spent his entire unemployment allowance on gambling and drink, leaving his family destitute. In court, his wife accused: 'I've been married nineteen years and the only thing that fears you is this place. You think only about your own skin and not me.'[81]

Other cases which resulted in court proceedings in Salford during the late 1930s involved men who were in relatively low-paid jobs, receiving wages close to or below Rowntree's revised poverty line, the 'human needs' standard. Significantly, men who were charged with neglecting their families tended to take a very high proportion of their wages for spends, even in a 'moderate' week. In January 1939, John Hart of Ordsall was placed on probation on a charge of neglecting his two children in a manner likely to cause them unnecessary suffering or injury to health. He was in regular work on wages of 55s. a week, 40s. of which he usually handed over to his wife. His regular spends of 15s. amounted to nearly 30 per cent of his weekly income. However, the complaint against him in court was that on three occasions in December 1938, he had gone to a dog track and lost all his wages. An officer from the NSPCC, summoned to investigate the third incident found only a quarter of a loaf, half a bottle of milk and a small portion of sugar in the house.[82] Another man earning 52s. a week who received a sentence of a month's imprisonment in May 1938 admitted that he usually tipped up only 30s. to his wife, keeping 22s., over 40 per cent of his income, for himself.[83]

Isolated reports of court cases illustrate the severe domestic problems caused by men who failed to tip up their wages or unemployment benefit. However, given the paucity of the statistical data relating to household budgeting, it is impossible to gauge the average levels of spends expected by working-class men with any precision. Moreover, the vast majority of cases where male spending caused hardship did not reach the courts. Women in these families faced an obvious dilemma: court proceedings were a last resort, and women endured enormous sufferings before turning to the law.[84] Some struggled to manage the home while attempting to hide evidence of domestic problems, for the sake of the family's respectability. In other cases, marital problems were public knowledge, and women depended on support offered by sympathetic neighbours.[85] In some instances, rows between married couples could spill out into the street, and women were sometimes forced to confront their husbands in public houses. Although pub vaults were open to men only, women flouted convention in attempts to shame their husbands. As Mrs Mullen recalled, in Ordsall:

'One [woman] plonked two kids on the counter. Said, "Here y'are, you look after 'em"...'.[86]

For some men who were heavy drinkers, alcohol dependency must have explained, at least in part, the 'craving' for beer. This perhaps makes such behaviour less culpable, although the consequences for their families were none the less disastrous. Drink and gambling were the forms of leisure most likely to feature in accounts of disrupted family relationships. Either activity could become a serious drain upon household resources. This points to the survival of an older, nineteenth-century pattern of leisure activity, centred around the pub and the betting pitch, during a period more often associated with the development of novel attractions in commercial leisure. Some men, like Mrs MacLeod's husband, frequented pubs during the inter-war period while rejecting the appeal of alternative entertainments:

What sort of arrangement did you have with him about money? Did he tip his wages up?

Well, I'll tell you what arrangement I had. If he didn't call for a pint, I got it. But if he did, I didn't. Put it like that. He was a very generous man.

[*Mrs L.M.*: Treating somebody else in the pub.]

Is that where his money went though? Was it on drink? I know that a lot of the men were spending a lot of money on betting as well.

No, he wasn't a gambler. He'd have a bet, but no, he wasn't a gambler at all. He liked a game of darts and cards in the pub, but he was a boozer. He drank.

Did he have any other sort of hobbies or anything like, did he go to the football or anything?

Did he hell! It was the pint pot.

Whereabouts did he do his drinking?

All over. Where you could find him.

How would you try and get the money off him?

Well, I'd try and find him if I could.

Would you look for him in a pub?

Yes, 'course you would. You'd look all over. If you found him, you got something, if you didn't, you got nowt.[87]

A number of respondents gave similar descriptions of fathers whose interests were confined to drink and gambling, and oral testimony is confirmed by autobiographical accounts of Manchester and Salford during the 1920s and 1930s. Harry Watkins, who grew up in Hulme, declared that:

Excepting for Dad's years in the army, the only times he went outside Manchester were on charity outings from the beerhouse. And as far as I know he never went to a cinema or theatre. He did not possess a book and never read one, except perhaps the booklets which contain horse-racing information.[88]

Whereas women and young people turned increasingly to the cinema during the inter-war decades, many among the older generation of men proved deeply conservative in their choice of leisure. Although some historians have spoken of a transformation of leisure during the inter-war period,[89] the appeal of more modern leisure activities was to a significant extent age- and gender-specific. New dance halls and cinemas may have appealed to working-class youths, but they made less impression upon men like Mr Watkins' father.

What remains of the accusation that drink and gambling were among the principal causes of poverty? Certainly, viewed through the family economy, male spending on leisure at the expense of the housekeeping budget restricted wider improvements in working-class lifestyles. Rises in real wages over the course of the early twentieth century did not, therefore, automatically translate into a simple improvement in living standards. However, the principal causes of poverty between 1900 and 1939 were low and irregular wages, the life-cycle, sickness and unemployment, and many of the families of men who spent heavily on drink or gambling were already living below or close to the poverty line. In this sense, spending on leisure tended to exacerbate, rather than 'cause' poverty.

The role of poverty as a brake upon leisure activities is much easier to document. The 'traditional' working-class leisure activities – the pub, sport, gambling, cinema and the seaside holiday – were all regulated by financial constraints, and the denial of leisure was an important element of the burden of poverty. Yet within this framework, participation in leisure hinged upon competing notions of masculinity: some men saw themselves primarily as breadwinners, and chose to lead family-orientated lifestyles; others identified with the masculine spheres of pub vaults and sport, and placed their own desires before the needs of their families. Men with comparable incomes thus had widely different leisure patterns.

three

Women: Housekeeping, leisure and independence

Gender was central to the division of leisure in working-class districts. Some of the major spheres of popular leisure, especially sport, were overwhelmingly male-dominated, and in this sense, working-class men tended to enjoy a significantly higher standard of living than their wives. None the less, although the vast majority of women had less experience of leisure than their husbands, women did frequent cinemas, music halls and, less frequently, pubs. The general neglect of women's activities in studies of leisure has meant that women's lifestyles have been only partially explored by social historians. The principal surveys in this field have been at best marginally concerned with gender differences, and the tendency for feminist historians to focus upon women's role as household managers has meant that leisure activities have still been largely obscured.[1]

Household management was, of course, the main preoccupation of working-class women. Men were usually considered to have the right to expect a certain amount of money as spends, which could be freely devoted to beer, cigarettes and gambling.[2] In contrast, as Elizabeth Roberts has shown, women were expected to put the needs of their families before their own.[3] Indeed, in Salford's working-class neighbourhoods, self-sacrifice was the essential virtue of a 'good' mother, as Mrs MacLeod remarked: 'If you were a good mother you looked after your kids. You didn't bother about anything else. As long as your kids were all right.'[4] Freedom of movement for married women was severely restricted by responsibility for running the home, so women throughout working-class communities enjoyed fewer opportunities to socialize than men. Moreover, married women who went out to work to supplement their housekeeping budgets enjoyed control over the use of their own wages, but the burden of combining paid employment and housework meant that in terms of their ability to participate in leisure, they were often little better off than women who did not go out to work. For any woman with a young family, childcare was a constant burden and working-class mothers could find themselves with very little free time at all during the early years of marriage.

Some working-class couples socialized together, sharing nights at the cinema or in the pub. Many others, however, went out separately, and in these families, women usually had much less experience of leisure. 'Bad' husbands, who spent heavily on drink and gambling, were unlikely to spend many evenings out with their families. Significantly, however, even 'good' husbands, who spent only moderate amounts on leisure, could still spend much of their free time in the company of other men. 'Good' husbands were those who provided a steady income, and took only an acceptable portion of their wages for themselves. They could still enjoy a much fuller social life than their wives, and this testifies to the relatively low demands made upon men in working-class neighbourhoods.

Women's leisure was often therefore an independent sphere. Women met in pubs, and shared trips to the music hall or cinema. Once a year, pubs organized a day trip for women, often to the Cheshire countryside, and for some working-class housewives and mothers, this was the only day in the year when they could take a break from family duties. However, women's lifestyles, like those of their husbands, were subject to the impact of the poverty cycle and unemployment. Women's social lives were maintained within a framework of financial, domestic and moral constraints, and this chapter examines a number of women's activities in relation to these everyday restrictions. The discussion is mainly concerned with activities which took place outside the home and, as a result, less attention is paid to the fragments of leisure, in brief conversations with neighbours, for example, experienced by women during their daily routines.[5]

Time and money

In working-class families, responsibility for balancing the weekly budget and running the home usually lay entirely with the housewife. Whereas men had spends, which could be freely devoted to leisure, women had to take money for drink or entertainment out of their housekeeping budgets. They had no separate spends, and any money spent on going to the cinema, for example, had to be taken from the resources available for feeding, clothing and housing their families. In poor homes, women therefore faced the dilemma of whether to spend on themselves or their families. Women with low housekeeping budgets faced immense difficulties in making ends meet, and spent less on leisure as a result. As the Salford Mothers' Guild reported in 1933, women in local families often had more urgent priorities:

'Many of the mothers of Salford are suffering from under-nourishment, and I am afraid that many of them are starving themselves in the attempt to feed their children properly.'[6]

In interviews, the division of leisure according to gender is reflected in descriptions of women who appear to have had very little experience of any form of commercial entertainment:

> *Can you remember anything about what your parents did on a Saturday night?*
> *Mrs Ryan*: Well my father used to go and see his friends.
> *Mr Donaghy*: He used to go for a pint.
> *Mrs Ryan*: But my mother never did.
> *Mr Donaghy*: Mother never went out. Sometimes, she'd go to the pictures, but [she] very seldom went out.
> *Mrs Ryan*: Very rarely went out.[7]

A strong sense of the separate roles of women and men underpinned family relationships, and even children held firm views on 'a woman's place'. In 1908, youth workers in Manchester found that:

> ... the bigger lads, like the smaller, often ... affect to care little for their sisters, and indeed may regard them as creatures of an inferior species ... finding their proper destiny as household drudges when work in the mill or factory ends for the day.[8]

Forty years later, Stancliffe and Muray were struck by the prevalence of the same attitude in Ordsall. They were concerned that teenage girls in the district appeared to have few interests beyond the pictures and their housework:

> One wonders how many of them fall into line with the male view expressed by the boy who, when asked whether his sister went to any club, said: 'No, she's either out courting or in the back kitchen where she belongs!'[9]

These attitudes were embedded in working-class custom. In Manchester and Salford, for example, Friday night was widely known as 'bucket night'. Mrs O'Brien described Ordsall during the 1920s and 1930s:

> It was a crime if a girl went out on a Friday night.
> *Why was that?*
> .Well, you used to have to clean the flags [pavements]. What they call 'bucket night', training the young girls ... your hearth, they used to do that with a bluestone ... You were all allotted a job each on a Friday night.[10]

As a result, dance halls flourished on Mondays, Wednesdays and Saturdays, but not Fridays.[11] Walter Greenwood described 'bucket night' as he attempted to set the scene for *Love on the dole* in Hanky Park:

> ... the pavements have a distant resemblance to a patchwork quilt.
> Women, girls and children are to be seen kneeling on all fours in the
> streets, buckets by their sides, cloth and stone daubing it over the
> flags, then washing it into one even patch of colour.[12]

By the 1930s, Friday night was alternatively known as 'Amami night', after
a popular brand of shampoo. As Mr Oliver recalled, the appearance of a
woman on a Friday night or Sunday dinner-time could arouse resentment
among men drinking in Salford pubs:

> Women them days were nondescript people. Women were nothing.
> Friday nights, and Sundays, you never saw the women out, whereas
> now they all are, they're all throwing darts, it never happened. Friday
> night was Amami night, they called it. Do you know what that is?
> *No, I don't.*
> Amami was a famous shampoo. Well, they were supposed to stay in
> and wash their hair. And if a woman came in, you'd see everyone look,
> 'What's she doing out tonight?' No women were allowed, especially of
> a Sunday dinnertime, if they came in your company, a woman,
> 'What's she doing here?' 'Get her out of here!' That was the attitude,
> they didn't say it, but that was the attitude ...[13]

Just as the duties which fell to teenage girls on bucket night set them apart
from their brothers, women were expected to devote themselves to the
wifely duty of running the home, leaving their husbands free to go out.
The demarcation of time was clearly important in maintaining gender
differences in the standard of living: freedom of movement for lads and
men was secured through responsibilities and restrictions imposed upon
women and teenage girls.

For women, access to leisure was widely restricted by the lack of both
time and money. The autobiographies of working-class women who were
active in the socialist movement illustrate how women's social lives were
constrained by the weight of their household duties. Hannah Mitchell, who
was born in 1871, was active in the Independent Labour Party and the
women's suffrage movement in Manchester and the surrounding area at
the turn of the century. She pointed out with a bitterness based upon her
own experience that the burden of washing and cleaning, and the 'tyranny
of meals' left women who were housewives and mothers little time for
themselves, even if they did not go out to work.[14] For women like herself
who were politically active, time spent campaigning was a source of friction
within marriage, as husbands resented their wives for spending time away
from home. Alice Foley, who was born 20 years later, worked as a trade
union official in Bolton, but found that meetings held at the end of the
working day needed to be brief: 'Time was a main factor, for if talks
dragged on married women grew restless about possible irate husbands
awaiting their delayed evening meal.'[15] In this sense, for women in paid
employment, time after work was not 'free' time. The restrictions imposed

by domestic routines and their husbands' expectations denied women access to leisure as well as the ability to participate in trade union meetings.

Mrs MacLeod described the pressures upon the time of women who held full-time jobs while raising a family during the inter-war decades. Her own husband tipped up little of the money he earned, and she worked for 31 years in order to provide for her family. During the Second World War, after her husband joined the army, she began to go to the pub at weekends. With his army allotment, on top of her own earnings, her income was sufficient to allow a surplus for the first time. During the early years of her marriage, however, her social life was more restricted. She did attend the cinema, but even a night at 'the pictures' was hard to manage:

> A treat for me was a glass of beer and a cig. I used to go out for a couple of gills on a Friday night, that was during the war. Before that, it took you all your time to get out. The pictures was my treat. You couldn't afford it. You didn't bother. And more or less, you didn't have time. I used to take the children to my mother's [and then] go to work ... 8 o'clock you started, 6 o'clock you finished. Well by the time you collected your children, took them home, gave them their tea, washed them for bed, got your husband's tea, you had no time. I did my housework of a night. And you were working Saturday morning.[16]

Oral testimony suggests that the growth of commercialized leisure barely affected the weekly routines of some Salford women.[17] Few accounts fail to stress women's commitment to the welfare of their families.

Women with large families could be trapped at home by their responsibility for minding the children. When married couples went out together, they either had to take their younger children with them, or find someone who could manage the home in the mother's absence. This role often fell to the eldest daughter, as soon as she was old enough to assume the responsibility.[18] Occasionally, men were willing to look after the home during evenings when their wives went out, but life was more difficult for those women with less sympathetic husbands. Women with very young children could be effectively imprisoned in their own homes. In her survey of the lives of working-class wives published in 1939, Margery Spring Rice asserted that:

> When there are a lot of young children it is miraculous when any real leisure is procurable. Many women say they cannot leave the children in the evening; a woman in Blackburn says 'Never go to Market or Cinema. Sister used to come and look after the children and let me go out, but has now removed from the town'. She is 35, has had six children of whom the first one died, and is in extremely bad health ... Her house is very old, damp and dark, but she says she never goes out.[19]

As Mrs Mullen commented, for women confined to the home: 'Your entertainment was your children.'[20]

Women also tended to assume the role of carers within the family. In some instances, great sacrifices were made, as Mrs Edwards recalled:

> ... my two aunties, they never went out for years. They looked after my grandma, they wouldn't leave her at night, and they never went out at night till she was ninety-two, and I thought it was marvellous.[21]

Few examples are found of men who behaved in this fashion. More often, a contrast is drawn between the behaviour of mothers and fathers, as by Mrs Rankine:

> He liked his pint ... don't get me wrong, he wasn't a drinker. But he used to like a pint ... I think he was a bit selfish to be quite truthful.
> *What about your mother, did she go with him?*
> No, she never drank ... my mother looked after her mother and that's how it went.
> *Was there anything that your mother did in the evenings or the weekends?*
> No, she loved her home. Her life was her home ...
> *What about the cinema?*
> Now, that's one place we used to go. The Carlton on Cross Lane.[22]

As feminist historians have shown, the desire to be a good mother and an efficient household manager did tend to dominate women's own perceptions of their role within the family. However, there is also evidence that the denial of leisure was a source of intense frustration among women who had little choice other than to confine themselves to the home. Margery Spring Rice cited the case of a woman who declared:

> I believe myself that one of the biggest difficulties our mothers have is our husbands do not realise we ever need any leisure time. My life for many years consisted of being penned in a kitchen 9 feet square, every fourteen months a baby, as I had five babies in five years at first, until what with the struggle to live and no leisure I used to feel I was just a machine, until I had my first breakdown, and dark as it was and hard as it was it gave me the freedom and privilege of having an hour's fresh air. And so truly I know this is the lot of many a poor mother ... So many of our men think we should not go out until the children are grown up. We do not want to be neglecting the home but we do feel we like to have a little look around the shops, or if we go to the Clinic we can have just a few minutes ... It isn't the men are unkind. It is the old idea we should always be at home.

Although some women found regular opportunities for leisure:

> Such cases however are the exception. It is much more usual to read that in effect such leisure time as there is is spent in some sedentary occupation as a rest from the long hours of standing – and that it is spent entirely in mending. Mrs. E. of Forest Gate, East London, is 38

and has six children. She says firmly that she gets no leisure till the evening when the children are in bed and then 'I just sit still and say, at last a bit of peace and quietness'.

When women were asked to describe their 'leisure' activities, they often named sewing, knitting and mending as their most common pursuits. This led Spring Rice to comment:

Leisure is a comparative term. Anything which is slightly less arduous or gives a change of scene or occupation from the active hard work of the eight hours for which she has already been up is leisure.[23]

Moreover, whereas the shortage of pocket money sometimes left men with the problem of killing time, for women, the struggle to make ends meet left little time to become bored. In order to save money, clothes were continually refashioned and household items renovated, and any spare moment could be put to use.[24]

Drink and respectability

The predominance of men was the single most important factor that shaped the character of pub life. The sexual division of leisure was constantly reinforced as men sought escapism via the 'shortest way out of Manchester': through the door of the pub vault. Yet despite this depth of male privilege, attitudes towards drinking varied enormously among working-class women, and patterns of pub attendance among women were more complex than any simple contrast between male indulgence and female exclusion might suggest. The following examination of women's lifestyles and attitudes draws attention to the contrasting notions of feminine respectability which prevailed in the working-class districts of Salford and Manchester during the early twentieth century. Few women ever failed to lay claim to respectability: the category was a subjective one, which could be redefined to justify very diverse patterns of behaviour. Only a tiny minority of women rejected the moral code of respectability entirely. They are discussed in the conclusion to this section.

It is impossible to provide a quantitative assessment of pub attendance among working-class women in Manchester and Salford between 1900 and 1939. However, a series of surveys conducted elsewhere, summarized in Table 3.1, did attempt to measure the extent of drinking among women. All of the surveys confirmed that pubs were predominantly masculine spheres. However, they gave different estimates of the overall extent of drinking among women. Mass Observation suggested a figure of 16.0 per cent, based upon a sample of 7172 people drinking in a range of pubs in Bolton in 1938–39.[25] Rowntree's estimates for York suggested that the figure was significantly higher. His own study conducted during the late 1930s suggested that in pubs in the older part of the town, catering for the 'poorer' classes, the figure was 26.0 per cent.[26] Significantly, his estimates

Table 3.1 Pub attendance among men and women in York, London and Bolton, 1900–39

Survey date	Area	Men (%)	Women (%)	Public house type, or location
1900	York	63.8	36.2	Slum district
1900	York	69.9	30.1	Thoroughfare, poor district
1900	York	85.0	15.0	Border of working-class and residential districts
1933–34	London	76.1	23.9	Unknown (sample of eight)
1938–39	York	74.0	26.0	Older parts of town, poorer customers
1938–39	York	79.5	20.5	More respectable, better-off clientele
1938–39	York	74.2	25.8	Modern, town centre or new estates
1938–39	York	58.5	41.5	Hotels, rarely frequented by working classes
1938–39	Bolton	84.0	16.0	'Wide' range
1938–39	Bolton	78.7	21.3	Town centre
1938–39	Bolton	87.5	12.5	Main road

Source: Calculated from data provided by B.S. Rowntree, *Poverty: A study of town life* (London, 1902 ed.), pp. 315–26; H. Llewellyn Smith (ed.), *The new survey of London life and labour* (London, 1935) Vol. IX, pp. 253–4; B.S. Rowntree, *Poverty and progress: A second social survey of York* (London, 1941), pp. 351–3; Mass Observation, *The pub and the people* (London, 1987 ed.), pp. 38, 135.

for certain districts at the turn of the century were higher still. In two pubs in 'poor' and 'slum' districts, the proportion of female customers was 30.1 and 36.2 per cent respectively, although women were likely to stay in pubs for shorter periods than men.[27] It is certainly possible that if Mass Observation had focused upon similar pubs in their study of Bolton, their survey might have yielded markedly different results.

The various studies do not, therefore, allow direct comparisons to be drawn, and it would be dangerous to assume that drinking among women decreased between 1900 and 1939: the limited evidence available suggests that, if anything, the reverse was the case. Rowntree claimed in his second survey that the numbers of women who habitually frequented public houses were increasing, but the differences between the samples he used in 1900 and 1939 undermine any attempt to measure change over time.[28] Retrospective testimony occasionally indicates that women drank more frequently after 1918, but in the absence of quantifiable data it is difficult to provide a firm assessment.[29]

Oral evidence does, however, suggest that in Salford, women's drinking was often concentrated in the lounges and women's rooms of the street corner 'locals' in the poorer districts of the city. The pubs chosen for Rowntree's two surveys were likely to reflect this realm of women's leisure and, on this basis, it appears that the proportion of women in pubs in working-class areas was likely to vary between 20 and 40 per cent. As Mass Observation's study emphasized, men always outnumbered women in pubs, but Rowntree's research suggests that drinking among women may have been much more common in some working-class areas than in others, and this would match the weight of oral testimony, which reveals that attitudes towards drink among working-class women were extremely – perhaps surprisingly – diverse.

Oral evidence has to be used carefully. In interviews, it is commonly asserted that prior to 1939, all the men in Salford drank while all the women stayed at home. These sweeping judgements testify to the predominance of men in pubs, but closer questioning reveals that many women did drink. However, respondents whose mothers did drink often stress that women drank only modestly. They were expected to devote themselves and their resources to their families, and heavy drinking would clearly have undermined a woman's status as a good mother.

The barriers against women's drinking were reflected in the lay-out of pubs, which were divided into separate rooms, as Mr Pearson described:

> The men had the vault, the women used to go in the 'room'. Well, the room was a bit posher, a piano, a bit of singing, anybody [who] fancied getting up could give a song, I've done it myself many a time.
> *So in the room, you'd get men as well as women?*
> Oh aye, some'd take their wives out, take their sweethearts out if they were courting.
> *It was just the men in the vault, was it?*
> In the vault, aye, very rare you got a woman. You got an odd woman in that could play crib ... It wasn't nice, like. It wasn't thought of nice anyway, a woman being in the vault.[30]

Segregation within pubs was maintained by convention. Women risked men's disapproval, and the censure of other women, if they entered a vault. In some pubs, landlords actively enforced gender divisions. Mr Perry's father-in-law was the landlord of the Peeping Tom in Ordsall. Prior to 1914, his father-in-law refused to allow any women to drink in the bar parlour of the pub.[31] A few pubs even barred women altogether. Mick Burke, who grew up in Ancoats, sometimes drank in 'Harry's Bar' in Newton Street: 'There were no women allowed in the pub and all the characters used to collect in there.'[32]

Segregation was designed to enforce the double standard whereby men who drank themselves would not tolerate drinking among women. Robert Roberts' father drank heavily, yet 'strongly disapproved of beer-taking women'.[33] Some husbands displayed a violent hostility to their wives' presence in pubs. Mrs MacLeod, for example, described an incident which took place in Greengate, when she called in for a drink with two friends, one of whom left her washing in a pram outside the pub:

> ... we called in the Nodding Donkey for a gill. It was Christmas time and Aggie was on her way [to getting drunk] ... So we got three gills. Well we were sat round. All at once, Aggie's husband came, 'Come on, out'. [She was] in a right state ... so she went. Doris said, 'My husband, let him do that to me and I'd sort him out'. Well, next thing, her husband's face was over the partition ... 'What do you want'? She says. And he was like a weed. She was big enough to eat him. So he said, 'Come on'. 'Don't you dare order me out like that. I'll come when I'm ready'. He said, 'You'll come now'. And she came now ... So we got outside. She said, 'You've showed me up – you wheel that carriage home'. And she left him to wheel the washing home ... Next morning she came into work with a black eye.[34]

Some husbands effectively attempted to control the movements of their wives. In contrast, women generally allowed their husbands a much greater degree of freedom, even if approval was withdrawn in cases where men started to neglect their families.

Working-class mothers who wanted to drink in pubs faced the additional difficulty of finding someone to mind their children. Prior to the First World War, women sometimes overcame this problem by taking their children with them. Mrs Ormond was taken to the Britannia Inn in Ordsall as a child during the 1900s:

> We'd be sat there, we daren't move ... 'don't say anything. Don't talk'.
> *Would there be other children in the pub as well?*
> Oh yes. But you had to behave yourself. You didn't have babysitters in those days. Used to drag the kids out with you.[35]

She declared: 'Of course, children were allowed in in those days.' In fact, children were banned from pubs under the 1908 Children's Act. However, it appears that this legislation had only a limited impact prior to 1914, and during the First World War the restrictions were still widely flouted in Salford and Manchester. According to Theo Simpson's 1915 pamphlet *The underworld of Manchester in war time*:

> On Saturday, September 4th, I visited a number of houses in Regent Road, Salford, six houses in Market Street, and side streets adjoining, and three houses in Oldham Street, and they were packed out, and there was no chance to sit down. Of the people present quite as many were women as men, and in some cases women were in the majority, and quite young women ... In many of the licensed houses children were running in and out, the Children's Act is almost ignored. In one house with a long lobby there were three perambulators and babies, and a number of older children running in and out.[36]

Children rarely feature in accounts of pub life after 1918, which suggests that the Children's Act did eventually pose another obstacle for women who wanted to socialize in pubs. Ironically, though, the belief in beer as 'food', widely used by men to justify their spending, was shared by some working-class mothers. The 'feminine' bottled beers, especially Guinness and stout, were held to be good for the health. Mrs Holden's mother usually drank at home:

> ... they were a great believer that stout was very good for you, especially if you had children. Because it was good for your blood, and if you were nursing a child, then that made milk for your child. So, my mam, whenever she could, she'd have stout.[37]

The barriers against women drinking were very considerable. However, in the face of this entrenched double standard, women's behaviour and beliefs varied enormously, and it is possible to use oral evidence to reveal a range of distinct yet widely held attitudes towards drink among working-class women. Some were unlikely even to enter a pub. To have done so would have threatened their own self-images as good mothers, as in the case of Mrs Tanner's mother:

> She never went for a drink until the war and then she didn't drink, but you know how people socialised during the war. She'd go in on the odd occasion, but we used to think it was terrible, my sister and I. Women going in pubs, we used to think it was absolutely awful, and we used to say to my mum, 'You'll never go in a pub will you, mum?' And she used to say, 'No, will I heck! What makes you think that?'
> *Why was it that you thought it was so bad for women to go in?*
> Well it was, those days. I mean, they didn't drink, they didn't go out then like they do now. Well, women now they're liberated, aren't they? You used to go out with your husband, but they didn't go out on your own like they do now. They can walk into a pub now and no bother, full of confidence.[38]

Many women, like Mrs Tanner's mother, did not drink at all prior to the Second World War. Her reluctance to drink was shared by Mrs Emerson, who, during the early period of her marriage, would stand outside pubs while her husband went in for a drink:

> *Did you go to the pubs?*
> Me? No, I never went to the pubs.
> *Was it mostly the men that went?*
> It was the men that went to the pubs. The women didn't go out to sup like they are today. It was all the men. The women were all at home, minding the children. And they hadn't to call them their husbands in those days, if they were talking anywhere, they'd say, 'Oh, I'll have to go, my master'll be in in a minute.'
> *The master?*
> Always call them the master, yes.

Which were the most popular pubs round you?
King Billy, that was opposite, the Park Hotel, the Regent. As the
years went by I used to go in them. I didn't drink at all when we got
married, but my husband he used to like a drink, he wasn't a drunk-
ard, but he liked a drink. And I stood outside sometimes while he
went in for a glass of beer. And in the end he said, 'Why don't you
come in, you can have a lemonade or a shandy'. So I went in, but I've
never been a drinker.[39]

It is fairly common to find examples of this second arrangement,
whereby women only drank if they accompanied their husband to a pub.
Under this arrangement, men 'took their wives out', usually on a Saturday
night.[40] The husband would pay for his wife's drinks out of his pocket
money, whereas she provided his food out of her housekeeping. However,
this meant that the wife was dependent upon her husband's generosity,
and as Mass Observation noted, many men chose only to treat their wives
at the weekend, keeping the rest of their 'beer money' to spend on themselves during the week. Mass Observation also found that some couples
tended to split up after entering a pub together. The wife drank in the
'best' room, while her husband chose the taproom or vault. In such cases,
the husband still paid for his wife's drinks at the bar.[41] Of course, the
husband's control over his pocket money was enough to ensure that in the
majority of homes, men enjoyed a higher standard of leisure than women.
    Although many married women depended upon their husbands to buy
their drinks, oral testimony provides a third series of cases, in which
Salford women drank independently, if modestly. Mrs Cunliffe's mother
drank in the Britannia Inn in Ordsall:

What about your mother, did she ever go for a drink?
Well, she had a friend who used to say, 'Are you there, Margaret?
Well I've got a few coppers, I'll take you for a gill'. She said, 'Well I
can't pay for one back because I've not got the money'. She said, 'No, its
all right, I'll pay for it for you'. They used to have one and come out.[42]

Mrs Aitken was also keen to stress that her mother, who was a regular in
the King William IV, the 'King Billy', in Ordsall during the 1920s, spent
little of her housekeeping on drink:

She'd put tenpence away ... it was tuppence ha'penny a glass of mild.
Now she would never allow anybody to treat her because she couldn't
treat back. And Monday, Wednesday, Friday and Saturday, she had a
glass of mild on each of those nights ... she'd go in at 8 o'clock, and
she'd stay till 10. She'd had that one drink.[43]

She indulged herself once a year, on the women's outing organized by the
pub landlady. This pattern of modest consumption was also encountered by
Carl Chinn, in his Birmingham-based study of the lifestyles of working-
class women.[44]

Pub outing, King William IV, Ordsall, 1920s. The country scene backdrop
was draped over the pub door.

In contrast to cases where women drank regularly, others tended to
drink only on special occasions, such as birthdays or holidays.[45] Mick
Burke's mother, an Irish street hawker living in North Manchester,
celebrated Whit Week in some style, as a holiday in Ancoats when her
domestic chores could be momentarily forgotten:

> The only time she had off was Whit week, when the house would be
> stocked with food and we all had to help ourselves. She'd say, 'It's my
> week this week', and be on the booze all week, made up like the first
> lady in the land.[46]

Other women drank only at home. Mr Johnstone claimed that respectable
women never drank in pubs:

> ... a lot of people, especially women, did their drinking at home,
> 'cause women in pubs was very, very rare. Its only a fairly recent inno-
> vation that. No normal self-respecting woman would be seen dead in
> a pub.[47]

Yet this was just one conception of female respectability. It was not all-
embracing; women who did frequent pubs also took pride in their homes
and families and would likewise have considered themselves respectable,
according to their own understanding of the term.

Occasionally, women frequented pubs while their husbands stayed at
home, in a striking reversal of the standard relationship within marriage.

Mrs Anderson lived in the Hope Street district of Salford. Her mother drank regularly, although moderately:

> She used to go of a night, the pubs closed about ten o'clock then, so she would go about half past nine ... She always used to make the excuse that she couldn't sleep unless she had a drink. And sometimes when it got [to] the middle of the week and she'd be counting her money, how much she could afford to go, sometimes my dad'd say, 'Here's fourpence, go and get a drink', 'Or else I know she'll be tossing and turning all night' ... every night she used to go and just have a couple of drinks. Then she'd come in and start telling us the tale of what'd gone on in there.
> *Did your father not go to the pub with your mother?*
> Very, very rare my dad went out. Only if my brother used to come down of a weekend, or anybody related to the family used to come down and they used to say, 'Are you coming across'? He'd go across, but only weekends, never bothered during the week. Never complained about mam going. If she wanted to go, she went. But dad was always content to sit in, and with him a furnaceman, it was hard work, he used to always be asleep ... he'd watch us, he was smashing, he was a smashing dad. Where mother used to clout us, he used to sort of screen you.[48]

Although such cases are relatively rare, this extract is by no means unique.

The ambiguous role of drink in the lives of working-class women is perhaps best illustrated by revealing the range of points raised by one respondent. Mrs Daly, who was born in 1925, described the Clarence Inn in Greengate. She lived in Durham Street, and the pub on the corner provided a focal point for the street's communal life. As a child, she spent evenings sitting outside the pub talking with her friends. They were attracted by the noise and singing within, and at weekends men in work would occasionally fling a handful of coppers in the air as they departed, leaving the children to scramble for them. Mrs Daly was well known to the landlord and landlady, Mick and Chrissie Crew, who served her with bottles of mild from the 'outdoor' for her to take home to her parents. She was familiar with the interior arrangement of the pub, and described the practice whereby men in the vault bought drinks for their wives, who were sitting in the other rooms: '... the men used to send their wives over a drink. "This is for Mrs So-and-so", "This is for the wife".' Her own mother's determination not to be left at home by her father was quite explicit:

> *Did your mother mind if your father went to the pub, or if he spent a bit of money on drink?*
> She did. If she knew he was there, she'd be there. Because she used to say, 'What's good for the the goose is good for the gander'.

Mrs Daly associated heavy drinking by her parents with fierce domestic arguments which sometimes ended in violence. She portrayed her father as the victim in these domestic quarrels: '... my mother'd fling the first thing she got her hand [on] at my father ... he was taken to hospital with a split open head'.

A number of the women in neighbouring families also drank, and in a number of the families in Durham Street, gender roles were reversed:

> ... some chaps didn't drink ... their wives used to go out drinking ... but the husbands never minded, they used to look after the children, put them to bed, they'd sit on the step and they'd be talking. Some of them couldn't afford a paper, my brother brought one home or my father, they all used to borrow the paper.[49]

In a further reversal of Brian Harrison's accusation that in Victorian England working men were driven to drink by nagging wives,[50] Mrs Daly recalled a woman in Durham Street who turned to drink as a result of her husband's behaviour:

> ... a lady in our street used to get drunk on a Saturday, because her husband never came home. She used to say, 'He's gone to his brothel', so, she couldn't stand it, she used to get herself drunk and go to bed.

Whereas Mrs Daly's own mother once put her father in hospital, in this neighbouring family the woman was the victim of domestic violence:

> ... he used to come home of a Sunday night, he used to smack his wife around something awful ... they had the police there, and the ambulance, [to] take her away, she was stitched all over the place ... If they hadn't taken him I think he'd have killed his wife ... We used to have to take [their children] in ... my brother used to get [the son] and I used to get [the daughter] and let her sleep with me and my sisters ... every weekend there was trouble there.

Greengate was frequently regarded as the roughest area in Salford, and Durham Street was one of the poorest in the neighbourhood, yet even within a single street, there were sharp contrasts between the behaviour of neighbouring families. Moreover, although gender divisions were as firmly rooted in Greengate as anywhere else in Salford, this testimony suggests that the partial reversal of established customs did not threaten the basis of family relationships.

Whereas drinking among women was justifiable for at least sections of the working class, such tolerance was rarely extended by social observers. Evangelical commentators could be fierce in their condemnation. Simpson complained bitterly in 1915:

> On Monday, September 27th, I went to see the wife of a Marine, who is on one of our large Battle Ships. She lives in Hulme, and I am doing my best to keep her off the drink. When I saw her she said,

'Oh, you should have been in the street ten minutes ago and you would have seen a sight. Five women, who had just come out of [the] Public House, were very drunk and were shouting and singing, as good as a Pantomime.' This Public House is notorious for harbouring women drinkers, they can stay any length of time. I have been in it, and once took a friend. We found one room full of women.[51]

Simpson's indignation is seldom reproduced in oral testimony, yet retrospective descriptions of life in Salford and Manchester provide a series of examples of unwomanly women, notorious for their drinking, fighting or heavy gambling, who openly failed to conform to the styles of behaviour expected from women in working-class neighbourhoods. This confirms that leisure was central to the separate gender roles accorded to women and men. Gender roles were not flexible enough to permit serious violations, and women who flouted the established moral codes in working-class neighbourhoods were soon categorized. Only a tiny proportion of women are described as having behaved in this way. They were clearly unusual in that they adopted the leisure patterns usually associated with 'bad' husbands. Mrs Emerson described a woman who lived in Ordsall:

... a woman used to come round selling fish out of Lynton Street. She just had a box on three wheels and they used to call her Mary Ellen Hughes. And any time she sold a bit of fish she'd be in the King Billy buying beer with the money. She was a real character ...[52]

She was well known through the police columns of the *Salford City Reporter*, with over 40 convictions for drunkenness by the inter-war period. Similar 'characters' are recalled in other districts. In Greengate, the street fights described by Mrs Bennett sometimes involved a local woman known as 'Little Ginny':

Mrs Bennett: You'd see many fights down Greengate. I've been late for Sunday school many a time.
Mr Bennett: Oh aye. Saturday night there was always fights.
Mrs Bennett: And Sunday dinnertime. I've set out early for Sunday school, I've been late, I've been watching the fights down there. A woman called 'Little Ginny'. It was regular ... you'd watch her.
Who did she fight?
Mrs Bennett: She was that drunk, she'd fight anyone who came near her. The police'd go near her, and they'd leave her alone. And she was only little, wasn't she?[53]

One of the most notorious characters in Manchester and Salford was described by the novelist Anthony Burgess, who spent part of his childhood in the Golden Eagle, a pub in a tough district in Miles Platting, North Manchester, where his stepmother was landlady:

There was a fearsome character known as Nancy Dickybird, whose violent approach was signalled by runners – 'Nancy's coming'. The

Nancy Dickybird, once the terror of the Manchester Police, served 173 terms of imprisonment, now a modern miracle
AS SHE WAS.

Nancy Dickybird, once the terror of the Manchester Police, served 173 terms of imprisonment, now a modern miracle
AS SHE IS.

Nancy Dickybird, 'Terror of the Manchester police', then pride
of the Salvation Army.

main bar would clear on her entrance, and my stepmother would greet her with a truncheon and knuckledusters. There was an extensive armoury available for defence, including two army revolvers complete with ammunition. Nancy would sail into an ecstasy of foulness, urinate on the floor and then leave.[54]

Not surprisingly, Nancy 'Dickybird' is commonly recalled by people who lived in North Manchester during the 1920s. With 173 convictions for drunken and disorderly behaviour, her reputation as a terror of the Manchester police spread throughout the districts of Angel Meadow, Collyhurst, Miles Platting, Harpurhey and Moston. A series of community myths still surround her activities, and various explanations for her nickname are put forward.[55] Mary Bertenshaw, for example, recalled that as a child, she regularly saw Nancy arrested by two policemen when drunk. On one occasion, she followed her to Willert Street police station in Collyhurst, where she heard the 'beautiful singing' which led to the name 'Dickybird'. She later saw her singing in a Salvation Army band, when her appearance was the cause of some astonishment.[56] For the Salvation Army, of course, Nancy Dickybird was a prize convert. Her notoriety made her an impressive ambassador, and the Salvationists encouraged her on speaking tours of Manchester, and beyond, up to her death in 1931.[57]

Frank Doran described another woman living in Miles Platting who posed difficulties for the police:

> ... when drunk [she] could square up and fight like [a man]. She would stand at her front door, swearing at the neighbours, and even the police used to get a rough handling. They knew her, and when on patrol would dodge past if they could, especially if on their own or pick up a mate later on and run her in. A big ginger haired copper was the only one who could handle her alone. She would go inside for him, or let him take her in if he insisted that the Sergeant was due. The strange thing about her, when sober, she was spotlessly clean and so was her house.[58]

For her neighbours, this drunken behaviour was, without doubt, 'rough' in the extreme. Yet even so, she appears to have maintained a private air of respectability which survived her public reputation, and this provides further confirmation of the subjective nature of 'respectable' values.

It is easier to gather evidence concerning women who were renowned for public displays of drunkenness, or for fighting, than to obtain information about women who failed to perform the domestic tasks expected of women as household managers. Eleanor Rathbone commented upon the general difficulties encountered in attempting to obtain information concerning domestic budgets in households where either parent spent heavily on recreation. This was most difficult of all in homes where it was the woman's spending at stake:

> ... of drinking and betting habits among women we have even less record. Those who are conscious that 'they would have a good many gills to put down' naturally will not keep budgets, and perhaps for this reason the wife in most of the households studied seems decidedly the better of the two parties. Some of them spoke strongly of the harm done among their neighbours by drinking parties, in which the women take turns to fetch and pay for a gill of beer.[59]

Clearly, statistical surveys were unlikely to uncover the full extent of drinking and gambling among women, and retrospective sources likewise provide few examples of women whose spending on leisure undermined their families' living standards. In interviews, respondents continually stress that it was much more common for men to behave in this fashion, and there is no evidence to dispute this assertion.

Yet cases dealt with by welfare workers provide occasional glimpses of women who spent heavily on gambling. Charles Russell cited cases from the *Annual Report of the Manchester City Mission* in 1914:

> Children's clothes are pawned for money to bet with. One woman, with seven children, begged for money for the children's dinner; she got sixpence, and then 'put it on a horse'! In another case, while the

missionary was praying in a house, the buy came to the door with the sporting paper: the woman got up from her knees and bought the paper, though she had just said that she had nothing to buy food for the children. Her excuse was that she wanted to win.[60]

In my own sample of 60 oral history interviews, only one respondent provided a comparable case. Mr Pearson had an aunt in Hulme:

She was a real hard gambler, she had the gambling bug ... many a time she'd have the bookie's wife on her hands and knees praying that the favourite'd get beat, she'd got that much running on the favourite ... she was a real ardent gambler.
Did her husband ...
Her husband never gambled.
Did he mind about his wife gambling?
Yes, very much so, as a matter of fact, he got that way, he would give her no wages, he did all the shopping, he saw to all the paying of bills and all that.
Normally the women used to do that, didn't they?
That's right, but that's what he had to do to keep his house going, keep his children ... She had the bug, she was really bitten with it.[61]

In her study *A woman's place*, which draws upon a sample of 160 interviews, Elizabeth Roberts also found just one case of a family where gender roles were reversed in this fashion. In that instance, the wife drank, but her husband assumed control of the family budget.[62]

Cinemas

Whereas women were barred from the vaults of pubs, and women drinkers were subjected to 'moral' disapproval by some working-class men, there were no social barriers against women attending the cinema. In fact, as Charles Russell remarked in 1914, the cinema, which offered a cheap and comfortable night out, was especially attractive to women.[63] By the inter-war period, the cinema was by far the most popular form of commercial entertainment in Britain, and a series of surveys conducted during the 1930s showed that the majority of adults going to the 'pictures', in some towns as many as 75 per cent, were women.[64] The popularity of the cinema tended to overshadow the music hall and the cheap theatre which, in Manchester at the turn of the century, had also catered for predominantly female audiences. During the 1900s, it was estimated that 75 per cent of the gallery audiences at cheap theatres in working-class areas of Manchester were women. Groups of mill girls and older women, sometimes accompanied by their children, were prominent in the theatre crowds. Similarly, working-class women who attended the Ancoats music halls often took the younger members of their families, sometimes even infants, along with them as this was the only way that many young mothers could manage an evening out.[65]

Manchester and Salford were at the forefront of the development of the cinema industry, and picture-houses were built throughout the working-class districts of the two cities. By 1914, Manchester had 111 cinemas, with an additional 17 in Salford. This combined figure was considerably higher than any other provincial city.[66] The enormous popularity of the cinema, even in the poorer areas of the major cities, prompted many contemporary observers to assert that by the 1920s, everyone was going to 'the pictures'. The Conference on Christian Politics, Economics and Citizenship held in 1924, heard that:

> The cheapness and accessibility of the moving pictures make it poss-
> ible for even the poorest members of the community to indulge in
> this form of enjoyment ... Both the cinema and the wireless open
> a new world of interest and give rest and recreation to enormous
> numbers of people who live and work in adverse conditions ... The
> 'pictures' are too solidly established as the pastimes of millions to be
> dismissed in a passing reference. In drab streets ... in grim and sordid
> surroundings they give the light and colour for which all humanity –
> not only the educated portion of it – craves, and finds often only in
> the public house, and there only in part. They feed the imaginations
> of those who are too tired or too unskilled to read; they provide a seat
> for those who have no room at home to sit. The picture-house
> provides an escape from routine; it is somewhere to rest; somewhere
> to talk and make friends, and somewhere to make love for those who
> have no other place to do these things.[67]

Among the vast audiences at cinema shows was a new group of working-class cinema devotees, often women, who attended a number of films each week. In 1914, Charles Russell pointed out that:

> I know a highly respectable widow, the mother of grown-up sons, who
> makes a regular practice of going to a picture theatre, or sometimes
> a music-hall, five nights a week, and I understand there are many like
> her.[68]

Retrospective testimony reveals many such cases. Robert Roberts, for example, recalled that: '... we knew of parents who went there four times a week, regularly, for years'.[69]

However, the pastime was far from universal. As late as 1937–38, the Manchester University Settlement study of a district in Ancoats showed that 17 per cent of families never used the cinema, while a further 33 per cent attended less than once a week. The survey included a detailed analysis of cinema attendance (see Table 3.2). Just as poverty restricted women's ability to socialize in pubs, some women were simply too poor to go to the cinema. Unless they were 'treated' by their husbands, women who wanted to go to the cinema had to find the admission fee out of their

Table 3.2 Weekly use of the cinema in Ancoats, 1937–38

Households with:	Never go	Less than once	Average once	More than once	Total
Eldest child under 10	13	28	24	14	79
Eldest child under 14	6	5	24	4	39
Eldest child over 14	6	26	21	17	70
Three adults	1	9	8	5	23
No children under 20	28	38	26	14	106
Total	54	106	103	54	317
Percentage	17.0	33.4	32.5	17.0	99.9

Source: Manchester University Settlement, *Ancoats: A study of a clearance area. Report of a survey made in 1937–1938* (Manchester, 1945), p. 10.

housekeeping. Although cinema prices were low, this was sometimes impossible. Margery Spring Rice's survey of the lifestyles of working-class wives during 1939 included an account of:

A woman in Sheffield who is very poor, lives in a slum house, and has four children, is in extremely bad health. She says she must rest sometimes during the day – and she sometimes plays cards or ludo 'as that is cheaper than the pictures – I have no money for pictures'.

Other women in her survey had never been to the 'talkies':

Another Leeds woman says 'never get out except to shop; have never been to the talkies'. Mrs. T. of Derby ... 'sits down for feeding the baby, but takes her own meals standing. She is in very poor health, having had bad kidney trouble with the first and third babies ... Her surroundings are squalid, and there is no water or sink in the house ... She has never been to a talkie'.

Spring Rice was struck by how many women declared that they never went to the cinema. This was a common plight, although the women writing these accounts were clearly aware that they were missing out. Spring Rice concluded:

Naturally there are some who seem to get more out of life than others; but almost without exception it is those who have very few children, one, two, or at the most three, and who for this or some other reason are in much better financial circumstances, and who are able to get more real rest and change of scene and to employ their leisure in some way which suggests an interest in outside things. But there are not more than half a dozen who speak of politics, literary interests, study any sort of music. The cinema is very rarely mentioned, and many women say that they have never been to the pictures ... An overwhelming proportion say that they spend their 'leisure' in sewing and doing other household jobs, slightly different from the ordinary work of cooking and house-cleaning.[70]

Spring Rice's account confirms that the poverty cycle was important in determining whether married women had the resources necessary to participate in commercialized leisure activities. Walter Greenwood suggested in *Love on the dole* that trips to the cinema, a regular feature of the social lives of single working women, became 'luxuries' after marriage, and oral testimony provides similar accounts of the predicament of young working-class mothers. Ms Osgood's mother began to go to the pictures only once her children were old enough to go out to work, and could therefore contribute to the family income: '... when we started to leave school ... my mum used to sometimes come with us, because there was that little bit more coming in the house. She could afford then, to go out, and go to the cinema.' Similarly, in Mrs Daly's family, her older brothers had more spends than her mother:

> *Did you ever go to the pictures when you were young?*
> Not unless m'brother treated my mother and I.[71]

Yet the poverty cycle was not the sole cause of poverty in women's lives. The Manchester University Settlement study of Ancoats showed that the families in the district who did not use the cinema included households with no children aged under 20, as well as families with dependent young children.[72] Women whose husbands were unemployed or out of work through illness, or those with 'bad' husbands who provided little in the way of housekeeping, were likely to enjoy little access to commercial entertainment, alongside young mothers trapped by the poverty cycle.

When women with young children did manage to find money for the pictures, they often took their children with them, just as Manchester mothers had taken children and even infants to the music hall:

> *What about going to the pictures? Who would look after your children?*
> *Mrs MacLeod*: You took 'em with you.
> *Mrs Mullen*: Under your shawl.
> *Would you have to pay separately, if you had two or three children to take in?*
> *Mrs MacLeod*: Well you'd pay for one and smuggle the other two in. Pay for one, pay for yourself.
> *Mrs Mullen*: You'd get 'em in somehow.
> *Have you done that?*
> *Mrs MacLeod*: Oh I have.
> *Mrs Mullen*: I've done it.
> *Mrs MacLeod*: You had to do.
> *Was it a common thing for women to take their children with them like that?*
> *Mrs MacLeod*: Always with them, the children.
> *When you went to the cinema when you were married, would you generally go with your husband, or without him?*

Mrs MacLeod: If I went with my husband, he'd be missing in the pub next door if there was one.

Mrs Mullen: In those days, the working-class man didn't want pictures, or football mad, it was beer.

Mrs MacLeod: Just beer, yes.

Mrs Mullen: The average, I should say. I mean probably there was the exception.

Did your husband not have any interest in the pictures?

Mrs MacLeod: Did he heck! No. That was the only pleasure we had really, pictures?[73]

It is fairly common to find accounts of women who attended the cinema without their husbands. This was the case in Mrs Anderson's family. Her father was not interested in the cinema, unlike her mother:

> He couldn't care less about pictures. She loved the pictures. She used to go to the Alexandra on a Monday, and then on a Wednesday she'd go again because [the programme] changed. And then on a Thursday she'd go to the Carlton on Cross Lane ... She used to like the love tales, anything that made you cry.[74]

Her family lived opposite Robert Roberts' corner shop, and it is possible that her mother is one of the parents who went 'regularly, for years', to whom Roberts referred in *A ragged schooling*.[75]

In contrast, many other couples did attend 'the pictures', and the rise of the cinema in the early decades of the twentieth century certainly contributed to an overall increase in the proportion of married couples who spent at least some evenings together. Mrs Holden's parents went to the cinema once a week:

> We had one called the Gem and my mother and my dad used to go every Wednesday night ... it was only sixpence for the back rows and twopence for the front rows, they were all forms [benches] and if it was a good picture, they used to squeeze as many as they could on a form. They used to keep hutching 'em up until they [were] almost holding on to each other ... that was a real treat for them to go to the pictures. I used to stay in and mind the children.[76]

A number of other respondents described how they went regularly to the cinema with their husbands, and could recall other couples, including their parents, who attended the cinema together.[77] Couples could also take their children. The cinema, like the music hall, provided families with an opportunity to spend their leisure time together, whereas by the inter-war period, there are few references to children accompanying their parents to pubs.

There was a hierarchy of cinemas to match the hierarchies of pubs and dance halls in Manchester and Salford. The Salford 'super-cinema', the Carlton, ranked high above the older 'bug huts' and 'flea pits' of the city. The older cinemas were themselves ranked according to respectability, as in Hanky Park, where the Scala was rated above the Empress. Status divisions operated within as well as between cinemas. In Mrs Tanner's view, at the Salford Palace: 'I think it was threepence downstairs, that was for the impoverished people. If you could afford sixpence you went upstairs in the balcony.'[78] However, these divisions did not correspond with any fixed social divisions within the working class.[79] When husbands and wives did go to the pictures together, they frequently attended different cinemas from week to week, taking the best seats in the plushest cinemas when they could afford to do so. As Mrs Holton recalled, the most opulent cinemas in the two cities were the 'super-cinemas' in the centre of Manchester. She contrasted a trip to one of the grander Manchester cinemas with a visit to her local cinemas in Ordsall:

> That was *the* night out, going to the cinema. If I went to the pictures in town [Manchester], that was an event. Because we had so many local cinemas we didn't need to go farther afield, but we felt we'd gone out if we went to what we called posh, the Odeon and the Gaumont. I mean they were flea pits what we had [in Ordsall], the Borough and the Empire and the King's. [We] sat on wooden forms in the King's, Saturday afternoon, twopence for the cinema and a half penny for an ice cream egg. Saturday night if your parents were very rich that week, you could book [to go to the Manchester cinemas]. They'd book to sit at the back, that was the fourpennies or three-pennies seats, and if you were lucky they'd treat you to go at the front, and you could turn round and wave to your parents in the posh seats.[80]

Her comment that visits to Manchester were occasional events, while her parents could afford to book seats if they were 'very rich that week', suggests that families took their place in the hierarchy of cinemas according to how much spare money they had from one week to the next.

Cinema was immensely important as a source of entertainment and escapism, and for working-class women, films provided glimpses of romance and glamour in lives dulled by poverty and the burden of housework. In Robert Roberts' view, cinema shattered the 'stifling parochialism' of Edwardian Salford:

> Cinema in the early years of the century burst like a vision into the underman's existence and, rapidly displacing both concert and theatre, became both his chief source of enjoyment and one of the greatest factors in his cultural development. For us in the village the world suddenly expanded.

Previously, as Roberts' mother had pointed out, dance halls provided working-class women with their only brief contact with romance before they were clamped down by marriage and child rearing. By the time of the First World War, however: 'Many had a lifetime's affaire to come with the "silver screen".'[81] During the 1930s, Hollywood romances found eager audiences in the working-class districts of Salford and Manchester. As Mrs MacLeod remarked:

> ... if there was a good picture, you got to know about it, you made an effort to go and see it ... used to only be about thrippence ... It used to be a treat when there was a good picture. You used to break your bloody heart crying.[82]

Fortune-tellers and spiritualists

Women's networks extended beyond the channels of mutual aid through which women exchanged food and practical assistance to see each other through lean periods. In Manchester and Salford, spiritualism and fortune-telling also featured in women's networks, although this realm of women's experience has not been explored in histories of leisure. Spiritualists attracted women of all ages, although it was rarer for men to attend their meetings.[83] Mrs Phelan told how the pastime was a fixture in her mother's weekly routine:

> I'll tell you what the older people used to go to. Spiritual hall.
> *What were they?*
> ... seances and that ... when the Band of Hope went out of Dawson Street, Norman England ... used to have a spiritual hall there ... 'Course, as children we used to make fun of it, but my mother went regularly, every Monday. She used to go to one in Florin Street [in Hanky Park], over a coalyard.
> *Do you know how much your mother paid to do that?*
> I don't think it was above tuppence.
> *And how long would she be in there for?*
> Oh, a good hour. She buried her sister when she was young ... She got typhoid fever, she died. And my mother used to go hoping she'd see her. That's all she used to go for.
> *Did people have a lot of belief in it?*
> Oh yes.

Norman England is remembered as an immaculately dressed man whose spiritualist church prospered during the 1930s.[84]

However, as Mrs Phelan's account indicates, other spiritualists operated on a more makeshift basis. Richard Heaton likewise noted that 'In the bad times that kind of person flourished either in their own home or above coalyards or stables. The girls went straight from work to the seance, to be given false hopes for the future.'[85] Similarly, Robert Roberts described a man who 'ran seances as a sideline in one of the parloured houses nearby' in *A ragged schooling*.[86] Spiritualism and fortune-telling were among the most basic forms of penny capitalism during the inter-war period, requiring no capital outlay on the part of those who worked at home, and oral evidence provides numerous examples of Salford women who exploited the popular taste for fortune-telling.

Mrs Mullen worked at Frankenberg's rubber works in Greengate in the 1930s. She described a woman, popular among her workmates, who read fortunes from cards in her room in the Greengate Dwellings, a nearby tenement.[87] Mrs MacLeod also worked at Frankenberg's, but unlike Mrs Mullen, she lived in Greengate and knew the area intimately. Her account of the same fortune-teller was revealing:

> She got false teeth ... and she was in Taylor's the grocers, and she said, 'Do you like my teeth, Mr Taylor?' 'Oh', he said, 'They are nice, Emma'. She said, 'I've got it off them bloody fools from Frankenberg's, telling 'em their fortune'. She used to charge a tanner.[88]

On one occasion, Mrs MacLeod visited 'Madam Rosa', another well-known Greengate fortune-teller, but their meeting caused some embarrassment:

> *Mrs MacLeod*: Madam Rosa used to be at the bottom of Greengate. You know what her name was? Mary Davies. Yes, it was Mary Davies. I went to her once, that was fortune-telling. They were all at it in Frankenberg's, 'She's very good'. I went to her, I said, 'You're Mary Davies, aren't you?' She said, 'Annie, don't tell anybody, will you?' I said, 'No'. So I said, 'I didn't know you did this'. So she said, 'Yes'. She was like a gypsy, and she was off a proper good family, her.
> *Mrs Mullen*: She used to make the money, though.
> *Mrs MacLeod*: She was good an' all, wasn't she?
> *Mrs Mullen*: She used to do your cards or your palm.[89]

Although retrospective accounts are laced with scepticism, a number of respondents still recalled predictions which proved to be accurate, and attitudes towards both fortune-tellers and spiritualists were, and are, ambivalent. Mrs Cooper visited a number of fortune-tellers during the early years of her marriage: 'I had no children. I was married, but [had] no children. [She said]: "You will have one boy and no more". I had four on a run, and then I had another one after ...'. A second prediction was more accurate: '... "you shall have eight children". I didn't ever want any kids at all. By God, I did.'[90]

Mrs MacLeod described a visit to a spiritualist hall in Salford, which she attended with a group of her workmates from Frankenberg's:

> *Mrs MacLeod*: May wouldn't believe us when we told her ... I said to her, 'You've been singing and you've been talking foreign languages'. She said, 'Don't be so daft'. I said, 'You have, you've been off, under'. She still wouldn't believe us.
> *Mrs Mullen*: Probably paid her to do it.
> *Mrs MacLeod*: No, I don't think so, she was with us.
> *Mrs Mullen*: I never believed in it.[91]

Attitudes varied greatly, even within households. Mrs Phelan recalled that her mother braved her father's weekly ridicule when making visits to a spiritualist, but it is clear from her account that for her mother, the trip was a valued form of recreation.[92]

In 1906, James Haslam published a series of articles in the *Manchester City News* describing spiritualist activities in the city. One of his most scathing accounts featured meetings conducted by backstreet 'table-rappers' where questions to the 'spirits' were answered by the rapping of table legs against floors, usually providing the responses which the audience were eager to hear.[93] Haslam's account closely matches a scene in *Love on the dole*, in which Walter Greenwood depicted a woman who held spiritualist circles and fortune-telling sessions in a house in Hanky Park. Greenwood's own cynicism is not disguised and the scene in the novel is highly comical. Yet the attitudes attributed to the novel's principal female characters range from credulity to contempt, with a middle line combining scepticism with the pragmatic view that there is enjoyment to be had. Spiritualists and fortune-tellers provided entertainment and escapism for women, and for those who attended as sceptics, they were, as Greenwood suggested, 'just a bit of fun'.[94] As meeting places for working-class women, they were alternatives to the masculine republics of pub vaults, gambling schools and billiard halls.

Although it is clear that working-class women suffered greater restrictions than their husbands – in terms of both time and money – leisure was by no means an exclusively masculine domain. Despite the stifling effects of poverty, many women did attend cinemas and pubs, and patterns of female behaviour were perhaps surprisingly diverse. This is best illustrated in an examination of attitudes towards drink, which reveals a wide range of feminine notions of respectability. The unequal distribution of leisure was most apparent among married couples. Prior to marriage, young women enjoyed much greater freedom and financial independence, and for a spell in their late teens, they were relatively privileged as consumers of leisure. Leisure among young, single workers forms the theme of Chapter 4.

four

Young workers: Parents, police and freedom

In Britain, the emergence of a distinctive 'youth culture' has commonly been seen as a feature of society since the Second World War. The social history of leisure has produced relatively few challenges to this assertion: generational differences, like gender divisions, have rarely been examined in any depth. Thus, as David Fowler has remarked, the 'teenager', with freedom to spend on leisure and clothes, is widely regarded as a product of the post-war 'age of affluence'.[1] By the 1980s, however, historians found this periodization increasingly difficult to accept, and recent work suggests that that elements of a 'teenage' way of life can be traced back well beyond 1939.[2] In Manchester and Salford, generational leisure patterns were well established in working-class districts at the turn of the century, and this chapter examines the independence of young workers in the spheres of income and leisure.

As Rowntree recognized, the period between starting work and getting married was one of the most prosperous stages of the life-cycle for working-class people. These years represented a brief phase of relative affluence, as young people were usually earning, but were not burdened with the costs of running a home. Young workers expected to have a certain amount of disposable income, and this was particularly important for women, who, once married, no longer had money which could be regarded as 'spends'. As a consequence of this financial independence, leisure was widely associated with youth throughout the early decades of the twentieth century. Prior to 1914, working lads and girls formed a sizeable proportion of music hall audiences, and in the expansion of the world of commercial entertainment after the First World War, young people figured prominently in the development of the dance hall and cinema industries.

Manchester offers a set of unusually rich sources for the study of leisure among working-class youths. During the decade prior to 1914, Charles Russell published a series of accounts of the lifestyles and attitudes of young males in the city, including the 1905 study *Manchester boys*. During the 1930s, a number of students and researchers at Manchester University conducted investigations into the leisure activities of local working-class youths. This chapter draws upon studies of adolescents and the cinema by A. Fielder, leisure among girl wage-earners by Joan Harley, and leisure among young workers in Hulme by H.E.O. James and F.T. Moore.[3] These surveys offer a useful statistical record of the importance of commercial entertainment, especially the cinema and dance hall. Used in conjunction with oral testimony, they provide a basis for a detailed examination of leisure among young workers.

The Manchester studies also draw attention to the range of street-based customs which were equally important in the social lives of young people. Informal activities, such as taking part in the Sunday evening 'monkey parades', accounted for at least half of the leisure time of young workers, although these communal pastimes also tended to bring youths into conflict with the police. The attempted regulation of leisure by the police, and the additional constraints imposed by family discipline, provide a broad context for the following discussion. Moreover, although youth was the period in which gender differences in terms of spending power and independence were least pronounced, sexual inequalities are still apparent in any examination of youth culture.

Family economy and family relationships

Although young workers expected a degree of financial independence, they still played an important role within the household economy. Moreover, it is clear that in the majority of families, rules governing the behaviour of young people were laid down by their parents, and this confirms that young workers were not free simply to spend their leisure time, or their wages, as they chose. They gained a measure of freedom through going out to work, but while living at home, they were still bound by the financial and moral codes of working-class family life.

Traditionally, children living at home handed their wages over to their mothers, receiving a proportion as spends in return. In the 1930s, as Walter Greenwood recalled, this arrangement was maintained in many working-class families in Salford:

> Although the old custom was slowly dying there were still many young men and women who 'tipped up the wages' to their parents and received 'spends' in exchange, plus their food, clothing and shelter.[4]

Surveys of working-class expenditure during the period before 1939 do not provide the basis for a statistical assessment of the levels of disposable income enjoyed by young people prior to marriage. A number of surveys confirmed that young people living with their parents usually kept back a portion of their income for themselves, but failed to reveal how much money was retained as spends.[5] In Manchester, the University Settlement's survey of Ancoats in the late 1930s asserted that young people tended to enjoy higher standards of dress and leisure than their parents, especially their mothers. In Ancoats, wage-earning sons and daughters did not usually contribute the whole of their earnings to the household exchequer. Instead, many chose to assert their financial independence and thus mirror the behaviour of fathers in many households. Of the surveys concerning the leisure activities of young people in Manchester, only Joan Harley's study contained information concerning levels of disposable income. She found that among a group of 108 girls aged between $14\frac{1}{2}$ and 19, drawn from predominantly (though not exclusively) working-class areas, the level of weekly spends ranged from 6*d*. to 6*s*. 6*d*. On average, they had spends of around 2*s*. 3*d*. per week.[6]

The most useful of the poverty surveys is Rowntree's *Poverty and progress*, researched in York during 1936. He provided details of a number of individual family budgets, and his evidence showed that even in the 31 per cent of working-class families described as living in poverty, young people tended to keep much more money as spends than their parents. In such families, levels of spends among children varied enormously, from a shilling or less, to occasional figures of 10*s*. or above. The higher figures were often found in cases where there were a number of wage-earning children in one family. Much higher disposable incomes were found in some of the working-class families living comfortably above the poverty line. In some such families, young people in their twenties, who were still living at home, could claim a pound or more as spends. In this latter group, consisting of older children in relatively prosperous working-class families, disposable incomes could be way above those available to the majority of young people from working-class families. Rowntree's case studies provide a series of glimpses of household budgeting arrangements, but it is difficult to draw a precise assessment of levels of spends from his somewhat fragmentary evidence.[7]

Although oral evidence does not provide an alternative fund of statistical data, interviews reveal two structural factors which were important in determining levels of disposable income among the young and single: age and gender. Young workers usually handed over their entire wage packets to their mothers when they first started work at 14.[8] They became more independent financially in their late teens, when they began to keep a higher proportion of their wages for themselves. They still took their meals at home, but were now responsible for buying their own clothes, so their disposable incomes were not devoted entirely to leisure. Older children usually decided for themselves how much money to hand over to their mothers, although it appears that young men tended to keep more for themselves than their sisters. Perhaps not surprisingly, oral testimony is often most detailed when respondents describe the arrangements they held with their mothers upon starting work, when they were expected to hand over their wages intact. Some respondents were more vague when asked about the higher levels of spends they retained in their late teens, preferring instead to emphasize their contribution to the family resources.

Mr Prescott described how many Salford parents accompanied their children when they went to try to secure their first job:

> When I started work, it was for seven and six ... on Blackfriars Road, making garments ... my mam took me, and [the man] said, 'Start this afternoon'.
> *What would you do with your wages when you were earning?*
> You used to give them all your mother.
> *Did you not keep any back?*
> No, because they knew what you were getting, because they took you for the job then, if you understand what I mean. So you couldn't say, 'I'm getting so-much', because they knew.[9]

Shared ties of neighbourhood and occupation appear to have led to the adoption of standard rates of spends among girls when they first started work. Mrs Jackman and Mrs Henderson were both born in Salford in 1895, and held their first jobs in Haworth's mill in Ordsall. They each started work on wages of 2s. 6d. per week in the 1900s, and they described an identical arrangement, whereby they handed their wages over to their mothers, receiving 3d. back as spends.[10] Clearly, it is possible that in areas like Ordsall, where large numbers of local people worked in the same mills and factories, and rates of pay were common knowledge, arrangements over young people's wages were customary: it appears that for girls starting work at Haworth's during the 1900s, 3d. for spends was the 'going rate'. Significantly, Walter Greenwood suggested that custom was equally important to young men who were unemployed in the 1920s. They would expect 6d. or 1s. as spends.[11]

Older children who were in work were more likely to assert themselves, taking their spends out of their wages before handing the rest over, and keeping a higher proportion for themselves. Mr Saunders explained how household arrangements changed as young workers reached their late teens:

> I can tell you my first job. I was fourteen years of age, I left school in 1924, and I went working for the British Petroleum, that was right at the corner of Trafford Park ... I was a nipper on there, and my wages were seven and six a week ... when you got your wages on a Friday night ... I'd give it my mother ... She'd take five shillings out and give me half a crown.
> *What about when you got a bit older, once you'd been working a couple of years?*

> Well you got a bit wider, didn't you? You started opening your wage
> packet and giving your mother what you thought was right and keep-
> ing the rest yourself ... at that time you could have been earning
> fifteen shillings a week, or maybe seventeen and six, you'd give your
> mother ten shillings. That's how you worked it.[12]

Young men in their late teens began to adopt the pattern of behaviour
commonly found among married men, deciding for themselves how much
of their wages to contribute to the home, and how much to keep for their
own use. As Mr Saunders hinted, as much as 40 per cent of the weekly
wage could be taken as spends. The position of mill girls also improved
considerably before they reached 20. As a former Ancoats mill worker
pointed out in 1904, most had the resources to enjoy themselves, attending
music hall performances, for example, more regularly than they could after
marriage.[13]

Although young women in their late teens tended to have less in the
way of spends than their brothers, they still became more independent
financially as they got older.[14] This usually meant keeping a higher portion
of their wages as spends, but at the same time they became responsible for
buying all their own clothes and paying their own fares to work, so their
disposable incomes were not spent on leisure alone. Moreover, many young
people retained a strong awareness of the importance of their contributions to the family economy, as well as a desire for independence. Mrs
Gilmour was born in the Adelphi in 1916:

> I got six shillings [a week] with the sewing factory ... and then from
> there, I went for twelve shillings a week to [a manufacturing chem-
> ist's], and then we got bonuses as well. So if we were lucky we came
> out with about eighteen shillings, twenty four shillings a very good
> week.
> *Can you remember what the arrangement was with your mother?*
> Yes, I used to get eight shillings a week, and I used to have to buy all
> my own clothes, pay for my own holidays, and I gave my mother the
> rest ... I had the eight shillings and she had all the extras, or any
> overtime. And if I went on my holidays, she always got my week's
> wages. I'd saved up enough money so that she wouldn't be short of a
> week's wages.[15]

Like their parents, young workers were still vulnerable to poverty. Jack
Lanigan, who was born in Salford in 1890, suffered bouts of unemployment
during the 1900s, while living in his step-sister's home. He had little money
for food, let alone leisure: 'I went to my young lady's home every evening
because there I could have a cup of tea and something to eat, which I did
not have with my step-sister, being too ashamed to eat from her table.' Not
surprisingly, many of the descriptions of leisure in his autobiography are
laced with references to poverty.[16] Even among youths, the world of
commercialized entertainment was restricted to those with sufficient funds.

Miss Johnson started work at a Manchester printing works for 5s. a week in 1913, a year or so after her father had died:

> *What did you do with the five shillings?*
> Turned it up, and got coppers [laughs].
> *Can you remember what your mother let you have back as spends?*
> Oh very little, we only had coppers. She was good, mind you, she had to work really hard to bring us up, she had everything to pay.
> *Did you take your whole wage packet home to your mother?*
> Oh yes.
> *You wouldn't take your spends out before?*
> No, I took nothing out. She used to give me so much ... she was really old-fashioned. And she expected your wage packet untouched. Then she'd give you spends out of it.
> *Did your sister turn her wage packet over as well?*
> Supposed to do, yes. She got married when she was twenty-three, and she didn't turn it up, she was saving up to get married so she didn't pay much at home.
> *Was she spending a lot on herself as well?*
> Oh no, she was saving up to get married. And she clothed herself out of what she got, bar big things like coats, my mother got those, but smaller things y'had to buy yourself.[17]

Mrs Sugden's father tipped up little of the money he earned to his wife, leaving her to bring up their five children.[18] Mrs Sugden was the second eldest child, and when she started work as a roving tenter at Haworth's mill in Ordsall, she was under unusually heavy pressure to contribute to the home:

> *How much wages did you get when you started off?*
> The first week's wages was seven and six. And out of that I had to give the lady that was teaching me the job half a crown.
> *So did you tip your wages up?*
> Well you had to do, didn't you?
> *What did your mother let you have back for your spends?*
> A shilling.
> *Was that a regular amount when you were working?*
> Yes.
> *Did your mother have anyone else bringing any money in at all?*
> No, only me and my brother. And my brother went in the army. There was only my wages, and her own, what she earned for cleaning for people.[19]

In families where the father was a heavy drinker or gambler, it was not uncommon for teenage children to become involved in disputes over money, even though their mothers usually bore the brunt of family rows. Mr Brookman's father was a violent man. They both worked for the

Broughton Copper Company, based in the Adelphi, although the family lived in Lower Broughton:

> He actually hit me once in work and knocked me out. And every time I got my money, those days, I think I got about five shillings, he even actually tried to come and get that off me, so that he could go boozing. Luckily for me, there were two blokes there that knew my mother, and they said they'd protect me every weekend, and make sure he didn't get the money.[20]

Young people could be heavily affected by friction between their parents, even if, in money terms, they were relatively well-off within the family. Interviews provide further examples of families where fathers, seeking money for drink or gambling, stole from their children or even pawned their children's best clothes.[21]

Accounts of parental violence are by no means rare. Despite contemporary fears surrounding the alleged collapse of parental responsibility in working-class families, young people in Salford, especially girls, were often subjected to a strict code of behaviour by their parents.[22] Rules commonly governed three areas: the times that young people came in at night, the places they went and, among girls, the use of make-up. In some cases, young people did defy these parental strictures, but breaches of parental authority could be met with violence, even in the cases of children who were about to be married. Mrs Sugden described her family life in Ordsall during the 1930s:

> *What about Peel Park, would you ever bother with going up there?*
> We used to go walks to Peel Park, especially at night. And we've had to chase all the way home because it's been getting on for nine o'clock, when we've come out ... and then I've got a good hiding for being out there, turned nine o'clock when I got in. My father was very strict on time.
> *What about lads compared to girls, was there any difference in the time you had to be in?*
> No, the lads, always in, just the same, but girls was worse. If I stayed out late one night, you'd got to stay in for a week or a fortnight, so I had to run home. I used to go there every night, I'll be honest, ladding it. Meeting lads in the park.

On the eve of her marriage, her parents, especially her father, were just as strict:

> I'd get a good hiding if I was in late ... very strict, my parents.
> *Was that one of your parents, or both?*
> Both of 'em, particularly over timing, you couldn't stay out late. In fact, a week before I got married, I got dragged round the house [by] my hair, by my father, 'cause I was in late, a fortnight before I got married. And I was twenty then.

Do you know where you'd been?
I'd been to the pictures, and in town.[23]

Mrs Cooper's father hit her when she arrived home late after a trip to the Blackpool Illuminations:

> I came in at half past twelve. But the coach had come in late. And my [father] broke my nose and blacked my eye. And I left home. I went to my husband's mother, and we got married at the Christmas ... I was married at under eighteen.[24]

More research needs to be done before historians can speak with any real authority about the extent of domestic violence during this period, yet my own sample produced a number of similar examples, so extracts cited here are far from unusual.

Dance halls

The growth in popularity of the dance hall has been seen as a symbol of a new freedom among working-class youths during the 1920s.[25] However, even in the 'roaring twenties', dance enthusiasts, especially girls, were still subject to parental discipline. The two most popular halls in Salford were the Empress, in Pendleton, and Dyson's, known locally as 'The Jig', a 'low-class' dancing room situated in Robert Roberts' village in the centre of Salford. Mrs Sugden attended the Empress:

> I was never allowed to go dancing. My father used to say they were no good, [people] that went dancing.
> *Did you ever go without telling your father what you were doing?*
> I'll tell you what I have done, I've thrown my shoes over the yard wall, and my mate's took 'em round to her house, to get ready, to go to the Empress in Pendleton, to learn dancing at Saturday afternoon. Till my dad caught her picking the shoes up in the entry. Coming out of the pub, he saw her [with] my shoes in her hand. He said, 'What're you doing with them'? She said, 'I'm waiting for your Ada ... we're going to learn dancing at the Empress'. My dad says, 'She's going to learn nothing ...'. He took 'em off her, I wasn't allowed out that week.[26]

This prejudice was shared by Mrs Cooper's father: 'One day I came home late, and my dance shoes were on the back of the fire. Went on the fire, no arguing. "You'll get T.B., dancing the way you do".'[27]

Robert Roberts avoided Dyson's, which he considered 'low', and instead attended the Empress during the 1920s. Here, he claimed, the sons and daughters of the skilled and the unskilled danced together for the first time. For Roberts, this was part of the break-up of old social barriers within the working class. However, oral testimony reveals that parents from a variety of working-class backgrounds still attempted to prevent their children going 'jigging' during the 1920s and 1930s. Some, like Mrs Sugden, were the children of skilled workers. Others, however, were from the families of labourers. Mrs Fletcher's father worked as a timber carrier on the Salford docks. He attended Salford Central Mission, and would not allow his children to go to the pictures, apart from Sunday School cinema shows. He also prohibited dancing:

> *You said that your dad didn't like you going dancing?*
> Oh no, thought it was terrible.
> *Why?*
> I don't know. We daren't go. I did used to go on a Saturday afternoon and it took all my spends. I used to go to a place called the Empress in Pendleton and it used to be a shilling to go in. Well I only got a shilling spends.
> *How old were you then?*
> Fifteen or sixteen ... I daren't tell my father I went.
> *What did you tell your father?*
> Oh, we'd gone out shopping, or we'd gone looking at the shops ... once or twice I went to a place called Dyson's in Liverpool Street. My father would have killed me if he'd have known. It was a right dive ...[28]

Dyson's stood well below the Empress in the social hierarchy of Salford dance halls. Each hall had its own rating: there were shabbier halls than Dyson's in Salford, but for the most glamorous halls, Salford youths made the short trip to Manchester city centre, as Mr Rowlings recalled. In Salford:

> ... there was one called the Broadway, and it was only a large house, with a wall in between knocked down, and it used to be murder in there, they'd be packed, sweating cobs ... most of them were just a three-piece band, a piano, drums and clarinet ... you had to go up town [Manchester] for anything on the really decent scale, and then we used to go t' Ritz.[29]

Miss Osgood avoided the local Salford dance halls like the Empress. During the Second World War, she travelled further afield, to Manchester, Monton and Sale: '... that was the ultimate in elite, the Sale Lido. Oh yes, the Jew boys used to go there, all the lads with money ... I was a bit snobbish, [the local] dance halls were a bit low-class in my estimation'.[30]

The 'dance train' is perhaps the most poignant symbol of the relative privilege of young workers within working-class families. Whereas parents, particularly mothers, often went without holidays, living out their lives within the confines of Manchester and Salford, the dance train carried the young and single to Blackpool, to Saturday night dances at the Tower ballroom. Mr Saunders went on these trips around 1930:

> The dance train. Every Saturday night, half a crown return. You'd go roundabout six o'clock in the evening, all young, and fancying yourself

and all that ... At Blackpool, you'd have your shilling to go [into the ballroom] and you'd pick a bird up. And it was crowded that train, every Saturday night ... you'd come home at night, girls on it, you'd be pulling the bulbs out of the socket ... all that patter ... In darkness, and you've got a bird there and all this. And back in Salford between two and three Sunday morning.[31]

In some contrast to the cinema, dancing provided an opportunity for working-class youths to develop skills of their own. Accomplished dancers were highly respected, and could gain considerable local reputations, so it is perhaps unsurprising that many young people devoted a good deal of their leisure time to the hobby. Both sexes were drawn to dance halls by the associations between dancing, courtship and fashion. Moreover, oral testimony suggests that like the cinema, dancing, especially in the more glamorous commercial halls, provided an important means of escapism. Mrs Statham and her husband were keen dancers during their courtship. She told how: 'I was in my heaven going to a dance'. For her, the dance halls in Manchester city centre were a world apart from the cramped terraces of Salford, but for any young woman with the obligatory long dress, social distinctions counted for little inside the halls.[32]

Of course, often young people attended dances in the hope of 'picking-up' a partner of the opposite sex, as Mr Rowlings confirmed:

Who did you go to dances with?
Well you'd go in gangs hoping to pick somebody up when you were there. That was the normal procedure, you might go out with your mates and finish up taking a girl home from the dance hall ...[33]

Oral testimony suggests that it was conventional for lads to ask girls to dance, and with much emphasis placed upon dancing prowess, those girls who were good dancers could expect to be asked up most frequently. Girls did not usually approach lads, although one dance per night, introduced as a 'ladies' excuse-me', provided a brief opportunity for girls to take the initiative.[34] Girls who were not approached by lads danced with each other. Mrs Gilmour explained the difference between Devonshire Street ballroom in Cheetham Hill, Manchester, which she only visited once, and the Ritz in Manchester city centre:

It wasn't the same thing, because I went [to Devonshire Street] with a friend and we were sat there and a boy came up, you used to say, 'Could I have this dance?' They'd ask you. But this boy [just whistled.] And I wouldn't. And you weren't supposed to refuse anybody ... it was bad if you refused to dance with anybody. And I wouldn't get up. [I said:] 'Do you mean me? I'm no dog'. Anyway I didn't dance with him ... But that's the type of thing you would get in that type of place. They weren't all like that, but you did get that element ...[35]

Showing off your first pair of silk stockings, Ordsall, 1920s.

As this account suggests, the refusal of an invitation to dance was considered bad behaviour.

The young men who attended dance halls sometimes had more than dancing or courtship in mind. During the 1920s and 1930s, the halls were also occasionally the scene of confrontations between rival street gangs. Mr Wilkinson, who served in the Salford police throughout the inter-war period, recalled gang fights which took place at the Empress:

> In Church Street, Pendleton, that's where Hanky Park was, there used to be the Empress and many, many times we had a gang going and breaking up the parties, the dancing girls and the dancing fellers. *Where were they from, the people that were causing the trouble?* Usually come from Swinton, and get fighting down here, or vice versa, we'd have somebody going up from Salford, in a clique, and finding out their dance halls up there ... *Would the police have to go into the dance hall to break it up?* Yes, I've done that. We had a lad named Chandler who was a bit handy, and the majority of times when anything'd happened, you'd

find that Johnny'd been in there. Having a punch-up.
Where was he from?
He was from Hanky Park. But he was knocking about with a girl from
Swinton, so occasionally he'd go up there. Or vice versa, we'd have
somebody from Swinton coming down into [the] Salford area.
Did he have a gang from Hanky Park?
Oh yes. Like you got a gang from Swinton.[36]

Mr Lomas described two incidents which took place during the 1930s at the
Devonshire Street ballroom in Cheetham Hill, which was one of the closest
halls for residents of the Salford districts of Greengate and the Adelphi:

> There were rival gangs, and I remember one instance, I went to
> Devonshire Street ballroom, me and a friend of mine from the
> [Adelphi Lads] Club, and there were two girls, all in lovely dance
> frocks, and nobody was dancing with them. We were strangers up
> there. So we started dancing with these two girls. And they were good
> dancers. We danced nearly all night with them ... [at] the end of the
> night, normally you asked them, could you take them home? We
> didn't ask them, we just walked out, just behind them. And as we
> walked out, there was a gang of about eight chaps followed us out. So
> I said to Albert, 'I think we're being followed' ... And we took to our
> heels and we flew down Devonshire Street ... They'd have murdered
> us if they'd have got hold of us. One of the girls was going out with
> one of these lads and they'd fallen out. We didn't know ...
> *Did you ever see any trouble at a dance hall?*
> Yes, this gang was involved, and one or two more people, and I know
> one of them went to prison for about nine months for affray. I
> remember seeing one feller get hold of a lad and hitting his head on
> the garden wall. I thought, 'Oh my God, get out of this'.[37]

Dyson's hall, 'The Jig' in Liverpool Street, Salford, possessed a particularly
strong reputation for violence. Ewan MacColl claimed that by comparison,
dances held at the Workers' Arts Club in Salford offered two advantages:
they were cheap, and they were safe:

> ... dances there were very cheap, cost thruppence to get in. And there
> were no fights at them, which was unique. There was a big dance-hall
> near by called 'The Jig', but the fights there were incredible. If you
> went there you took your partner with you. If you walked across the
> floor to ask a girl to dance and she was, say, a member of the Percy
> Street mob, a dozen blokes would converge on you. And you were
> lucky if you got out without being beaten up.[38]

His account was confirmed by Mr Oliver, who described fights between
gangs of youths from the Ordsall and Hope Street districts which took
place at Dyson's, and Steve Humphries drew similar accounts of dis-
turbances in Salford dance halls in his portrayal of 'street gang sex' during

the 1930s. According to Ray Rochford, one of Humphries' respondents, youths with 'hard' reputations frequently started fights to avenge insults, imagined or real, directed at their girlfriends.[39] Not surprisingly, a number of local dance halls employed bouncers during the 1930s, and 'Nipper' Cusick, one of a string of well-known Salford boxers, worked on the door at Dyson's.[40] The sporadic dance hall clashes of the 1920s and 1930s in fact posed fewer problems for the police than the 'scuttling' gangs of the late nineteenth century. Scuttling clashes, between rival neighbourhood gangs, provoked a moral panic during the late-Victorian period, but the scale of youth violence appears to have declined after 1900, even if violence was to remain a feature of the youth scene in the two cities.[41]

Cinemas

During the 1920s and 1930s, film-going was without doubt the most popular form of commercial leisure among young people. Joan Harley's survey of leisure among girl wage-earners in Manchester in the mid-1930s revealed that the majority of girls aged 14–19 attended the cinema, on average, once a week. Between a quarter and a third of the girls in her predominantly working-class sample in fact attended twice.[42] In 1939, the Manchester University psychologists James and Moore, using a mixed and slightly older sample, found that it was common for young people in the Hulme district of South Manchester to attend up to three films a week. Oral testimony confirms that youths were the most frequent patrons of cinemas in Manchester and Salford, and a number of respondents could recall going to see two or three films each week during their teens.[43]

James and Moore insisted that watching films should be classified as a group, rather than an individual, activity. They argued that a good deal of group activity accompanied the actual watching of the picture. Young people went to films with their peers, or in couples, with James and Moore suggesting that 'much love-making goes on in the cinema, [whereas] congested home conditions and the lack of motor cars rule out this possibility [elsewhere]'. Similarly, Joan Harley pointed out that Manchester girls attended films in order to meet their friends, and to have the opportunity of meeting members of the opposite sex. Harley claimed that: 'quite a number of girls will see the same film twice rather than go to a less familiar cinema where they do not know the people who go'. Similar points are made in interviews, and in literary depictions of working-class life. Walter Greenwood, for example, gave a colourful portrayal of 'the noisy hilarity inside the Flecky Parlour' in *Love on the dole*, in an account based on the Empress cinema in Hanky Park.[44]

It is not difficult to demonstrate that Hollywood had a significant impact on youth fashions in working-class districts by the 1920s. Recent work on London, by Sally Alexander for example, suggests that films were highly influential in shaping the identities carved out by young people. Similarly, in Salford and Manchester, young people of both sexes copied the appearances of their favourite stars. Mary Bertenshaw's autobiography provides a clear illustration of the role of films in shaping the fashions adopted in North Manchester around 1918:

> I was becoming more conscious of my appearance and I spent my spare money on threepenny tins of Eastern Foam Cream, or a twopenny tin of Phulnana Face Powder or maybe a small bottle of Ashes of Roses. After a good scrub at Red Bank Baths I felt as glorious as Theda Barra.
>
> The highlight of the week for us was Friday, which we all called Amami night, after a new lovely hair shampoo; each Friday night after washing my camisoles and bloomers and doing the housework I shampooed my hair and, when it was dry, tied it in a bun fastened with a Woolworth's tortoiseshell comb – didn't I just look like Clara Bow.[45]

Although it is easy to demonstrate the impact of the cinema upon fashion, it is impossible to gauge with any precision the influence of cinema upon young people's attitudes. Despite the widespread contemporary fear that 'immoral' films led to declining moral standards, a survey of 'Adolescents and the cinema' conducted in Manchester by A. Fielder in 1932 suggested that young people were far from passive spectators. Fielder asked a sample of local working-class youths what they thought of the films they saw. He immediately found that they were a critical audience. They were quick to recognize poor films, and had strong ideas on the type of features they preferred. Films won approval if they were judged to offer excitement, humour or good music and singing, but were disliked if they were seen as 'impossible' [too unrealistic], or dull and boring. Moreover, while many lads and girls possessed photographs of their favourite actors or actresses, they were not universally star-struck. Fielder's question, 'Have you any fault to find with cinema shows?', prompted one 18-year-old to declare: 'Joan Crawford and her huge eyes bore me stiff.'[46]

Cinema was clearly important in presenting images of life beyond the working-class districts of Manchester. However, local youths were quick to criticize portrayals of other classes on the screen. Fielder made a specific attempt to measure the impact of the portrayal of the 'higher ranks' of society in films, but found that many youths simply questioned the realism of the films. Responses included 'Such pictures are definitely untrue' and 'All a lot of rot'. Scarcely any of his respondents declared that they formed a favourable impression of the upper classes, and the following remarks were common: 'They are all hypocrites'; '[They] are not always happy'; 'I prefer our own ranks'; 'It is a lazy and boring life'; 'They are to be pitied'; 'They are snobbish'.[47]

Historians have sometimes argued that cinema was a conservative force in inter-war society. Films are seen as having supported the status quo, either explicitly or implicitly, and some weight is implicitly given to the fear expressed by contemporary left-wing critics that films provided a new opiate for the people. Tony Aldgate, for example, has argued that British cinema during the 1930s formed: 'a further significant factor in contributing to the remarkable stability of British society during this period. It reflected and reinforced the dominant consensus ...'.[48] The comments drawn from Fielder's survey could be used to suggest that films bred a fatalistic sense of satisfaction with working-class life. However, the comments can be interpreted in other ways. The tendency to question the accuracy of screen toffs suggests that working-class youths were far too cynical for attitudes ever to be simply channelled by Hollywood. Tracing the formation of social consciousness is one of the most difficult and sensitive of the tasks undertaken by the social historian, and care must be taken in discussing the ways in which the attitudes of young people were formed. However, undue emphasis upon the role of the cinema can easily obscure the importance of experiences at home, on the streets, and at work, in forging young people's outlooks. Joan Harley worried that films glamorized love and marriage, but the nature of domestic life in Manchester and Salford was likely to breed scepticism to temper romance.[49] What is certain is that films provided enjoyment and relaxation, as well as a couple of hours of escapism, and contemporary commentators agreed that the cinema was a central feature of leisure among working-class youths.[50]

Corner gangs

Despite the growth of the cinema, communal, or informal, leisure activities accounted for most of the leisure time of young workers. James and Moore found that, on average, young men aged 21 had 18 hours of leisure spread over the weekday evenings. Six hours, or 33 per cent of this free time, was devoted to cinema shows, making 'the pictures' by far the most popular form of commercial leisure. However, their category 'talk' accounted for an average of 9¾ hours, or 54 per cent of the time available for leisure. In this category, James and Moore included the forms of communal leisure upon which the social lives of young people most depended. 'Talk', in their survey, described time spent in gatherings with friends, principally on the streets of Hulme.[51] Their findings are widely confirmed by oral evidence, which suggests that a similar pattern of leisure activity existed among young people in Salford and North Manchester. For many young workers, there was no alternative to the streets. Few had the inclination or the resources to spend all their free time in the cinema, and the cramped 'two up, two down' homes of Salford, and Manchester districts such as Ancoats and Hulme, could not accommodate nightly gatherings of youths.

Street corner gatherings were predominantly, but by no means exclusively, male spheres. Joan Harley found that time spent walking and hanging around the streets was also of considerable importance to working-class girls:

When they go out in the evening, they walk in the streets of their own neighbourhood. There are nearly always certain streets in every district which are used as promenades by the young people of the locality.

On weekday evenings, time on the streets was spent mingling with corner lads, as suggested by some of the comments made by girls in Harley's sample:

On Tuesday I went with the boys.
Thursday talking with the boys.
On Thursday I went a walk with three girls and stood to speak to two boys.
On Tuesday I go a walk on the road.[52]

Although girls spent time in street cliques, they had more domestic responsibilities than their brothers, and consequently spent less time at the street corner. Mrs Rowlings grew up in Ordsall.

On the next corner was Johnny Ainsworth's pawnshop. Well they used to sit on that step, singing.
Was this the lads, or was this girls as well?
The lads, and it'd be girls an' all, but some of the girls had to get in early.[53]

The male members of street corner society were known locally as 'corner lads':

... your own mates were classed in those days as corner lads, because they used to stand on the street corner. They were all fancy singers, or thought they were ... there used to be yodellers amongst 'em, and harmonising. I thought we were brilliant but the neighbours didn't. Used to [say], 'Why don't you bugger off home?'[54]

Although young men who were dance hall regulars, sporting fashionable haircuts and clothes, were sometimes known as 'jazzers', the term 'corner lads' is much more common as a description of young males during the inter-war period, reflecting the centrality of street activities in youth culture as late as the 1930s. In contrast, the labels attached to young people from the 1950s were more often a reflection of commercial influences, of styles of fashion and music: 'Teddy boys', 'mods', 'rockers' and 'punks'. 'Corner lads' were known for their own regular spots, which became their single most important venue for leisure. Throughout Manchester and Salford, working-class lads were known through their membership of street corner cliques: as Ewan MacColl remarked in his account of violence at dance halls, trouble was caused by gangs like the 'Percy Street mob'.

Time spent in street corner gangs was mostly spent talking and messing around.[55] Topics of conversation ranged from the everyday affairs of

Corner lads in Peru Street, the Adelphi, 1933.

Manchester and Salford to the more glamorous world of Hollywood: discussions of work, school and family affairs mingled with talk of dancing, fashion, films and film stars.[56] Among lads, gambling was another of the principal street activities, as Mr Paterson described:

> Wherever you lived, you congregated round one corner in your street or somebody else's street, and that's [who] people called corner lads ... And that's where you'd do your gambling, your carding, playing brag or owt ... same as Percy Street [in Ordsall], we had the corner lads there, one at the top end of Percy Street and one at the bottom.[57]

Social observers tended to see this as time wasted, but retrospective sources suggest that the social relationships of young people were formed and maintained through corner gangs, as well as at dance halls and cinemas. Robert Roberts stressed the economic function of street gangs in *The classic slum*, where they formed:

> ... an open-air society, a communal gathering which had great importance socially, culturally and economically ... During each nightly meeting the young worker, once fully integrated, listened, questioned, argued and received unawares an informal education. Here work-a-day life beyond his personal ken came up for scrutiny. Jobs in

factory, pit, mill, dock and wharf were mulled over and their skills explained. From first-hand experience, often bitter, youths compared wages, hours, conditions, considered labour prospects, were advised on whom to ask for when seeking a job and what to say. All this was bread and butter talk vital at times to the listener, talk that had an economic scope and variety to be heard nowhere else.[58]

Street corners were also places where courting couples were introduced. Mrs Jepson was born in Salford in 1922:

> I used to go and sit on the St John's wall up on Liverpool Street. I used to go there because the boys that I knew went and sat on this wall ... you'd go with a friend ... You knew that if some [other lad] was attracted to you, they'd come talking to these boys ... and of course, as conversation grew, you sort of were drawn in ... They'd say, 'Get her to talk to him' ... [59]

Youths who stood in street corner gangs were vulnerable to police harassment, on charges of loitering, or obstructing the footpath. Police interference could arouse great resentment among youths. 'Lounging' or 'loitering' was a commonplace activity, and although illegal, was widely viewed as a victimless crime. In popular opinion, youths who were charged with loitering offences were held to have been doing no harm at all. This could pose serious problems for the police, who were caught between pressure from moral entrepreneurs, to clean up the streets, and pressure from working people who resented interference with established customs.

In 1906, the Manchester police found themselves under heavy criticism, when allegations that they were harassing respectable youths were raised in the local press. Letters to the *Manchester Guardian* testified to:

> ... the deadly results which may follow from recording a conviction against a youth, the trail of which will always be over him and implant him with a sense of injustice from authority, which is surely a great factor in determining the accused's future relations to the state.[60]

In March 1906, magistrates dismissed the case against two lads who were brought up by the police for standing at a street corner. In court, the lads claimed that they had 'nowhere else to go'. A *Manchester Guardian* report prompted further correspondence:

> I have often noticed how in the more crowded parts of the city, whenever any boys are together as soon as they see the police constable they run. This is a most lamentable state of things. What is the use of doctors, philanthropists, and social workers constantly striving to improve the conditions of city life when the police make our boys into criminals because they prefer the fresh air instead of the atmosphere of their small and too often insanitary homes?[61]

A City of Manchester *Police instruction book*, issued in 1908, warned at some length that officers needed to 'exercise tact and discretion' when dealing with youths on the streets of the 'thickly-populated districts', adding that cases should only be taken to the courts as a last resort. Problems continued, however, perhaps inevitably given the nature of working-class housing during the inter-war decades. The *Salford City Reporter* noted a case which reached court during May 1930:

> When a youth of nineteen years was before the magistrates at Salford City Police Court yesterday on a loitering charge, it was stated that the family of father, mother and six children sleep in one room in a house in West-Wellington Street, Salford.[62]

Oral testimony confirms that obstruction charges remained a serious source of friction between the police and working-class youths. Moreover, personal reminiscences confirm the assertion that prosecutions for standing on street corners bred lifelong resentment. This was highlighted in an interview with a man born in Ordsall in 1916:

> *Were the police generally much in evidence around the area?*
> The local police were really shocking around this area. You couldn't stand on a corner in those days, waiting for your girlfriend or your mates, you'd be moved on ... The only conviction I've got in my life is for that ... I was sat on a wall right outside our house and the wall lies back, it doesn't interfere with anybody walking up Eccles New Road ... there was bags of room, and I was sat on the wall and he came and booked me, this policeman ...
> *Did he not just warn you?*
> Oh no, he just booked me and that was it. No argument. I played hell at court, but it made no difference. I got a five shilling fine.
> *Were many people arrested?*
> Oh yes. If you remonstrated. If three or four of you were stood in groups talking, a policeman walked up. 'Come on now, move on.' If you remonstrated, that was it, you were booked immediately. No harm in you whatsoever.[63]

However, in the vast majority of cases, police disruption was evaded. Lads and girls vacated their corners when beat constables or detectives appeared in view, returning as soon as the police had passed. In this way, corner gatherings remained an integral part of the social lives of young workers. Police harassment was a serious issue for those individuals who were caught and fined, but was not enough to drive corner gangs off the streets of Salford districts like Hanky Park:

> *When you were in Hanky Park, did the lads congregate on the street corners?*
> *Mr Phelan*: Oh aye, that went on.
> *Can you remember the police moving them on?*
> *Mr Phelan*: Oh yes, used to come round ... On Clarendon Road, I was

stood there that time ... 'Don't hang about else I'll pinch you'.
Was there any resentment if the police moved them on?
Mr Phelan: No, I don't remember ... what you'd do, you'd go round the
street and come back again. He knew that. You weren't causing any
trouble ... You'd just congregate and talk, talk about anything, maybe
football ... In fact, if you saw him, you'd go yourself [to avoid the
police].
Would girls meet up as well as lads?
Mrs Phelan: Oh yes, [to husband] that's how I met you, wasn't it? The
corner lads brought you.[64]

Even when 'rowdyism' did occur, the police were unable to apprehend
more than one or two among a gang of youths, as in the following incident
in Ordsall during August 1920:

> Seeing a crowd of youths in Robert Hall Street, Salford, late on Friday
> night, Police-constable Howard investigated and found they were
> singing, playing a banjo, dancing, and creating a terrible noise. As he
> approached they ran away, but later they returned and commenced
> the racket again. He rushed and succeeded in arresting Harry Single-
> ton, aged 21, of New Bury Street, Salford, who was now fined 20*s*. or
> thirteen days for being drunk and disorderly.[65]

The arrest was clearly made with some difficulty, while most of the
revellers escaped.

Street football among children and youths was also vulnerable to police
raids. Corner gangs persisted in organizing games and would attempt
to dodge the police, but occasionally players were caught. Mr Lomas
described an incident which took place in the Adelphi around 1926:

> They used to book you for playing football in the street ... I remem-
> ber playing in Briggs Street, there must've been about ten a side, and
> the two goalkeepers must have been two of the smallest in the
> company. The [other] boys were about fifteen, sixteen, and I was ten
> or twelve and the other goalkeeper was the same age. And one detec-
> tive came one way, and the other came the other way, and that was
> the only two ways out. They herded us all to the side along the wall.
> And then he said to the other goalkeeper, 'Come here, you. How old
> are you'? He said, 'Twelve'. And he gave him a winger across the
> earhole. 'Now', he said, 'Get off'! So I thought, 'I'm going to get the
> same here'. I walked up, I said, 'Twelve'. His hand went up, and I
> ducked. And he kicked me. Lifted me about two feet off the ground ...
> *Do you know what happened to the older lads?*
> Yes, they all got fined.
> *So he let you off the fine?*
> Well these lads were working. They'd made a good cop. They got
> about twenty lads there, and if the lads had all run they could only

have caught two, when you think of it.

Were they plain-clothed detectives who did that?

Yes. In fact the two detectives that were noted for it, I know their names. They were called Lamb and Neary, and they were two tough cops really. They used to lead the raids on [gambling schools] of a Sunday.[66]

Police interference could sometimes draw hostile crowds, and the Salford districts of Ordsall, Greengate, the Adelphi and Hanky Park all had reputations as places where local adults were prepared to 'tackle' the police. In oral history interviews, Salford people frequently declare that the police would only ever patrol these districts in twos or threes.[67]

Monkey parades

The most notorious youth custom in Manchester and Salford was the 'monkey parade'. Whereas corner gangs mainly congregated in the side-streets of the working-class districts, the Sunday evening parades saw youths take over many of the main streets across the two cities. Promenades were well-established in nineteenth-century Manchester, along Oxford Road, Market Street and Stretford Road during the 1860s, for example, and the persistence of parading underlines the importance of communal leisure forms in working-class culture.[68] The label 'monkey parade' was commonly used by the 1920s, and the term is often used in oral history interviews, although the terms 'monkey run' and, more rarely, 'monkey walk' are also mentioned.[69] In the early twentieth century, Regent Road, Eccles New Road, Cross Lane, Ellor Street, Eccles Old Road, the Crescent, Lower Broughton Road and Littleton Road were all among the regular Salford parades. There was a further set of parades throughout Manchester, but Salford youths tended to stay in their own city on Sunday nights, joining the parades near to their own districts.

Charles Russell described the central Manchester parades during the 1900s:

On Sunday evenings there are three main points of attraction for working lads – Oldham Street, Market Street, and Stockport Road ... From Hulme, from Ardwick, and from Ancoats they come, in the main well dressed, and frequently sporting a flower in the button-holes of their jackets. But the motive is not so much that of meeting their friends, as of forming an acquaintanceship with some young girl. Girls resort to Oldham Street on a Sunday night, in nearly as large numbers as the boys ... [The boys] exchange rough salutations with the girls, who seem in no way less vigorous than the boys themselves, and whose chief desire, one would think, was to pluck from the lads' button-holes, the flowers which many of them wear.[70]

Young people walked up and down the main streets, in twos or in groups, with the aim of 'clicking', or pairing off, with members of the opposite sex. Oral evidence suggests that as in dance halls, gender roles were in fact in evidence on the monkey parades, where lads were usually expected to take the initiative by approaching girls. Mr Saunders met his wife in the parade along Eccles New Road, favoured by youths from Ordsall:

How would you get someone's attention on the monkey run?
You'd just chat 'em up ... she might have been looking in a window ... and you'd just go and start chatting, 'Do you fancy that, love'? and all this. And you've not got a penny in your pocket.[71]

If girls were not expected to make the first move, they were far from passive in the process of 'clicking'. Mrs Fletcher also went on the parades along Eccles New Road:

What would happen when you got to the run?
Just parade with our eyes all over, 'Oh, there's so-and-so. Look who they're talking to' ...
Who would make the initial move?
The boys.
Could the girls help that along in any way?
Oh by all means.
How would they do that?
You'd be looking round and looking round ... then we'd walk a bit more and we'd look again, then all at once we'd go into a shop window. Well invariably they'd come up to the shop window to us. Nobody had more lads than Nellie and me. We had a good time.
Would any girls go up to a boy, or would they normally wait?
I don't think so. Well we never did, because it degraded you really ...[72]

The parades, like dance halls, were tabooed by some parents, like Mrs Cunliffe's mother:

They called it the monkey parade. All up Regent Road on either side were lads and girls ... till they got to Cross Lane, then Eccles New Road, that's where they picked these lads up. My mother copped me once with a lad, and I got a damn good hiding. 'I'll give you playing with lads' ... And I wasn't allowed out for a couple of weeks after, to go with my friends. All the lads used to say could they walk with us.
Did you have a girlfriend that you went with?
Yes ... they used to shout, 'Lily, are you coming out'? And my mother'd say, 'Where are you taking Lily'? So I said, 'Only a walk up Regent Road'.[73]

'Picking up' was also widely known as 'stragging', as Mrs Grady recalled: 'We used to call it stragging of a Sunday night ... we used to be eyeing all the fellers. Monkey parade they called it.'[74] Middle-class commentators found the term offensive. In 1908, the Manchester youth workers Charles Russell and Lilian Rigby remarked that:

> 'To strag' is to send out a tame pigeon which will fly round other cotes and bring other pigeons back. 'A stragging pigeon' is a well-known term to certain lads, and the expression is horribly used as an alternative to 'picking-up', and is in itself an indication of the extra-ordinarily low estimate in which girlhood and womanhood are held.[75]

They were probably unaware that working-class girls also used the term. Few respondents were so prim in their descriptions, and oral testimony provides more positive assessments of the parades, as lively scenes of public sociability. Mrs Anderson recalled:

> We used to go up there to try to pick up ... you used to go arm-in-arm. You used to say, 'There's two lads over there, let's go over there' ... you'd keep walking past, backwards and forwards ... it used to be alive, Cross Lane and Ellor Street ...[76]

The most unusual parades were held in the art gallery situated in Salford's Peel Park. As Mr Gilmour recalled:

> Peel Park. The art gallery was the main monkey run.
> *Was it?*
> Yes. And they used to dress up in their finery, whatever they had, and they'd go to Peel Park and they'd wander round the park, the avenues, but the art gallery was a great monkey run, walking up and down there, sitting on the bench, pretending to look at the pictures.
> *Mrs Gilmour*: Watching the girls go by.
> And watching the girls go by ... when they get to seventeen or eighteen, and onwards, they'd start to do this.
> *That's inside the museum?*
> Yes, that was a great place for it ... that was a monkey run in Salford, definitely.
> *Mrs Gilmour*: We used to go and sit in the museum, and say, 'Oh there's so-and-so coming in.' Then you'd go out and you'd walk through the park.[77]

As this extract suggests, the monkey parade also served as a fashion parade. 'Sunday best' clothes were displayed by those who could afford them, but as Charles Russell noted in 1905, the boisterous public life of working-class youths was vulnerable to poverty, and lads without best clothes, or whose Sunday clothes were in pawn, would stay at home rather than parade in their working clothes. Jack Lanigan made the same point when describing the North Manchester parades around Rochdale Road and Boggart Hole Clough during the 1900s: 'At the Clough on Sundays would be the usual parade, for those who could sport a new dress or a suit. Those Sunday afternoons would be enjoyed by those who could take part.'[78]

By the 1920s, indigenous working-class youth fashions were augmented by American styles. Mr Lomas was a member of a highly fashion-conscious gang from the Adelphi during the early 1930s:

> If you could afford it, you had trousers with a twenty-four inch bottom, with an inch turn-up. And if they were anything under twenty-four inches, you didn't want to know them. That was the fashion. You also used to have your hair cut in a special style, what they call a 'jazzer's' haircut. And if you went dancing, that was the recognised rig-out. Bell bottom trousers with a twenty-four inch bottom, and haircut to match.
>
> *What about a hat?*
>
> The hat was a a stetson. And the one that I wore was what they call an 'at-a-boy'. That was like a stetson and you pulled it low down, like a gangster effect. And a black belt, and a short belted overcoat.[79]

Other affluent young men paraded in cadies, with black ebonite walking sticks, according to the fashions of the day.[80] However, the poverty noted by Charles Russell in 1905 was by no means absent from the lives of young people in Manchester and Salford during the inter-war period. Mr Paterson went on the monkey parade on Eccles New Road when he was aged 18 or 19, during the early 1920s:

> *Was there any fashion, clothes that the lads would wear on the monkey run?*
>
> I can't describe it, more or less, I was rough and ready, I never had money to buy suits of clothes ... I didn't take much interest in clothing, 'course there would be special suits, but I couldn't name it, not now.[81]

The parade to Boggart Hole Clough in North Manchester was described by a woman who grew up in Collyhurst. Fashion was of as much importance in Collyhurst as in Salford, but was often highly improvised:

> We used to walk to the Clough and then walk back ... to the edge of Weaver Street, that was near town – and walk back again to the Clough. And there was droves! You had to walk in the middle of the road, there was that many, walking up and down and laughing and talking. A lot of them did it to click, you know – try and find a boyfriend. And we did that for hours and hours, till about ten o'clock. That was our Sunday night pleasure. And they called it the Monkey Walk. And you know the toreador hats – with the tassles? My friend and I got one of those. It was only about five shillings. We walked up and down the monkey run with these toreador hats and we thought – ooh gosh – the tassle hanging down! And sometimes we hadn't even got money to buy powder. It was a tiny box and it was only about twopence. So we used to put flour on our face. With these fancy hats on – flour on our face! We did that for years, every Sunday night. Two hours of walking up and down. And you hadn't two ha'pennies for a penny in your purse![82]

Like street corner gangs, the monkey parades were subjected to sporadic police harassment. In 1924, the Salford magistrates declared that they were going to stamp the parades out, and over 20 youths were fined between 5*s* and 10*s*. for obstruction during February and March. Police testified to the rowdy behaviour of youths who had taken to: 'walking abreast on the footway singing "Yes, we have no bananas', [as] foot-passengers were jostled into the roadway'.[83] In the view of one constable: 'They call it the "monkey's parade" on Sunday evenings, and I am quite satisfied that it deserves that name'.[84]

Police harassment is a common feature of retrospective accounts of the Salford parades, and Mr Lomas described the parade along Lower Broughton Road:

Would it be busy on a Sunday night?
Yes, in fact, the police used to march up and down and move you on if you stood [still], they wouldn't allow you to stand on the kerb, you had to stand in the road, and then nine times out of ten the police used to come along at a certain time and move you on. They wouldn't let you stand still. You had to be walking.
Did you ever see anyone booked on the monkey parade?
Oh yes, they got fined half a crown for loitering.
Did you know anyone that that happened to?
Yes, I do. I remember a lad who belonged to the [Adelphi Lads] Club, and they told him to move on, and as he stepped back, he stepped into the road. There was about six [lads] and they took two of them. He was fined half a crown.
Was that his sole offence?
He did nothing wrong. All he did was stand still at the corner of Broughton Lane. And when he was told to move on, because he wasn't sharp enough, sort of a bit annoyed about it, they got booked.[85]

However, youths dodged the police on the parades, just as they did on street corners. As Mrs Fletcher remarked:

... there was always police on, plain clothes. We could spot them a mile off and we'd be off down the back, down Winford Street. We'd come back when they'd gone ... they were very keen about this Eccles New Road business, because nobody [else] could walk along it, because of the lads and girls that were there ... I remember the police coming. We gave false names ...[86]

Despite police initiatives the monkey parade remained an important part of the urban youth scene during the inter-war period.

In Salford and Manchester, the Sunday opening of cinemas and dance halls was prohibited prior to the Second World War. Yet the popularity of parading cannot be explained solely in terms of the restrictions upon commercial entertainments during the Sabbath.[87] The monkey parade provided a valuable alternative, a communal form of leisure, in which participation was free, at least for those whose Sunday clothing was adequate for public display. Jeffrey Richards found that in Birmingham, cinemas did brisk business when they opened on Sundays for the first time in February 1932, yet the 'Sunday parades' of young people appeared undiminished, which suggests that cinema-going was added to rather than substituted for existing activities.[88]

With its heavy accent upon 'picking-up', parading was a different activity from attending the cinema. As a means of meeting unattached members of the opposite sex, it was unrivalled. The monkey parade was cheaper and less formal than the dance hall, and conducted on a much larger scale. Mrs Fletcher recalled parading with some affection:

> I think the monkey run was the happiest days of my life ... We hadn't much money, we couldn't afford to go anywhere in the sense that we couldn't afford to go dancing, because if we went dancing on a Saturday afternoon, that was the limit and we'd no money left. We weren't allowed out during the week, we were only allowed one night a week out. And by the Saturday we had to be in by 10 p.m. and on a Sunday we had to be in by 9.30. So we couldn't go so damn far between 7 and 9, could we? Nevertheless it was good while it lasted.[89]

As James and Moore found, as late as 1939, the principal pastime of young workers in Hulme could be classified as 'talk', which largely consisted of walking or hanging around in groups on the streets. The monkey parade was one of the central activities in this category: 'The parks on fine Sundays, the herb-beer shops, but above all the streets, for play, for lounging and for promenades, especially the Sunday evening "pick-up parades", these are the scenes of Talk ...'. Among lads in work between the ages of 14 and 21, 'talk' was the supreme weekend leisure activity, even on Saturdays, when the local cinemas were open. On Saturdays, working lads spent on average 15–20 per cent of their free time at the cinema. 'Talk' accounted for 40–50 per cent, and a series of other activities favoured by youths which would have fitted this category, such as street gambling, are discussed in Chapters 5 and 6.[90]

In 1939, the monkey parade clearly remained an important custom. In Manchester and Salford, the character of the parades changed very markedly during the Second World War, and in interviews, the threat of the blitz and the arrival of US servicemen are both recalled as having disrupted the traditional monkey parades. However, younger Mancunians describe Market Street in the city centre as a parade during the late 1940s,[91] and even during the war years, a form of parading continued in Market Street and Salford's Broughton Lane. As Mrs Daly recalled:

> ... it was Market Street that was the monkey run then, Market Street was the place for the Yanks. I [was] never allowed to go up that way at all ... they used to come round Bury New Road, down Broughton Lane ... they used to whistle after y', but my father used to bring us

in, the girls. All the fathers used to come out and bring their daughters in, tell the Americans to clear off.[92]

Throughout the early decades of the twentieth century, young workers enjoyed a measure of financial independence, and a degree of freedom from domestic responsibility. The period between starting work and getting married represented a distinct stage in the life-cycle, in which it was relatively easy to find time and money for leisure. Young workers turned to novel forms of commercial entertainment, like the cinema, alongside traditional, nineteenth-century urban customs such as the monkey parade and, in this sense, the broader division of leisure, into commercial and informal activities, was mirrored in the diversity of working-class youth culture.

five

Streets, markets and parks

In *The classic slum*, Robert Roberts described the side-streets of Salford's Hope Street district as a 'great recreation room'.[1] This chapter examines a cluster of street activities which together formed an important element of working-class culture, ranging from the spectacular to the mundane, from impressive displays of street theatre in the annual Whit walks to everyday pastimes like 'sitting out' on the doorsteps and talking to the neighbours. Street customs were an important feature of the communal life of working-class districts, as neighbourhood ties were formed and maintained through socializing, in streets and street-corner pubs, as well as through women's mutual support networks.

Street culture offered a range of communal leisure activities, and a series of alternatives to commercial attractions such as the cinema. In contrast to the cinema or dance hall, street activities usually cost little or nothing, so poverty was less of a barrier to participation. Although adult pastimes like sitting out appear more mundane than youth customs such as the monkey parade, they were equally important as activities which accounted for much of the free time available to manual workers and their families. Markets and parks were also important venues for communal gatherings. For many working people, the weekly leisure cycle included touring the market areas on a Saturday night, and walking or sitting in the parks on Sundays and weekday evenings.

These activities were all free, and considered alongside the wider range of street culture, constitute a communal, or informal, sector alongside the commercial sector which has been well documented in surveys of working-class leisure. Moreover, it is in the communal sector that the continuities in urban leisure patterns are most apparent. Many of the street activities discussed in this chapter can be traced from the early or mid-nineteenth century to the mid-twentieth century. This forms an important contrast with the pace of change in the commercial sector, where the development of the music hall and film industries gave the impression that the nature of leisure was changing very rapidly around the turn of the century. Historians have commonly regarded the last quarter of the nineteenth century as a 'turning point' in the history of working-class leisure, but this periodization, based largely upon a consideration of the commercial sphere, obscures the prominence and persistence of communal leisure forms.[2]

Accounts of neighbourhood life are frequently riddled with ambiguities. Robert Roberts, for example, warned that:

> In our day some sociologists have been apt to write fondly about the cosy gregariousness of the old slum dwellers. Their picture, I think, has been overdrawn. There could be much personal unhappiness and fear of one neighbour by another ... Close propinquity, together with cultural poverty, led as much to enmity as it did to friendship ... In general, slum life was far from being the jolly hive of communal activity that some romantics have claimed.

Yet even Roberts recalled how:

> ... there were benign nights too, when neighbours gathered in little groups to chat ... It was the warmer days, above all, that people felt a glow of 'community', a sense of belonging each to each other that, for the time being, overrode class and family differences.[3]

These contrasting assessments can be traced through Roberts' work, which testifies both to the importance of community and to the limits of neighbourliness: solidarities and tensions co-existed within the 'classic slum'.[4] The first section of this chapter examines first positive and then negative depictions of community.

Street life and neighbourhood relationships

From the 1840s to the 1940s, descriptions of the custom of sitting out on the doorsteps underpinned representations of neighbourliness in working-class districts. In 1849, Angus Reach visited the operative quarters of Salford, and Ancoats, Hulme and Cheetham in Manchester:

> Every evening after mill hours these streets, deserted as they are, except at meal times, during the day, present a scene of very considerable quiet enjoyment. The people all appear to be on the best terms with each other, and laugh and gossip from window to window,

and door to door. The women, in particular, are fond of sitting in groups upon their thresholds sewing and knitting, the children sprawl about beside them, and there is the amount of sweethearting going forward which is naturally to be looked for under such circumstances.[5]

James and Moore described the scene in the streets of Hulme in 1939:

In summer family life overflows in to the street, people sit in the doorways and on the pavement. At most times of the year the children play in the street, and the adolescents talk at street corners and, after dark, make love in the 'backs', the narrow passages running between two rows of backyards and in the doorways and entries of shops and factories. Privacy and quiet are hard to find.[6]

Teenagers distanced themselves from their parents, adopting street corners as an alternative to their own doorsteps, but the scene described by James and Moore is essentially the same as the one portrayed by Reach. Adults, especially but not exclusively women, spent much of their leisure time simply 'sitting out', chatting to neighbours, with their children playing in the street around them. The streets were the main arena of working-class sociability, and during the warmer months especially, friendships were maintained on pavements as much as in pubs.

Music features strongly in retrospective accounts of street life. Mrs Daly described Durham Street in Greengate:

... there was no television, just a wireless.
Did many people in the street used to have a wireless?
Not many, no, a few did, a few didn't, but my mother bought one second-hand, and we had one of those old gramophones, and my parents came from Ireland, from Dublin and my mother brought a big harp over and we used to have that in the street, playing.

She also recalled the street parties which followed holidays and royal celebrations:

I think everybody got merry, and they'd be dancing and singing.
Would they dance in the street?
Oh yes.
What would they have for music?
They had their own music. One or two of us had the old gramophone ... had the kids winding it up while the mothers and fathers'd be dancing.

Wirelesses were sometimes shared with neighbouring families, to the benefit of those who could not afford them: '... you'd either go into the house, or they'd all go outside, if they put it on loud enough, sit on the front step and listen'.[7]

Women's networks, through which help was exchanged in periods of illness and severe poverty, were also largely street-based. In working-class

Sitting out in Liverpool Street, Salford – the 'classic slum'.

districts, women frequently helped each other through domestic crises, although such networks were often confined to women living in one section of a street.[8] Women's networks also provided a social outlet. Housewives snatched brief daytime conversations, although as Robert Roberts pointed out, gossip had an economic value as well as a social function:

> Gossip, that prime leisure activity of the time, played a vital role in a milieu where many, through lack of education, relied entirely on the spoken word ... that daily feature of the slum scene, the 'hen' party, did not function, as many thought, merely to peddle scandal; matrons in converse were both storing and redistributing information that could be important economically to themselves and to their neighbours.

When the weather permitted, household tasks, from peeling potatoes to breast feeding babies and combing and de-lousing children, were widely performed in the streets.[9] In this sense, neighbourhood life was much richer during the summer months.

However, retrospective accounts of neighbourliness, even during the summer months, are often far from sentimental. In Knott Mill:

> They used to sit at the doorsteps on chairs, and, to be blunt, in those days the condition of the houses was such that there was quite a lot of bugs in houses. And the heat, y'couldn't get to sleep, the bugs were everywhere, and the people were up until one or two in the morning ...
> *What sort of things would they do, would they just be chatting with each other or ...*
> Oh chatting, and reading the paper, and the kids'd be playing on the flags.[10]

Some families suffered so badly that they were forced to sleep outside. Mrs Daly described Greengate during the 1930s:

> In those days we had to sleep in the backyard because we had bugs, we had terribly hot weather ... and we all had to sleep in the backyard.
> *Was that the whole family?*
> Everybody in the street. And we had health visitors down and every-thing, used to give us sulphur candles and we used to burn these during the night while we were [outside], but we still got them, they came back from other houses ...

When her family slept in the house:

> ... if you came downstairs for anything, we used to have to come down with a lamp, and it [was] just like a carpet moving, big cockroaches, and they used to all go under the skirting board. And we all complained. And we had this health visitor ... we told her she'd have to come and actually see, but she could smell, you could smell the bugs and you could smell the beetles. And she told us to buy some mild beer ... and spread it down round the skirting boards ... the cockroaches used to like the beer, and they used to drink and then of course they'd get drunk and fall on their back and that's how you used to have to get rid of them. They'd die on their back.[11]

Problems were not restricted to the warmer months. In winter, families were confined to their homes, but the small terraces of Salford, Hulme or North Manchester provided little space for communal gatherings. As Richard Heaton recalled, in Salford at the turn of the century:

> Coal was out of the question for most families, except as a luxury now and again. In winter the whole family would be huddled around the coke fire, so it was not surprising many people had bronchitis and chest troubles after inhaling the fumes.[12]

The domestic sphere was often far from comfortable. Although reading, sewing and knitting were popular among many women, these private pleasures should not be seen as elements of a cosy domesticity. Similarly, hobbies such as carpentry were popular among men, yet the cramped nature of working-class housing again set limits to the pursuit of home-centred entertainment.

From the 1900s to the 1930s, housing conditions in Manchester and Salford were the cause of considerable anxiety among local social observers. A series of social surveys highlighted the social and health problems associated with slum housing, and the following account of conditions in Greengate in 1933 highlights the depth of problems in the older, central working-class districts:

> At No. –, Paradise Row, husband, wife and four children live and sleep in one room with one bed. The eldest girl, who is aged eleven, was sent to sleep with an elderly relative, but the doctor who attends the old lady says it is not healthy for the child to be there, so she will probably have to return home, and make a seventh person in the room. The walls are verminous ...
>
> At No. –, Sharratt Street, husband and wife and five children sleep in two small bedrooms. The house is very damp, and rats and mice cannot be kept out. The sanitary convenience has no door and is just opposite the back door. There is a down draught from the chimney with resultant soot and smoke.
>
> At No. –, Dixon Street, two tiny rooms, very damp, are occupied by a husband and wife and two children. The wife has been very ill with tubercular trouble and has been at Nab Top [isolation hospital] for some time, but has now returned. The husband also looks very ill and the children had whooping cough while the mother was away and are often ill.[13]

Conditions were much better in districts such as Ordsall, where the bulk of the housing was built between the 1870s and the 1890s, yet even here, leisure in the private sphere was largely confined to the back parlours of two up, two down terraces.

In the narrow terraced streets of working-class districts, even those indoors were exposed to the noise of the street outside. Neighbourliness and strife were often not far removed, and some people resented the animated street life of working-class areas, where personal or family quarrels could lead to slanging matches or fights. In 1896, Herbert Philips declared:

> I scarcely like to speak with disrespect of the homely practise of sitting out on the doorstep on a hot summer evening, but my experience at the City Police Court, where neighbours bring their personal quarrels for adjudication, leads me to think that this mode of taking the air gives abundant opportunities for what is technically called 'language', and must be very distasteful to decent, quiet people.[14]

Similarly, one of Rowntree's investigators, who spent a Sunday in July 1899 in a slum district in York, recorded:

> Majority of women standing gossiping in the streets are in 'deshabille'. Children simply swarm – dirty and ill-clothed ... In the evening there were several wordy battles between women neighbours, the language being very bad. Weather being very warm, men, women, and children are sitting on the pavement most of the evening.[15]

Religion was an occasional focus for differences. Mrs Statham grew up in Ordsall:

> *What would they do if they were sitting out, would they be chatting?*
> Oh yes, chatting, or watching the children or, if there was an argument with the children ... they'd have something to say. But generally chat with anyone passing.
> *So it's quite friendly then?*
> Oh yes. There was one part of the street, the top part of the street was seemed to be cut off from the other half of the street ... what I could gather, it was more Catholic at one end and more Protestants at the other end, and one old lady in particular was called an Orangewoman, and when it was Orange day, very bitter y'see the Orange and the Catholics, she'd put the Orange flag out and it'd cause rows in the street. They'd be rowing like anything ... but I knew the people at my half of the street very well.[16]

Religious tension was most likely to surface at Whit week when the rival faiths were celebrated in the annual 'scholars walks' in the two cities.[17]

When fights broke out in the streets, they quickly drew crowds. Fights between neighbours and brawls outside pubs at closing time were common occurrences, forming part of what Jerry White has termed the 'street theatre' of working-class neighbourhoods.[18] In Salford, there was a series of streets and pubs which were renowned locally for outbreaks of violence. As an Ordsall man recalled: 'You could name various streets and you could gamble Saturday night or Sunday night there was a brawl in the street.'[19] The St James in Ordsall had a reputation as a rough pub. Situated in the area opposite the dock gates known locally as 'Little Africa', on account of a handful of seamen and Maltese café owners who settled there, the pub was a dockers' haunt:

> *Do you remember any fights?*
> Oh yes, there used to be a lot of fights with the men. Lads used to fight in the street, and when the pubs let out there used to be fights. I've seen fights at the St James there, they were always fighting there, when the St James let out.
> *Did people used to come out to look at the fights?*
> Yes, they were always out watching it. They said,'Oh a fight at the St James's'. 'Is there another one'? 'Oh it's terrible down there'.[20]

Although the police kept watch on the most notorious streets, like Trafford Road, the dock road in Ordsall, the majority of street fights took place without disruption, as it was clearly impossible for the police to patrol all the pubs in the 'rough' districts of the two cities at closing time on Friday and Saturday nights.[21]

Street entertainers and working-class charity

The general neglect of informal leisure activities by historians has meant that itinerant entertainers have been largely ignored in the existing social history of leisure, yet in Manchester and Salford, street musicians were an important feature of city life throughout the Victorian period and the early decades of the twentieth century.[22] Street performances offered a means to combat poverty for some of the poorest members of working-class neighbourhoods, and itinerant entertainers appealed to the working-class tradition of providing charity for the poorest groups in society. As Jerry White has pointed out, the lower forms of busking were closely akin to begging.[23] However, the performances of more professional street entertainers provided a means to fill in leisure time for those with least money to spare for leisure. Audiences were not restricted to those who could offer payment, and street musicians and singers provided free entertainment for people with little access to music halls and cinemas.

Street performances took diverse forms in the two cities during the nineteenth century, with street singers and Italian organ grinders equally prominent in the ranks of itinerant entertainers. John Page described Manchester in 1858:

> ... street ballad singers have rhymes upon almost every conceivable subject, but the professional street singers ... know what subjects will suit certain neighbourhoods, and 'work' accordingly. In the districts where the weavers most abound a song upon anything or anybody connected with the loom finds its best market, and by the same rule Irish songs are sung and sold where they are sure to be appreciated. Many of the latter are extremely comic and are sure to attract a crowd of listeners ...[24]

These professional performances contrast with those of 'singing beggars', who appealed more directly to working-class charity. The lower street singers worked individually or as families, and throughout the second half of the nineteenth century, there were striking accounts in the Manchester press of parents who took their children to sing in the streets.[25] Fred Roberts recalled that in Miles Platting, Manchester, during the 1890s:

> There were a lot of street singers in those days; people were poor, very poor indeed. It was common to see a man and his wife coming along the middle of the road and two or three children trailing behind, singing for the odd ha'penny.[26]

During trade slumps and strikes, the ranks of street performers were swelled by working people who turned to street entertainment as a temporary means of obtaining relief. During the Lancashire cotton famine, unemployed Manchester and Salford operatives paraded the working-class streets of the two cities in bands, and the scene was repeated in 1893, when, during a coal strike, 'the streets of Manchester were invaded by colliers' using vocal and instrumental music to raise financial support. Collections were estimated to have raised £20 per day, for the relief of pit villages like Pendlebury on the outskirts of Salford.[27]

A more cosmopolitan tradition in street entertainment resulted from the growth of the Italian immigrant community. In Manchester, Italian street performers were a popular feature of city life from the 1820s. The first Italian organ grinders suffered an uneasy relationship with the law, especially over the issue of obstruction in the city centre, and, during the mid-1830s, the Manchester police briefly attempted to 'rid the streets' of immigrant street musicians. Yet despite this initial harassment, organ grinders remained part of the common scene in Manchester and Salford throughout the Victorian period. By shifting their activities to the side-streets of the working-class districts, organ grinders avoided police persecution, and a series of social commentators testified to the popularity of street music in the poorer districts of the two cities.[28]

Hugh Cunningham has argued that by the late nineteenth century, itinerant entertainers were losing their markets,[29] and the world of Victorian street life appears far removed from the more sophisticated mass entertainment industries of the twentieth century. Yet in Manchester and Salford, street performers maintained a strong presence in the sphere of working-class leisure throughout the decades prior to 1939. When William Jordan, for example, surveyed the itinerant musicians working in Manchester in 1901, he found organ grinders, mechanical piano players, German bands, 'nigger minstrel' troupes, evangelical hymn singers, women street singers and blind vocalists among the ranks of the city's street entertainers.[30]

The Italian quarter in Ancoats was the centre of Manchester's barrel organ trade. Performing bears and monkeys were kept in cellars in Jersey Street, and the main provincial organ manufacturer was located in Portugal Street.[31] Barrel organs were taken out by Italian families, and by men from other Manchester districts who hired them on a daily basis. Organ grinders worked throughout Manchester and Salford, and their performances were a popular form of entertainment in the two cities. In 1900, the Manchester authors C.E.B. Russell and E.T. Campagnac remarked that:

> Dancing may often be seen in the alleys and courts of the poorer parts of the Lancashire towns, and even in the side streets turning out of great thoroughfares. A crowd, not only of children, but of

Street dancing in Collyhurst, Manchester, 1904.

young men and women will gather round a barrel organ, and in a few moments many couples will have begun to dance.[32]

Street dances flourished in Manchester throughout the 1900s. The sight of dozens of young people performing polkas, waltzes and schottisches to music provided by Italian organ grinders was a common feature of city life.[33]

Oral testimony indicates that organ grinders retained a market in Salford and Manchester districts such as Ancoats, Collyhurst and Hulme throughout the early decades of the twentieth century. Mrs Cunliffe described Ordsall on the eve of the First World War:

What did people do when the organ grinder came round?
Dance in the street.
Who'd be doing that?
Well, neighbours.
The children?
The mothers, come out and dance ... my mother was one of 'em. She used to sing 'Sons of the Sea'. 'We are all British boys!'

Her mother had little access to commercial leisure, so the organ grinder's appearance provided a welcome opportunity to enjoy some free entertainment. Mrs Cunliffe remarked that as far as her own family were concerned, the organ grinder 'never got any money ... we were all put to'. However, working-class mothers, often tied to the home by financial and household responsibilities, provided a captive audience for street musicians.[34]

Mrs Sugden was born in Ordsall in 1915, and her account confirms that street amusements remained an integral feature of public sociability during the inter-war period:

> *Can you remember any of the organ grinders coming round?*
> Oh yes, the same one used to come round every Thursday night and all our mothers and fathers used to come out on the street dancing.[35]

Organ grinders were frequently employed on festive occasions in Salford, particularly at working-class weddings. Joe Toole told how:

> In the street where we lived a regular feature was the appearance of a blind neighbour who earned a living playing a barrel-organ ... Whenever a wedding occurred he had a standing engagement for that day. He played a repertoire of twelve airs over and over again, from the time the happy pair returned from the Church ceremony until everybody adjourned to the corner 'boozer' and he was given the word to cease.[36]

Mr Riordan's marriage took place in the Adelphi in 1922, and his wedding followed the same pattern: 'When I got married, I got a barrel of beer, and the feller was there with the organ ... From there, I was treating them all in the pub at the corner'.[37]

Organ grinders were aware that their performances held most appeal in the poorer districts. In 1905, Charles Russell remarked that: 'The best paying districts, and those from which the most regular incomes can be derived, are generally in the poorer quarters of the town and in places where the people come out to hear the music and dance to it.'[38] In Manchester and Salford, the link between poverty and the survival of street music persisted during the 1930s. Jerry White encountered a different trend in London, where:

> The growth of the wireless, more indispensable than the kitchen sink by 1939; the unabated popularity of the cinema; a desire for newness in almost every aspect of popular taste; rising standards of home comfort and a reduction of overcrowding in inner city areas – all conspired by the late 1930s to make street entertainers appear tedious and out of date.[39]

Yet in Salford, the poorest districts were still those most receptive to itinerant musicians during the 1930s. Mrs Daly described Greengate:

> *Did you ever see anybody bringing a barrel organ round the streets?*
> Oh yes, often ... people that couldn't afford wireless sets used to look forward to the music of these men, they used to give them money to stay outside their door, to listen to the music.

Would you ever find anybody having a dance to the barrel organ music?
Some of the women, yes. They'd have a few drinks of course ... They
used to pick their skirts up, and cock their legs up.
Did you know where the men who brought the barrel organ came from?
Never knew, no ... They used to come and stop at each street, and if
they got no response or got no money off anybody they used to move
on. But I think they liked coming to the top of our street because
most of us, well we had an old radio but most of the others didn't.[40]

A number of men in this street were out of work during the 1930s, so it is
possible that some of the families without wirelesses had been means-
tested. The decline of street-based leisure was clearly an uneven process: in
Salford, Italian organ grinders still worked the city streets in the summer
of 1939.[41]

'Singing beggars', a common sight in nineteenth-century Manchester
and Salford, also appear in many accounts of street activities after 1900.
Angel Meadow, the most notorious slum in Manchester, was known as a
haven for the 'lower' kinds of street singers and musicians, and the lodging
houses off Rochdale Road provided a base for those who worked regularly
in the two cities. Mary Bertenshaw's parents took over a lodging house in
Angel Meadow on the eve of the First World War, and she described the
trades of a number of lodgers who earned a living as entertainers, including a pavement artist, a ventriloquist who 'played the pubs' and a couple
who sang in the streets of Manchester, Rochdale and Oldham.[42] In 1904, a
street musician living in Angel Meadow could earn around 2*s*. 6*d*. per day,
although this was not enough to keep a family above Rowntree's poverty
line.[43]

Singing beggars pitched their appeal directly to the sympathy of their
audiences. Mrs Ormond described Ordsall on the eve of the First World
War:

People used to go up the streets singing songs. Women with babies in
their arms ... so's you'd give 'em a copper.
How did people react to them?
Well, some used to feel sorry for 'em, if they had a ha'penny or a
penny they would give it them, but some hadn't got it to give them ...[44]

Mrs Grady also grew up in Ordsall. She described a woman who lived off
Chapel Street in one of Salford's poorest working-class districts, near the
Flat Iron market:

What about anybody singing in the road?
Oh there were plenty who used to sing by the road. There was a blind
lady and she came round for years, and she was a poor old soul, she
used to have men's boots on. And she used to sing:

God have mercy and compassion
Look with pity down on me

There was hardly anybody that didn't give her anything. And my mother used to wrap her up a bit of food to take home, 'cause my mother was very soft like that ... she'd knock at the doors, and she'd shout 'God save all here'.[45]

Mrs Daly described a woman who toured the Greengate streets during the 1930s:

Was there anyone who came round the street singing?
There used to be a lady, she used to come round every night between five and six, and she'd be singing

> Oh please give me a penny,
> For I was rich like you,
> Now that I am poor,
> Please give me a penny,
> And I won't ask any more.

She used to sing that over and over again. Every night she came round. Just used to walk in the gutter.[46]

These extracts confirm that the Victorian custom, whereby the lower street performers appealed to working-class charity, persisted during the early twentieth century. In the inter-war period, charity was extended to street singers from among the ranks of the unemployed, and this provides a further explanation for the survival of street culture in Manchester and Salford during the 1930s.[47]

Retrospective testimony also provide glimpses of more sophisticated forms of street entertainment. Performing bears were used by a range of entertainers, including members of the Italian community in Ancoats, and Mrs Holden described a man who took a dancing bear around the streets of Bolton:

He wore a bright yellow blouse and green trousers ... and he came along, leading this bear on a chain ... it would come ambling up the cobblestones ... it would go on its back paws and sit up, looking at us ...[48]

From the 1910s, professional street performers who had previously taken their material from music-hall songs began to borrow additional ideas from the cinema. In Ancoats:

A young man dressed like Charlie Chaplin ... would have about 200 children all sat down on the kerb each side of the street and they would do everything he asked them to do. He sang and danced to a barrel organ which his partner played ... They used to cover all parts of the poor areas in Manchester.[49]

In this way, itinerant entertainers adapted to fashion, by exploiting developments in commercial entertainment. A few of the more adventurous performers appear to have made a relatively comfortable living during the mid-1930s. In Paradise Row, a street in Greengate:

Street entertainer, Chorlton-on-Medlock, Manchester, 1900s.

... there used to be a man and his two daughters ... and he used to go
out singing and his two daughters used to go out dancing. They used
to dance to their dad's singing ... I think they did pretty well really
because they were always well dressed when they used to go out ...
the girls used to go out dancing in the evenings, or go to the ice rink.
Or used to pass our street to go to the pictures ... so they must have
made a few bob.[50]

By performing in working-class side-streets, itinerant entertainers
usually managed to avoid police harassment. The Salford police tolerated
their activities, and even provided advice upon the most receptive neighbourhoods to performers who were unfamiliar with the city. Mr Wilkinson
served in the Salford City Police throughout the inter-war period:

*When you started working in the 1920s did you still have people taking barrel
organs round the streets in Salford?*
Well, yes. That was good, they used to say, 'Where's the Catholic
area'? Play hymns in that.
Where would you have sent them, if somebody asked you that?
I would have sent them down Whit Lane to St Sebastian's, or
Greengate ... They'd find where the Protestant area was as well.

Did you ever have to watch the people who brought the barrel organs round the streets for obstruction?
Oh no. They would get on a croft, they wouldn't cause any annoyance at all, those people ... down Regent Road [in Ordsall], they'd get in the side-street and play their organs there, so they didn't cause much trouble.
I didn't realise that the barrel organs had hymns on them.
'Course they had. They didn't always play them, there was jazz music as well, then they'd have them all round ...

He also recalled 'singing beggars':

You got these people, they were beggars really, some of them, they'd say, 'Where's the Catholic area'? And of course you'd tell them, they'd start singing Catholic hymns, and Protestant hymns. And they made quite a lot of money.
Would you have to watch them?
No, you didn't interfere with those people, really.[51]

In Manchester, street musicians were liable to be fined 40*s.* if they refused to move on after objections by a householder or police constable, and they were vulnerable to obstruction and vagrancy charges, but oral evidence suggests that police attitudes were generally lenient.[52]

Ewan MacColl provided a vivid account of the range of street entertainment in Salford during the 1920s and 1930s, and his testimony, which is worth examining in depth, confirms that street performers were far from redundant, especially during the period of mass unemployment from 1929 to 1933. MacColl outlined the theory of street singing:

... street singers had the technique of making the verse of a song last all the way from the bottom to the top of the street. The idea being that you don't sing too fast, because if you do you can't catch the eye of somebody so that they'll feel embarrassed or ashamed if they don't give you something ...

Salford witnessed choirs of unemployed fishermen from Grimsby and Hull, and groups of Welsh miners singing tear-jerking parlour ballads like 'Come into the Garden, Maud' or 'Just Plain Folk':

Sometimes they'd have a little placard which they'd carry with them saying 'We are Unemployed Welsh Miners', or 'Through no fault of our own we have no jobs, can you help us?' These weren't professional street singers – they were obviously men who felt embarrassed to be doing this, because they were singing to people who were as poor as they were. But it was only from the poor that they were going to get any kind of help at all.

Street musicians included men who played the 'rickers' (two bones held between the fingers to make a noise like castanets), organ grinders, piano accordionists, flute players and street pianists. Musicians were supplemented by occasional acrobats, escapologists, groups of tumblers, Punch and Judy men and even 'a chap who used to come round with a display of butterflies mounted in a portable showcase which he would show for a ha'penny'. MacColl's account shows that Salford hosted a vibrant street life as late as the 1930s.[53]

Street customs

In Manchester and Salford, the most spectacular occasions of street theatre were provided by the annual Whit walks. Popularly known as 'the scholars walks', churches and Sunday schools organized processions of children to Albert Square in Manchester, and around parishes throughout the two cities. The Protestant walks were held on Whit Monday, with Catholic walks taking place the following Friday. On either day, central Manchester was brought to a standstill by the processions. In Mrs Ryan's words, 'it was God save the King Monday morning and God save the Pope Friday afternoon'.[54] Indeed, as Steve Fielding has noted, the Catholic Whit walk was described in 1935 as 'in any year, no doubt, the biggest spectacle that Manchester affords'.[55]

The walks were hugely popular, drawing crowds in their thousands. Significantly, although the walks were expressions of rival faiths, many people went to watch both the Catholic and Protestant processions through Manchester. Mrs Easton's family lived in Ordsall. They were Protestants, but they made the trip from Salford to watch both the Whit Monday and the Whit Friday walks to Albert Square, and made a third trip on Trinity Sunday to see the separate Catholic procession held in 'Little Italy' in Ancoats: '... we always used to watch both Church of England and Roman Catholic, and on Trinity Sunday, the Italians walked round New Cross, top of Oldham Street. They carried a massive Madonna, full of lilies'.[56]

Although, as Steve Fielding pointed out, relations between Catholics and Protestants in Manchester and Salford were generally harmonious,[57] religious hostility did sometimes surface during Whit week. Mr Byrne lived in Paradise, one of the poorest streets in Greengate. Although the top half of the street was predominantly Church of England and the bottom half largely Catholic, he claimed that there was no animosity at Whit week. On the contrary, many people watched both processions.[58] Mr Pearson gave a very different account of a street in Knott Mill, Manchester, during the 1920s:

> *Was there a lot of rivalry between the Catholics and the Protestants?*
> There was, especially at Whit week ... And Whit Monday was a real day, walking round ... Market Street, Albert Square ... past the cathedral. Whit Friday was the Catholics. Now then, if Whit Monday was a glorious day and Whit Friday it rained, y'could gamble there'd be a scrap between the women.
> *Between the women?*

Between the women, yes. And in those days they had long hair ... there were two particular neighbours that were real bitter. One was ... a Liverpool Irishwoman, and another that was really, y'know, they really came to, hard, and I've seen 'em scrapping on the cobblestones ... the Liverpool Irishwoman's husband was a gentleman, his idea was nobody interfere, 'let 'em fight it out and finish it'. Then perhaps at the weekend they'd be pals again, in the pub having a drink.[59]

Even if open hostilities were short-lived, Whit week was potentially fraught with tension.

Domestic problems were also posed. For working-class mothers, Whit week meant a challenge: children usually needed new clothes to take part in the processions, as much emphasis was placed upon making a respectable appearance. Mr Slater took part in the Catholic walk with St Edmund's, Miles Platting:

But Whit Week had its bad times, Whit Monday and Whit Friday were 'Holidays without Pay' so this was where your mother had to perform a 'miracle' and keep the family for a week on four days' wages. She took in some washing, or went out to clean for a few shillings, or my father's silver lever watch was pledged to help out and redeemed at a later date.[60]

Some children never took part in the walks. Mrs Phelan's father was unemployed during the 1930s and tended to exacerbate his family's poverty by spending most of his unemployment allowance on betting. As a consequence:

When it was Whit week, we never had any Whit week clothes. We used to just look through the parlour window and see everybody else dressed up. That was my sister and I. But we always came back to the table for something good to eat. My mother never spent money on clothes, it always went on the table for food.[61]

Collective efforts were sometimes made to maintain the reputation of a parish. Mrs Ryan took part in the Catholic Whit walk with St James's, Pendleton. The St James scholars walked from Salford to Albert Square in Manchester, and care was taken to disguise the poverty of some of the children: '... if my mother had money and another child's mother didn't she'd buy it a pair of shoes or something like that'.[62] By contrast, on the eve of the First World War, when the children of St Bartholomew's in Ordsall walked round their own parish on Whit Monday, the poverty of the poorer scholars was put on display. As Mrs Cunliffe recalled:

Did you go to Sunday school?
Yes, St Bartholomew's ... and all my children.
So your parents were Church of England?
Always, we're John Bull, we are, t'backbone. When the scholars were

walking, I used to walk in my bare feet, and they used to put me right at the front of the band when we were going up Regent Road. We had no money, y'see ... the poorest children were sent straight to the front, and we all got clapped, people clapping it up.
How far did you walk?
Well, to the church. From the school, straight up Regent Road, along Oldfield Road, to St Bart's.
Did you have any special clothes to go on the walk?
Well, my mother used to go up the [Flat Iron] market and buy me a bit of a frock and it'd be sixpence ha'penny, the frock. And she used to wash it and iron it up, and it used to be lovely. And put a bit of ribbon round ...[63]

In the dockland community of St Bartholomew's in the era of the 1911 Salford dock strike, there was no escape from public manifestations of poverty.

May Day was another important point in the festive calendar. Again, much emphasis was placed upon the role of children. In Manchester and Salford, the custom whereby girls formed May queen processions flourished throughout the period before 1939. Girls chose their own queen, who was usually dressed in improvised finery made from lace curtains and tissue paper, and paraded their home street with a 'maypole', performing songs and dances in return for coppers from neighbours. In parts of the two cities, boys blacked their faces to form so-called 'nigger troupes' as an additional procession, and May Day therefore provided an occasion for working-class charity, as children who rarely had money of their own were treated with halfpennies and pennies towards a party.[64]

The processions aroused mixed opinions among outside observers. An article in the Manchester magazine *Faces and Places* in 1903 saw the ritual as a welcome sign of rural influences, and a much-needed diversion for poor city children.[65] By contrast, a school teacher who wrote to the *Manchester Guardian* in May 1923, complaining of a class of seven-year-olds who were addicted to the ceremonies, referred disparagingly to 'the fantastic little get-up of the grubby little May queens with their ubiquitous staffs of collectors'. When the class were asked to put some of their May Day songs on paper, one girl provided the following verses:

I am a likl May quenn,
I juth come from the wuz,
I brort a bunsh of rosese,
For you to see my love.

And if you do not like them,
I'll tek them back agane,
I'll tek them to the wuz,
And you won't find them agane.

A second song (now commonly heard in oral history interviews) was:

The Queen of the May, Manchester, 1903.

We come to greet you on the First of may,
And we hope you will not turn us away,
For we dance and sing our mary ring,
Around the Maypole gay.
For we all, for we all, sweet danties are we.[66]

In Ordsall, May queen processions were not restricted to schoolgirls. Women who worked at Haworth's mill in Ordsall Lane frequently describe how mill girls held their own ceremonies:

The Maypole [procession] were just mill girls. Well, they started at thirteen in there.
Did you do that yourself when you started at Haworth's?
Yes ... I was one of the young kids there, we went round for money for Salford Royal [Hospital].
Who organised that?
I was in the weaving shed, well your weaver organised it ... we used to go in someone's backyard practising ... and she'd get a bit of tissue paper for us to get dressed up.[67]

Mrs Cunliffe also described processions of girls from Haworth's: 'They used to go door to door, singing, all the little side-streets ... some'd give us nothing, [others] would say, "Sing for us first, before you get a ha'penny off us".'[68]

These accounts refer to the period before 1920, but the custom persisted at least until the early 1930s. Mrs Sugden worked at Haworth's during the inter-war period:

> They used to get a Maypole and dress it up, pick the smallest one for the queen. And they used to go round the streets at night.
> *So the mill girls went round Ordsall?*
> Where each of 'em lived, we'd go up their street. Oh aye, we were full of tricks.
> *How old would the girls be who were doing that with you?*
> About fifteen or sixteen. The older ones wouldn't have a go, we used to try and get 'em to have a go, but they wouldn't.[69]

The May Day procession allowed working-class girls to adopt the role of itinerant entertainers, performing in Salford's natural 'recreation room', the streets.

The May queen processions were restricted to girls unless a boy was recruited to carry the maypole. In the Ordsall and Hope Street districts of Salford, 'nigger troupes' provided an alternative May Day parade, in which boys predominated, although girls sometimes took part as well. In Ordsall:

> Now the boys had nigger troupes that day.
> *Nigger troupes?*
> Nigger troupes they called them. I suppose it's a crime to mention it now, but they would black their faces, they would borrow anybody's old clothes, trousers too long, they had to make themselves look funny. All old gear, anything like that, black their faces, old caps and things on. They'd go in a group, and sing daft songs like 'Paddy had a job on the railroad', just stand round and knock on the door. They'd open the door and they'd sing:
>
> > All you peaky lads keep away from me
> > If my girl sees you she'll only be after me
> > She's in Strangeways doing the time for me
> > All you peaky lads keep away from me
> >
> > I'm a collier by trade
> > And I wield a pick and spade
> > I can push a little wagon up a brew
> > I get fifty bob a week
> > And a wife and kids to keep
> > I'm a collier of Pendlebury brew
>
> ... if the nigger troupe got a copper, it was really from the man of the house, who saw the funny side of it.[70]

The teacher who wrote to the *Manchester Guardian* in 1923, complaining about the popularity of the May queen ritual, pointed out that:

A prime favourite with the 'nigger bands', who invariably accompany the procession, is an old rhyme beginning:

> There was a little nigger
> And he grew no bigger,
> So they put him in a wild beast show.

Another popular song among the city's seven-year-olds was:

> She's a ragtime soldier's wife,
> She's a ragtime soldier's wife,
> Early every morning she takes her stand
> At the pawnshop door with a bundle in her hand.
> She's a ragtime soldier's wife,
> In and out the pubs all day,
> She's half a dozen rings on her fingers,
> Out of another man's pay.[71]

The names adopted by the children, 'nigger' troupes and bands, and the first of the songs recorded by the school teacher, reveal a strong awareness of racial types. In Ordsall, where the dockside streets around Monmouth Street were christened 'Little Africa', black seamen were an established presence in the community. However, the stereotypes used among local children drew upon the alternative, music-hall figure, the 'nigger minstrel', which was central to the formation of racial stereotypes throughout Manchester and Lancashire.[72] The songs performed by boys on May Day reveal a second common concern. 'All you peaky lads' and the 'ragtime soldier's wife' satirize the relation between the sexes in a way which helps to explain the suggestion that in Ordsall, it was 'the man of the house who saw the fun of it'.

When asked if Bolton children formed minstrel troupes, Mrs Holden described a very different ritual, pace-egging, which also involved the blackening of faces:

> *Did you ever know of children teaming up for what they called the 'nigger' troupe, where they blackened their faces?*
> Oh yes, we used to call that pace-egging. That was on Good Friday, and we had a place at Bolton called Rivington Pike ... well, they used to go up there and they would all be black faces and they would all carry a basket of eggs ... they would go up to the top of the Pike and then they would all stand in a row and roll these eggs down ... and that's what they call pace-egging, and they would have their names on these eggs and the one that got to the bottom first would win ... And there was loads of children used to come from all over. And then when all that was done ... the pace eggers, they all had clogs on ... and they used to come round the streets and sing ... in a ring with these sticks, and these bells used to be jangling and their faces all black and their lips all red and whiten their eyes ... and all the street, they used to come out at the door clapping ...

Did you know anybody who took part in that?
Oh yes, anybody out of the street that wanted to do it could join in ...
any of the neighbours if they had a lad ...
What sort of age would they be?
Well, I wouldn't say old men, up to about thirty, thirty-five ...[73]

A century earlier, pace-egging was part of the calendar of popular customs in Middleton, a weaving village north of Manchester described by Samuel Bamford.[74] Mrs Holden's account shows that the custom was adapted in an urban context by the early twentieth century. The pace-egging ceremony was conducted on open ground, but was followed by street performances given by local men and lads rather than itinerant entertainers. This form of amusement was far removed from the world of commercialized mass leisure, but it took place in an industrial neighbourhood: Mrs Holden's home was situated in a mill district in Bolton, and she entered the cotton industry upon leaving school.

There is no documentary or oral evidence that pace-egging took place in Manchester or Salford at this time. However, one respondent who was born in Ordsall in 1914 was familiar with the ritual described by Mrs Holden:

Did you ever hear of pace eggers at Easter? I was told about it in Bolton and I've never heard of it going on in Salford.
No, it hasn't. No, the only thing about Easter eggs, which is what that comes from, in Bolton I think they used to hard boil the eggs and roll them down. And you had to, well its only because I've seen it in lantern slides ... Well I've seen them doing that, and the lads of course all had clogs on, but Bolton's a clog-makers' place.
Where did you see that slide?
At Dock Mission.[75]

Salford and Bolton are only seven miles apart, yet pace-egging was presented as another culture at the Dock Mission in the Ordsall district of Salford. Many historians have emphasized the uniformity of 'traditional' working-class culture, but oral testimony, by contrast, highlights significant local variations in popular custom, even between urban centres in South East Lancashire.[76]

Saturday night markets

In an essay written in 1904, Frank Jordan pointed out that, 'There are a great many people who live in and around Manchester, whose week is not, to them, complete without the Saturday night is spent in the very heart of the city.' The main attraction was the Saturday night market at Shudehill, which held a dual appeal, as a source of cheap food and free entertainment, which ensured that the Saturday night trip to 'town' was a central fixture in the social life of working-class families.[77]

The custom of touring the market areas on Saturday nights was immensely popular in Manchester and Salford from the mid-nineteenth century to the mid-twentieth century. John Page gave a vivid portrayal of the atmosphere at Shudehill during the 1850s. The stallholders were widely recognized as entertainers, and Page described the patter of a 'Cheap Jack' selling hardware by Dutch auction:

> Here is a concern in Shudehill, Manchester. The front of the van is hung round with guns, bridles, trays, rules, measuring tapes, braces, belts, handsaws ... The platform is occupied by a middle-aged man in a red plush waistcoat with sleeves, corduroy breeches, white stockings, and high–low shoes ... it is eight o'clock at night – a Saturday night in February. In front of the van, with the bright glare of the lamp reflected on their upturned faces, stand, at least, two hundred persons, mostly men – there are some women amongst them – and a good sprinkling of lads. I am a few seconds late to hear what 'John' has said to cause such a general roar of laughter ... [selling a pocket-knife] 'Remember, this is a well-bred knife, its father was a razor, and its mother was a butcher's cleaver ...'[78]

The Saturday night markets drew huge crowds during the second half of the nineteenth century. In 1870, it was estimated that 15 000–20 000 people made the Saturday night trip to Shudehill, although the majority sought to take their Sunday dinner home with them, which made Saturday night a time for essential food shopping, not a period of unbridled leisure. The price of foodstuffs dropped considerably by late Saturday, as the vendors lowered their prices to try and shift their stock before the market closed. 'High change', or the peak in trading, lasted until 10 o'clock, and working-class housewives, hunting for bargains, made Saturday evening the busiest time in the market all week.[79]

The entertainments on offer around Shudehill were impressive. In addition to the free spectacle provided by the traders, small-scale leisure entrepreneurs saw the Saturday night crowds as a good target, and new forms of amusement found their way into the variety of attractions which the market could offer. On a Saturday night in 1867, Shudehill was:

> ... alive with animation, and amid a blaze of gas all is life and bustle. In the outskirts of the market place you may have yourself accurately weighted and measured for one halfpenny. For the same sum you may receive a shock from a galvanic battery. You may then enjoy a few moments' sporting, by shooting at a target over a rifle range extending about two yards ... you have thrown in free of charge, an oral lecture ... explanatory of a great portion of your own interior, accompanied, at a short distance, by the strains of an energetic Scotch fiddler requesting you to 'come through the heather, around him gather, for wha'll be King but Charlie ...'[80]

Touring the market brought men and women together, in contrast to activities like drinking which tended to keep couples apart. Those with children in tow were usually the most careful shoppers, whereas courting couples, with fewer domestic responsibilities, treated the wander around the market as more of an excursion.[81]

Salford's Flat Iron market fulfilled many of the same functions as Shudehill, although the Flat Iron attracted a good deal of controversy between 1890 and 1939, when the market was finally closed. The poverty of the Flat Iron was much more acute, and more visible. The second-hand clothes dealers, operating on the open ground around Trinity Church, lacked any claim to respectability. The poverty of the Flat Iron was an embarrassment to Salford's civic pride. The location of the market, at the gateway to Manchester, meant that the corporation was unwilling to tolerate the outdoor traders, even though the market was also conveniently situated close to some of the poorest districts in Salford, like Greengate and the Adelphi.[82]

None the less, the market captured the imagination of a series of journalists who were impressed by its atmosphere, and the performances of the traders in hardware, crockery, cheap furniture and clothing. The market was a famous Salford landmark, described by one writer as a 'carnival of copper'.[83] Robert Roberts saw things differently:

> Those in greatest need found even the old brokers' shops too expensive: they bought everything from the local Flatiron market. Some writers since have found a certain romance about the place; it is hard to see why. The 'Flatiron' differed little from any other street mart in our industrial cities, except perhaps that, established close by a ganglion of railway lines, it lay constantly under the thickest smoke pall in Britain. It's frequenters then, could have looked sleazier, and the pathetic wares on sale even more grimy than most. In such places poverty busied itself.[84]

Despite the surrounding display of poverty, in the early decades of the twentieth century, the Flat Iron market featured a fairground as well as the trading area, with roundabouts, shooting galleries, boxing booths and a cheap theatre. Moreover, as at Shudehill, the traders were judged to be worth watching. In 1906, a journalist on the *Manchester Guardian* described:

> ... the auctioneer striding up and down the platform of his stall, by turns wheedling the people with a honeyed tongue, or with winks and sideways glances setting the women giggling and the men roaring, or browbeating them with his fiercer banter until he has them at his mercy. 'Some of ye don't come to buy, s'elp me ... ye come to pinch.'[85]

Markets also figure prominently in retrospective accounts of life in Manchester and Salford in the early twentieth century. This evidence provides more precise illustrations of the ways in which this custom fitted into individual family lifestyles than can be obtained from documentary sources. An evening spent around the markets and main streets could be an occasion for married couples to spend time together; it also afforded parents with young children the chance to go out as a family. In her auto-biography, Alice Foley recalled:

> The trip we loved best was to be taken to town on an occasional Saturday evening. Here was life at its gayest and rowdiest; the open shop fronts lit by paraffin flares, competing traders bawling their wares, and narrow streets crowded with buyers or gaping sight-seers. The poorest groups hung on until closing time, near Midnight, when one shilling parcels containing a rabbit, assorted vegetables and fruit, could be had, making sure a good Sunday dinner. The covered market was a mecca for the townsfolks.[86]

In homes where the struggle against poverty shaped leisure, as all other activities, this Saturday night custom retained the functions recognized by journalists in the nineteenth century. First, there were bargains to be had, particularly foodstuffs which traders had no means of storing over the weekend. This could be crucial to the household economy of the poor. Their poverty dictated that even Saturday night, the peak in the weekly leisure cycle, could not be free from domestic responsibilities. And yet, at the same time, the liveliness of markets and main streets was a source of entertainment in itself. As Foley pointed out, both shoppers and 'gaping sight-seers' were catered for by the markets.

Mrs Holden went to Bolton market as a girl, around the eve of the First World War, to buy food for her mother to cook for her family's Sunday dinner, the week's main meal. Her mother used the cheap meat to feed a family of nine living on one wage, and this account shows how trips to the market could play a vital role in the family economy:

> ... my mam would give me a brown paper carrier bag with a string handle and sixpence ... and about five minutes to ten I used to make my way to the market, and there would be crowds, all around ... the feller would have a great big table ... and him and his assistants would be stood in the middle of it. And they would have all these rabbits, and poultry, small chickens, hens ... all round on this stall, that they hadn't sold ... he'd shout, 'Who'll give me one and six for this lovely big fat hen?' 'Course it was soon snapped up. And then when he'd sold all his hens, he'd come down to his chickens and them would go the same. I was waiting for rabbits ... And as soon as ever he put the first big pair of rabbits up ... he'd say, 'Now then, look what I've got for you', and he'd walk around and show all these rabbits, held up by their back legs, he said, 'Now I've got a pile of rabbits here ... first bidders gets 'em'. And as soon as he says, 'Now who'll give me a tanner for this pair?' 'I will, mister! I will!' And I'd hand up the brown paper carrier, and he'd dump the two rabbits in. And I'd give him my sixpence and I was happy, I used to think, my mam will be pleased ... And do you know, she'd skin them rabbits, wash them, chop 'em all up into pieces ... She'd put these two rabbits in [a bowl] and two or

three big onions, carrots, and then she'd stock the coal oven up, and she'd cover this dish up, and she'd put it in the oven and let that cook slowly all night. And then, next morning, she'd make a whole dish of dumplings, and put them in this stewed rabbit, and that did all our Sunday's dinner and all our Sunday's tea, for sixpence.[87]

Salford's Flat Iron market, and Shudehill market in Manchester, have been widely described in similar terms.[88] Moreover, shopping expeditions from Salford to Shudehill were often shared between relatives or neighbours within the networks of mutual aid operated by housewives in working-class districts. Mrs Rowlings grew up in Ordsall, and she recalled joining her grandmother's shopping expeditions during the 1920s. They went to Shudehill for meat and vegetables, and the food was shared with her own mother, representing the main shopping trip for both women for the week.[89]

The market traders, known locally as 'spielers', were among the best-known characters in the two cities. Prominent among the stallholders at the Flat Iron market was Mary Newton:

> *Mrs Mullen*: They used to have a woman called Mary on the second-hand stall, and she'd bargain with these clothes, all second-hand. Everybody knew her.
> *Mrs Cooper*: She used to buy pawnshop bundles ... got them out. And By Jove, I don't care if there's anybody in Salford that's not been dressed up by Mary.
> *Mrs Mullen*: She used to pick something up and she'd [gasp]. And you'd think, 'Oh that's beautiful' ... she had it all off to a T.[90]

She was also recalled by Mrs MacLeod:

> They all had patter. Mary'd say, 'Here y'are, a pair o'knickers that Princess Marina wore' ...
> *Were they worth watching?*
> Oh aye, it was an entertainment. You used to stand there, you'd listen to 'em ... Mary could sell anything ...[91]

Mary Newton was one of a series of Salford celebrities associated with the market. When Janey Garner, the 'grand old lady' of the Flat Iron, died in 1938, a year prior to the market's closure, her death was recorded by the *Salford City Reporter*:

> Many people, including stall holders from the Flat Iron market, attended Salford Cathedral on Monday afternoon to pay their last tribute of respect to Mrs. Jane Garner, aged 85, of Deal Street, Salford. For over 60 years Mrs Garner had an Ice Cream Stall at the Flat Iron Market and she was one of Salford's best-loved characters, popularly known as 'Ice-Cream Janey'.[92]

Traders who sold by Dutch auction had a routine which thrived on audience participation. Miss Osgood described Flat Iron market in the 1920s:

A spieler at work, Flat Iron market, Salford, 1933.

Were there any characters amongst them?
Oh yes, especially the men that sold the pots ... and the men that sold shoddy goods, that were no good really, but they made you believe that you were buying fantastic things. They call them the spielers, and they had a way with them, they'd sell ice to Eskimoes, those fellers, the way they used to talk. And all the women used to fall for it ... they'd say, 'Right, so-many pounds of tomatoes there, am I asking sixpence?' And the women'd shout, 'No!' 'Am I asking fivepence even?' 'No!' ... he'd get as low as he could, with making a profit. And then you'd hear one woman say, 'I'll have that' ... he used to chuck 'em, perhaps she'd get a pound of tomatoes for twopence or threepence ... it was a way of life, all the women used to love to shout 'No!' ...[93]

The market was a place where married women among the shoppers behaved boisterously. There is nothing subdued in this routine. The stall-holders were entertainers, and recognized as such. In interviews, many people stress that it was the fact that the trip to Shudehill or the Flat Iron cost nothing which accounted for the popularity of the markets as a Saturday night rendezvous. As Mrs Bennett put it: 'You could spend a night [out] and not spend a penny'.[94]

The custom of touring the market districts on a Saturday night was widely shared by working-class youths. In 1905, Charles Russell claimed that 'nearly all Manchester lads' made the Saturday night trip to Shudehill, and certain comparisons may be drawn with the Sunday evening monkey parades. The tour around Shudehill provided another communal leisure form, in which participation cost nothing. Russell commented:

> Sometimes the chance of picking up a small bargain at one of the stalls is the attraction but on the whole it seems to be a desire to see their fellows and to talk over with other lads, whom they may not see again for another week, their various doings in the football field, or the successes and disasters of 'City' or 'United'. Working lads generally change into their Sunday clothes, or, in their own expressive language, 'toff themselves up', for Saturday night, and even if they have been to a concert, a theatre, or a music hall, will take a tour round 'the market' before finally going home ... Crowded as it is with young folk, mainly youths, surprisingly little disorder of any kind prevails; the lads are quite content to promenade up and down the long central avenue, meeting and talking with their friends.[95]

Working lads recognized the value of any form of free entertainment. In Joe Toole's words, 'The open market was a free attraction, and extremely welcome when you were broke.'[96]

The markets remained a Saturday night mecca for working-class youths during the 1920s and 1930s, attracting young people of both sexes, who were drawn by the 'carnival' atmosphere of the market districts.[97] Mr Peters went to Salford's Cross Lane market in his late teens, around 1930: '... we used to go round the market ... and watch all the other mugs spending the money. We couldn't, because we hadn't got any to spend, so you'd get a night's entertainment like that'.[98] Despite the immense popularity of the cinema and the dance hall among working-class youths, the expansion of commercial entertainment, even in the inter-war decades, did not destroy this older, nineteenth-century youth custom. Saturday night markets survived alongside the Sunday night monkey parades during the 1930s, which confirms that communal forms of free leisure continued to play a role in working-class youth culture.

The tendency among working people to gather in the central market districts of Manchester and Salford on Saturday nights was acknowledged by those concerned with trading opinions as well as those trading goods. When Frank Jordan surveyed the scene in Tib Street, close to Shudehill, on a Saturday night in 1904, he believed that he had discovered 'the most motley collection of gatherings ever seen'. Crowds surrounded two street preachers and, more surprisingly, a mathematician, a coarse critic of the teaching of the arithmetic in schools.[99] Political activists were also to be found in the ranks of Tib Street orators. Joe Toole, who was to become the first Labour MP for South Salford, served his political apprenticeship in Social Democratic Federation street meetings in Salford, while subsequently, in Manchester, 'at the corner of Tib Street and Market Street ... we used to run Labour meetings every Saturday and Sunday evening. Our platform was open to anyone, friend or foe – "let 'em all come", was our cry'.[100] Situated close to Shudehill, which attracted working people in droves on Saturday nights, the open air meetings were aimed at people on their way to and from the markets, as part of their night out in 'town'.

The custom of flocking to the town centre was common throughout the Lancashire cotton towns, where the market areas were crowded on a number of evenings, especially Saturdays, each week. As the North of England Society for Women's Suffrage observed in 1905:

> In the cotton districts during the summer months the workers spend their evenings out of doors, more after the fashion of continental than English towns, and on certain nights of the week anyone going into the market-place can get an audience of interested and intelligent men and women, varying from 600 to 1,000 and even 1,500, who will stand for an hour or two to hear the question discussed.[101]

Manchester's most popular debating ground was situated in Stevenson Square, again close to Shudehill. The Square had a history of open air meetings. According to Swindells, writing in 1907:

> For three-quarters of a century the square has been popular with open-air orators. Innumerable have been the causes advocated from improvised platforms. Religious gatherings representing most phases of religious thought, temperance and social reform meetings, and mass meetings of Liberals, Conservatives, Socialists and Chartists have been held there ... on occasions I have seen three or four separate gatherings grouped round speakers who have been advocating entirely different views.[102]

Stevenson Square retained its role as a debating ground during the inter-war decades, and in 1931, on the Sunday after the formation of the National Government, crowds estimated at 3000–4000 gathered to hear a series of Labour and Communist speakers discussing the news. Leading local orators included Jimmy Rochford, a Communist-turned-Catholic, and Kilgarrif, a former navy boxer, and Communist from Openshaw.[103]

Joe Toole described the 'propaganda pitch' in Trafford Road, the main dock road in Ordsall, which was one of the best-known debating grounds in Salford. By the 1930s, the area had been railed off by Salford Corporation, who, Toole claimed, feared the Labour and Socialist propaganda conducted there. In the early twentieth century, many leading British and international socialists had addressed the Trafford Road crowds, including Bernard Shaw and Liebknecht, while Toole himself heard James Connolly, leader of the 1916 Dublin Easter Rising, speaking on behalf of Ireland and the labouring classes. In Toole's view, the debates were popular because they provided another source of free entertainment:

When a man or woman with a shilling or two to spend at the end of
the week has bought the trivial luxuries that fall to the lot of those
who are always living from hand to mouth, time hangs heavily
between one Sunday morning and another, and that was one of the
reasons why the propaganda pitch in Trafford Road was so popular.[104]

In oral history interviews, the Flat Iron market and Manchester's Shudehill
are constantly described as central features in the social life of the two
cities. The Trafford Road and Stevenson Square debating grounds feature
strongly in the memoirs of the politically active, but are mentioned less
frequently in a wider oral history sample, and appear to have played a
smaller part in the array of outdoor entertainment in the two cities.

Parks

Manchester and Salford were at the forefront of developments in the
provision of public parks and open spaces. Parks were established in the
two cities from the mid-nineteenth century, and were in part designed to
provide an alternative to the streets as a site for working-class recreation.
Supporters of the municipal parks claimed that they would prove beneficial
to the health and contentment of the working classes. They also argued
that the custom of promenading in the parks would bring members of
different classes together, as Mark Philips suggested in Manchester in
1844:

... the mutual improvement of all classes must be the result, together
with a greater degree of confidence between one class and another;
for the more they mix with one another, and the more they see of one
another, the more they will understand one another.[105]

The parks were envisaged as arenas of 'rational recreation', where the
tensions of a new urban society might be partially alleviated. Philips and
Queen's Parks in North Manchester, and Peel Park in Salford were established by the 1840s: each was situated close to vast areas of working-class
housing.

By the early twentieth century, parks were well-established features of
the landscapes of the two cities. In Salford, Peel Park was widely used by
residents of the Adelphi, Islington and Hope Street districts, while Ordsall
Park catered for the dock area, and Buile Hill Park was frequented by the
people of Hanky Park, Seedley and Weaste. By 1915, the city possessed
over 30 parks and recreation grounds, while Manchester boasted a total of
70, covering 1480 acres.[106] However, despite the progress of the parks
movement, some of the central working-class districts of Manchester were
poorly served. The Ancoats and Hulme districts, among the most heavily
populated in the city, possessed no parks, as the pace of industrial growth
during the nineteenth century had accounted for all the available land in

these inner areas.[107] Hulme possessed hardly any open spaces, although as James and Moore noted, 'on the outskirts of the district there are two public parks where children can play and where, in the summer, people walk, listen to the band and look at one another'.[108]

The parks were heavily used, especially at weekends and on public holidays, when the larger public parks, such as Peel Park, and Heaton Park in Manchester, were crowded with visitors. When Salford's Buile Hill Park was extended in 1903, it regularly drew numbers of local people estimated at 10 000 or more.[109] Adults and young people went for walks in the parks, or simply sat out, while children spent many hours playing games, especially during school holidays. To an extent, therefore, the parks were a success. However, the families who took most advantage of the parks were those who already tended to share family-orientated leisure activities. Mrs Darby visited the Salford parks at weekends with her husband: '... we had a walk to Buile Hill Park, all the parks, we used to visit the parks a lot, and sit there if it was nice weather. Take the children with us ... he was a good family man, I had a very good husband ...'.[110] Families where one of the parents was a heavy drinker were much less likely to share in the weekend promenades in the parks, so the section of the working class most distant from the ideal of rational recreation was least susceptible to the aims of the parks movement.

Courting couples and married women resorted to the parks in search of peace and quiet. Mrs Holden, for example, did some of her summer-time courting in the rose garden of Bolton's Queen's Park, where 'we could be alone to talk and wonder what our future held for us. In the summer evenings and weekends after work, this Park was a "Godsend" to couples like us with no money and nowhere else to go.'[111] Married women visited the parks on weekdays, if their domestic routines left them time for an afternoon out. As Mrs Darby recalled:

> I used to take the children, when I came to have a family ... I had a friend, and she used to bring her friend, she had children as well.
> *Would you go during the week?*
> Oh yes, go through the week, day-time, husbands at work. Get back at tea-time ... we'd just get together, for company.[112]

More active forms of leisure were also catered for, and many working people were drawn to the parks by brass band performances, which were immensely popular throughout the two cities. Top bands, including the famous Besses o' th' Barn, were hired by Salford Corporation, and in July 1927, a band concert drew an estimated 25 000 people to Peel Park.[113] Many families would turn out whenever a performance was held. Mr Gilmour's family lived in the Adelphi, but his father attended recitals throughout Salford and North Manchester:

> The bands in the parks were a feature of town life.
> *Who went to listen?*

'Dancing in the park: Bandstand, Peel Park', looking towards the Adelphi and Lower Broughton, L.S. Lowry, 1925.

They'd all go. The adults would be leaning on the rails, enjoying it, and the kids would be running around, going mad.
Did your parents go?
Yes, my father was very keen. He used to travel all over, outside Salford, to these bands, Buile Hill Park, Boggart Hole Clough ...[114]

By the early 1920s, dance music was played at the evening performances in Ordsall Park and Peel Park, where enclosures for dancing were built around the bandstands. In 1923, over 20000 people paid the admission fee of *3d.* to the enclosures.[115] Dancing to the bands in the park is widely recalled in Ordsall:

> ... they made a concrete ring round the bandstand in Ordsall Park and put railings round it. At the time I'd started dancing, it was thrippence to go in and dance, you danced on the concrete. And all the people were crowded round the rails outside, watching. You used to get hundreds go to watch. There was no other entertainment, so Monday night, everybody was up to the park. Mother would throw her shawl on, and everybody would be down there. And they'd be playing all the popular tunes. It was really good, and that was all free, unless you wanted to dance and you paid your copper ... if you had a young lady you'd take her in and you'd dance on the concrete.[116]

Teenagers went to park dances in gangs, as an alternative to attending the commercial dance halls, and the bands played waltzes and popular songs instead of overtures and marches.

Among working lads, parks and open spaces were also widely used for games of football, rugby and cricket. As an apprentice, Richard Heaton, for example, spent hours playing in Peel Park, in teams drawn from gangs of youths living around Hope Street, Salford.[117] In the wake of fears over 'national fitness' at the turn of the century, municipal authorities were keen to encourage participation in 'healthy' sports, and new facilities were provided during the 1900s, and again during the inter-war period. In 1926, the Salford Parks Superintendent claimed that:

> Nature is medicinal and restores tone to the body and mind of the fatigued worker in an industrial community, and a liberal provision of open spaces and opportunities for participation in outdoor games will be reflected in the improved health and contentment of the present and future Citizens.

Bowls, tennis and golf were increasingly promoted in the city parks, and the municipal bowling leagues, in particular, were a success, drawing over 100 000 customers in 1929.[118]

The use made of the parks did not always match the rational recreation ideal. In Ardwick, Manchester, prostitutes paraded around a park close to the army barracks, while the band performances in Ordsall Park, although widely popular among local people, were sometimes frequented by prostitutes working on Trafford Road, the main dock road which runs along the edge of the park. As Mr Dobson recalled, 'about three parts of the way through the evening, when they'd had a few drinks, they'd come into the park with the seamen and carry on dancing'.[119] Recreation grounds and parks were also used for gambling. One of Salford's open spaces was even christened 'One o'clock park' by locals as it was much favoured as a venue for reading the midday racing papers, and illicit gambling schools were widely held in recreation grounds from the mid-nineteenth century until the 1930s.[120]

Although access to the parks was free, they were still beyond the reach of some working people. Young mothers, in particular, could find it difficult to manage a trip to the park due to the demands of housework and child-care. For such women, the home street remained a haven for leisure. Moreover, even in districts such as Ordsall, which did possess a park, children living some distance away were still confined to the streets for their playground.[121] Clothing was an additional burden. Respectability was at stake in the parks, and Sunday excursions required 'best' clothes. Parks could never replace the streets as a venue for working-class leisure, for they were simply not as convenient. For women in particular, leisure time spent on the doorstep was much less demanding. Streets were still the main 'recreation room', for children's games, the corner gangs of youths, and for sitting out and gossiping among adults, even though, for many families, time spent in the parks did provide an important break from home and street-centred lives.

six

Gambling

Gambling was one of the most pervasive of street activities. During the first half of the twentieth century, 'back entry bookmakers' operated throughout the working-class districts of the two cities, and their pitches were important features of the common scene. Despite a growing middle-class lobby against popular gambling, betting on horse races was one of the most popular working-class leisure pursuits. Informal 'gambling schools', held in the back streets in many working-class areas, formed a second arena for betting. Here, men gambled with coins in 'pitch and toss', with dice in 'crown and anchor', and on card games such as banker or pontoon.

In addition to these street-based activities, there was a host of traditional sports which were the focus of keen gambling. These included foot races, whippet races, pigeon flying and cockfighting, all of which served as occasions for betting in Salford and Manchester in the nineteenth and early twentieth centuries. Moreover, between 1900 and 1939, more modern forms of betting, on the football pools and at greyhound tracks, extended the range of gambling activities. Sport was a major preoccupation in the lives of working-class men, and popular sports were all closely bound to gambling.

In popular memory, gambling is widely associated with policing. Working-class gambling was the target of sustained legislative hostility from the mid-nineteenth century, and the 1906 Street Betting Act was specifically designed to stamp out cash betting on horse races as practised in the 'artisan' districts. In contrast, betting at the racecourses, or on credit through licensed bookmakers, patronized by upper- and middle-class gamblers, was given legal sanction.[1] Street gambling schools, another proletarian haunt, were illegal, and the character of street gambling was determined by its illicit status.

Despite the tightening of the class bias of the law, street gambling persisted on a huge scale in Salford and Manchester, as elsewhere. Under pressure from moral entrepreneurs, the local police forces were forced to take an active role against illicit gambling networks. However, an examination of the impact of police strategies only reveals the limitations of the police as an agency of control. Bookmakers and gambling schools used look-out systems to shield themselves from arrest, and during the inter-war period, it became increasingly apparent that relations between the police and bookmakers were heavily characterized by collusion. The exposure of allegations of police corruption posed serious difficulties for the chief constables of both Salford and Manchester, but despite mounting criticism, they were unable to enforce legislation which was widely perceived to be biased and therefore unjust.

This emphasis upon the limits of state authority contrasts with the work of social historians who have portrayed the police as the repressive arm of the Victorian state. Historians have tended to argue that popular culture was tamed during the nineteenth century, as its rougher elements were suppressed by a police force which grew in size and efficiency after 1850. Although it is widely recognized that police strategies sometimes met with resistance, much emphasis has been placed upon the transformative impact of policing, with Robert Storch arguing that it is impossible to understand nineteenth-century popular culture without keeping in mind 'the appearance of new conceptions of public order and social discipline, and the creation of new agencies of repression, regulation and constraint'.[2]

Gambling was popular throughout working-class society, across barriers of gender, age and skill. Although women gambled much less extensively than men, betting, at least on horse races and the football pools, appealed to both sexes. This is perhaps surprising, yet as Ross McKibbin has argued, gambling can be seen as a rational pursuit given the economic insecurities which governed working-class life during the early twentieth century.[3] Indeed, poverty and low wages tended to set the limits to the scale of working-class betting, imposing a more effective constraint upon popular gambling than any piece of legislation.

Local sources are extremely useful in a survey of gambling. A detailed combing of the Salford press, for example, provides evidence of shifts in police strategy and occasional insights into the organization of illegal gambling networks. Similarly, oral testimony is invaluable. Whereas the press tended to report the successes of the police, interviews provide a means of examining networks which were shielded from the law. This illustrates the weaknesses of law enforcement, taking the historian beyond sources compiled by the police themselves, as Raphael Samuel and Jerry White have shown in their studies of areas in East and North London.[4] Moreover, interviews with people who placed bets with back entry bookmakers or took part in gambling schools provide an alternative to the testimony of the 'experts', often anti-gambling campaigners, who provided much of the evidence at Parliamentary inquiries dealing with popular betting. This chapter employs oral and documentary sources to re-examine the role of gambling in working-class culture.

Back entry bookmakers and the police

Prior to the 1906 Street Betting Act, illicit bookmaking was frequently conducted in the side-streets in working-class districts, with look-outs posted on the street corners using a signal code to warn of the approach of the police. In 1900, Police-Sergeant Charles Bloomfield of the Manchester City Police listed the following gestures:

> Right hand raised to face – look out
> Handkerchief to face – the man on the beat
> Tying shoe laces – two plain clothes P.C.s about
> Hat raised – a stranger about
> A sharp walk from the corner – stop booking – danger[5]

The 1906 Act, which gave the police clearer powers to prevent loitering for the purpose of betting, drove bookmakers off the streets and into the back entries, or alleyways between the rows of terraced housing in working-class areas. In oral history interviews, the back entry bookmaker is a central figure in neighbourhood life from the early part of the century until the 1950s, prior to the legalisation of cash betting in 1960.

These illicit bookmakers operated from the backyards of terraced houses, with a clerk standing in the yard, dealing with the punters over the wall. People who wanted to place a bet would go down the alley and hand a piece of paper naming their fancy, along with their cash, over the wall of the yard. Both parties acknowledged the illicit status of the transaction: the punters used a nom de plume on their slips, and the bookmaker posted a look-out, known in Salford as a 'dogger-out', at both ends of the alley to watch for the police.[6]

When the police raided a bookmaker's pitch, they almost invariably arrested the man or woman posted at the end of the alley in lieu of the bookmaker. The look-out would not resist arrest, and after going to court, the bookmaker would pay his or her fine. Under this arrangement, the police filled their quota of arrests, while the bookmaker was safe from the threat of prosecution. This process was described by Mr Wilkinson, who helped to organize betting raids as a Detective-Sergeant in the Salford City Police during the inter-war period:

> A feller would be paid to stand there, and then occasionally the police would raid them. The bookie was very, very rarely caught, of course, because he was paying that man, when he got arrested, to hand over

ten pound. It was usually 'fined ten pound or fifty-one days'. Now the bookmaker wasn't in that at all. But the 'rubbing rag' was, the feller that was ... planted outside for the police to come. They didn't know who was coming, but occasionally we had a raid. And the feller would be caught and taken down to the headquarters, or to the divisional police office, and charged with 'loitering for the purpose of betting'.[7]

The police were well aware that street bookmakers were almost immune to prosecution. They made occasional raids, but were satisfied with arresting the look-out, leaving the bookmaker's pitch intact. This clearly fell far short of an attempt to enforce the 1906 Street Betting Act. As Table 6.1 shows, the annual level of arrests under the 1906 Act in Salford rose from between 100 and 200 between 1909 and 1914 to a level of around 400–500 after 1925.

William Bowen, who presented a detailed survey of betting in Salford to the Royal Commission on Lotteries and Betting in 1932, estimated that there were 200 bookmakers' pitches in the city, so even this higher level of police activity during the 1920s and 1930s meant that an individual pitch was unlikely to be raided more than two or three times a year.[8] Fines of £10, the figure given by Mr Wilkinson, were imposed for bookmaking offences throughout the period from 1907 to 1939. These were modest financial penalties compared to the potential takings at street betting pitches, although most of the working people who went to court on behalf of a bookmaker would have faced imprisonment if the bookmaker had failed to pay the fine for them.

Although sporadic police harassment was a feature of back entry bookmaking, the arrest of bookmakers' agents did little to foster respect

Table 6.1 Annual level of prosecutions in Salford under the 1906 Street Betting Act, 1907–38

Year	No	Year	No	Year	No
1907	69	1919	388	1931	466
1908	95	1920	512	1932	483
1909	102	1921	300	1933	430
1910	140	1922	213	1934	415
1911	192	1923	327	1935	395
1912	183	1924	655	1936	474
1913	194	1925	468	1937	432
1914	173	1926	502	1938	452
1915	55	1927	490		
1916	10	1928	503		
1917	8	1929	493		
1918	45	1930	520		

Source: Chief Constable's Reports.

for the legitimacy of the law or the authority of the police. Look-outs, often men without work, were regularly convicted for bookmaking, although their economic status was vastly inferior to that of a street bookmaker. Moreover, in working-class neighbourhoods, staged arrests were widely held to depend upon collusion between bookmakers and the police. Indeed, there is substantial evidence that in many instances bookmakers were tipped-off when a raid was due. The bookmaker would then employ a local man, or occasionally a woman, known as a 'jockey', to replace his regular look-out on the specified day, and the jockey would be arrested and taken to court. Mr Pearson 'stood out' for a bookmaker in the Hulme district in Manchester:

> I myself have been to court ... it was the normal routine, you stood out, and it was arranged between the bookmaker and the policeman ... the police sergeant would notify the back entry bookie, that he was going to be knocked-off that day. Well, he'd ask for some-body to stand out. Now, I stood out this particular day, and the routine was that I'd have a certain amount of money and a certain amount of bets in my pocket, and they always came in plain clothes. And then not far from the bookie that I was knocked off from was the police station, City Road ... Now then, the routine was to be taken in and the sergeant behind the counter would take your bets, and your money, then you'd go in a cell for about half an hour. After half an hour, two people would come along and they'd say they'd come to bail Mr Pearson out ... the next day you would go to court and you'd be called out, and the normal sentence at that time was a five pound fine. It didn't go on your record. It was just a wangle between the police and the betting people.
> *So it was arranged?*
> It was arranged, yes, I'd be there waiting for 'em to come and get me. I'd walk up Jackson Street towards City Road, and they'd be behind me. And I'll never forget the funny part of it. The bookmaker said to me, 'Now there's five shillings in there and that's for the sergeant behind the desk'. So these two fellers that've come to bail me out, they said to me, 'Has he given you a dollar [five shillings] for the police sergeant?' So I said, 'Yes'. 'We'll not give it him. We'll have that ourselves'. So, as I'm going out the police station, the big voice shouts behind me, 'Hey, haven't you forgotten something?' So right away I realised it was the sergeant after his five shillings.
> *Did you give him the five shillings?*
> Oh, I had to give it him ... otherwise he'd 've had me for summat else, some day.
> *Did the bookmaker pay the five pound fine?*
> Oh aye.
> *That was a lot of money, wasn't it?*
> It was a lot of money, yes, those days. And the young policemen on

the beat were a bit clever and they used to come round when ... they weren't expected to come round. Because ... if the bookmaker didn't grease the police, he got done more than he should have done. So the policeman used to come down, and he'd get half a crown off the book-maker.[9]

Retrospective testimony provides countless descriptions of this process, which appears to have taken a similar form throughout Manchester and Salford. Significantly, various levels of the local force are implicated in his account, from the plain-clothed detectives to the desk sergeant and the beat constables. The police had no need to use physical force in making the arrest, and, by walking behind the offender on his way to the police station, ensured that he suffered little loss of dignity during apprehension. In court, Mr Pearson pleaded guilty, with the bookmaker's son in attendance waiting to pay his fine. Mr Pearson did not even hand the money over. Occasionally, the pretence was exposed in court. In November 1920, a Salford man, asked how he was going to pay a fine of £10 imposed for illicit bookmaking, replied that he was 'expecting the bookmaker any minute'.[10]

In 1932, William Bowen described how the arrest of 'jockeys' followed a regular procedure:

He is given money and he is given slips, neither of which refer to that day's betting. He is then told to wait here until the officer comes along, who asks (it is almost a set dialogue): 'Which is it?' The man says, 'It's me'. The man is arrested ... he is allowed out on bail; he comes back the next morning; he is tried with a number of other men similar to himself; they all admit the offence ... They are fined £10. They receive the £10 from the bookmaker's clerk ... the fine is paid.[11]

However, relations between bookmakers and the police were not universally corrupt. If that had been the case, bookmakers would not have employed look-outs on a regular basis, as they would only have needed one when they had notice of a raid. Although references to collusion are a consistent feature of oral history interviews, a number of respondents also described occasions when the police attempted to launch surprise raids against betting pitches. Detectives sometimes adopted disguises, even posing as 'midden men', or refuse collectors, in order to penetrate a pitch to try to arrest the person receiving the bets.[12] Clearly, attempts were occasionally made to enforce the 1906 Street Betting Act, and bookmakers could not afford to operate without look-out systems. Moreover, although collusion may have smoothed relations between bookmakers and the police, a system which depended in part upon bribery could easily breed resentment among individual bookmakers or their employees, if they felt that they were being victimized by the police. John Hilton, who gave a talk on gambling during his BBC radio series in 1936, published the following extract from a letter he received from one of his listeners:

> I am the wife of a bookmaker's runner, he gets 1*s*. in the £ for horses
> or football pools as well. He has been taken from our very doorstep
> and dragged through the streets, because another bookmaker pays
> the Police to take him and make him pay £10 at the least ... I could
> fill a book with some of the dirty tricks that have been played on my
> husband, by men dressed up in dirty filthy rags, that decent workmen
> would not be seen in; they are called plain clothes policemen. But
> even if these said men of course must do their work you would expect
> them to do the job off their own bat, but they don't, they go and drink
> with the other bookies who pay them well, and then go straight to the
> little runner and as they call it, 'knock him off'.[13]

Relations between the gambling fraternity and the police could therefore
be characterized by conflict as well as collusion. Robert Roberts claimed in
The classic slum that 'Old bookmakers, talking of the time, state categori-
cally that they had to bribe the police frequently to stay in business at
all', and there is considerable documentary evidence to show that police
strategies towards street bookmaking involved extortion.[14]

In the 1880s and the 1930s, scandals erupted over the regulation of
bookmakers in Salford, and the subsequent debates in the local press are
an important source of evidence concerning police practice. In October
1885, Jabez Bradbury alleged that corruption was rife in certain sections of
the city police. At a meeting of the Salford City Council, he claimed that:
'the detectives had got from betting men scores of hundreds of pounds ...
They had thought more about extorting money ... than about doing their
duty ...'[15] The chief constable rejected the accusation in letters to the
Manchester and Salford press, but a special meeting of the Salford Watch
Committee found one sergeant and one constable guilty of extortion, and
both men were dismissed from the force.[16]

In 1932, a national scandal followed a speech made to an ecclesiastical
conference in Durham by Canon Peter Green, Rector of St Philip's Church,
Salford. He outlined the process whereby the police warned bookmakers of
impending raids, declaring that:

> I do not say that the police are all corrupt. Most of them are perfectly
> straight, and the uniformed men are almost untouched. It is the
> plain-clothes men and detectives – the great majority of whom are
> upright and honourable – but the temptations are strong and some
> of them are undoubtedly bribed ... A police officer will go to a book-
> maker and say: 'It is time you were on the carpet. Put a dummy at
> the end of the street at twelve o'clock on Thursday and I will take
> him'.[17]

The speech provoked a bitter controversy in the national and local press.
Peter Green was Canon of Manchester, so in reports in the national
newspapers, Manchester was implicated in his charges, although he was
known locally as a Salford figure. The chief constable of Manchester, John

Maxwell, the chairman of the Manchester Watch Committee, and the chairman of the Bench in the Manchester City Police Court, Nathan Laski, all challenged Canon Green to name his witnesses or state that Manchester was exempt from his accusations. In contrast, Major C.V. Godfrey, the chief constable of Salford, and Alderman Hughes, chairman of the Salford Watch Committee, refused to comment upon the allegations when pressed by reporters. The issue therefore developed as an exchange between Canon Green and the Manchester police establishment.[18]

After a week's furious correspondence, conducted in the letters page of the *Manchester Guardian*, the controversy faded, and in contrast to the incident in 1885, there were no bureaucratic repercussions. The Manchester Watch Committee declared its support for the city police, while the Salford committee ignored the allegations.[19] Canon Green did provide details of a series of cases, including incidents which he alleged had taken place in Manchester, in letters to the *Manchester Guardian*.[20] He claimed that the police knew that they could never stamp out street betting, and had therefore devised a policy to avoid the persecution of individual bookmakers or punters. If they raided a pitch without warning, punters would lose their wagers, and the bookmaker would risk losing his clientele. This would create hostility towards the police which could be avoided if a warning was given. Canon Green claimed that this arrangement was common knowledge in working-class areas, and warned that when the chief constable issued statements denying that collusion took place, 'Manchester simply laughs'.[21]

The following year, Walter Greenwood outlined the operation of a back entry pitch and the nature of collusion between bookmakers and the police in *Love on the dole*. Greenwood described a scene in which winnings were paid out on behalf of Sam Grundy, a bookmaker in Hanky Park:

> ... people ... flowed into the back entry through three openings, where, at each, an unemployed man unable to find any other occupation, offered himself ostensibly as paid sentinel to keep a look out for Two Cities' policemen, all of whom knew that at any day and at the appropriate time, law breakers could have been arrested by the score. For some reason or other their beats took them elsewhere than the back entry's vicinity during Sam's business hours. Though, occasionally, plain clothes men did come upon the scene to take away the sentinels whose fines were paid by Sam. Though Sam looked upon this expenditure as a kind of rent due to the law for permitting his transgressions.[22]

The novel was criticized, partly for its portrayal of the police, by the wife of a prominent Salford businessman in a letter to the *Woman Citizen*. Greenwood replied, tartly, drawing attention to this paragraph while adding: 'The Chief Constable's comment on this would be interesting'.[23] It was, however, a further three years before Salford's chief constable entered the public debate.

The next controversy, in 1936, followed the renewal of complaints that the Salford police were not doing enough to drive gambling off the streets. On behalf of evangelical organizations in the city, William Bowen approached the Salford Watch Committee to complain of 'the serious damage ... caused to the community' by the practice of street betting, and the arrest of stooges in place of bookmakers. In an interview with the *Manchester Guardian*, Bowen stressed that his charges concerned the efficiency rather than the integrity of the force.[24] However, the watch committee, which had refused to become drawn into the 1932 dispute, was forced to order an examination into the enforcement of the law against street betting in the city.

On this occasion, the chief constable, Major Godfrey, was obliged to write a special report, in which, hardly surprisingly, he concluded that collusion between his men and the bookmakers was 'impossible'. As proof that no corruption existed, Godfrey claimed that during 1934, 23 Salford bookmakers had been arrested under the 1906 Street Betting Act. He pointed out that under procedures he had introduced, only plain-clothed officers picked at very short notice were used in raids against betting pitches, while superintendents were encouraged to borrow men from other divisions when acting against bookmakers. Godfrey claimed that these extreme measures had been introduced not because it had been found necessary to prevent collusion, but to safeguard the force against suspicion.

Bowen's campaign, and the subsequent pressure upon the chief constable to tighten local enforcement of the law against working-class betting, led to an increase in attempts to prosecute bookmakers rather than their employees, which helps to explain why oral testimony describes both collusion and genuine attempts to raid pitches. Even so, the total number of arrests under the 1906 Act in Salford during 1934 was 414, which leaves 391 cases where the bookmaker escaped prosecution. This testifies at least to the efficiency of look-out systems against the police, but it is clearly possible that some of the cases involved collusion. Oral testimony is not precise enough to gauge shifts in police practice in one year, but the weight of available documentary and taped evidence suggests that bookmakers survived police harassment during the inter-war period through a combination of their own warning systems, collusion and the level of public sympathy they received. Of course, the extent of collusion may well have varied between different divisions within the Salford force.

Despite Bowen's criticisms of the Salford police, Godfrey showed that activity against bookmakers was maintained at a much higher level in Salford than in other cities of comparable size, as Table 6.2 shows. The failure to suppress street betting in Salford therefore represented defeat for an unusually vigilant police campaign. In Salford by the 1930s, the intensity of the local anti-gambling campaigns led by Canon Peter Green and William Bowen, and the canon's readiness to publicize allegations of police corruption, made betting an important test of police efficiency. The chief constable was obliged to maintain a high level of arrests in order to preserve the reputation of the local force. However, Godfrey

Table 6.2 Convictions under the 1906 Street Betting Act during 1934

	Population	*Convictions*
Salford	223 400	414
Bradford	300 900	16
Bristol	399 900	38
Cardiff	223 800	77
Coventry	182 000	0
Derby	142 300	0
Hull	315 200	24
Leeds	486 400	28
Leicester	241 300	2
Newcastle	283 600	53
Nottingham	270 900	4
Portsmouth	251 500	5
Plymouth	207 600	7
Stoke	279 900	2
Swansea	165 500	15

Source: *Salford City Reporter*, 10 January 1936.

conceded that: 'The great majority of the working-class do not regard betting as a crime, or even morally wrong.' The double standard of the law was well known and the 1906 Street Betting Act was resented, rather than respected, in the city. Consequently, according to the chief constable: 'the sympathy of the general public is always with the bookmaker against the police whenever a raid is made on a betting pitch. They are ever ready to assist the bookmaker and to obstruct the police by giving warning of their approach.' He acknowledged that the task of enforcing a law which failed to win the respect of the public was one of the most difficult facing the police. In this instance, popular hostility towards the law reflected the widespread working-class belief that betting was an acceptable practice.

The chief constable's report provided a remarkably candid statement of the difficulties encountered by the police. Godfrey concluded that the suppression of street betting was impossible. The sheer scale of the crime made it impossible to act against all the bookmaking businesses in the city, and piecemeal arrests did nothing to wipe out a highly profitable industry. His men could do nothing more than make limited arrests, and ignore the vast majority of the offences they observed. His only proposal was that the council should write to the Home Secretary to advocate the legalization of cash betting.[25] Gambling was a source of peculiar difficulty for the Salford constabulary. Other problems encountered in policing working-class neighbourhoods did not attract the glare of publicity, and therefore caused fewer anxieties for the chief constable. For example, although the police were unable to stamp out Saturday night brawls outside public houses,

Johnny Boden, Hanky Park bookmaker during the interwar years, and
Canon Peter Green, Salford's most outspoken anti-gambling campaigner.

these outbreaks of street violence affected only those living in the immediate neighbourhood, and rarely attracted the attention of middle-class
moral entrepreneurs.

Bookmakers and neighbourhood life

The standing enjoyed by Salford's bookmakers within working-class
communities can be partly explained by examining their role as employers.
In 1932, William Bowen claimed that a street bookmaker's clerk earned a
weekly wage of £3 in return for assuming daily responsibility for receiving
bets and paying out winnings. Moreover, each bookmaker's pitch required
the protection of two 'doggers-out' against the police, at a combined weekly
cost of 50*s*.[26] Look-outs were drawn on a casual basis from the ranks of
the unemployed, although a few achieved what was almost a professional
status. Mrs Daly described Joe McGrath, one of the best known in Salford,
who worked for a bookmaker in Greengate:

> ... he used to be a tall, well-dressed chap with a trilby and he used to
> be always dogging out for the police ... [he] was very quick on the

Table 6.3 Convictions under the 1906 Street Betting Act in Salford during 1920: Age profile

Age	Number convicted	Percentage of those convicted
60–69	6	2.6
50–59	16	6.9
40–49	59	25.3
30–39	55	23.6
20–29	93	39.9
10–19	4	1.7
Total	233	100.0

Source: Compiled from data in the *Salford City Reporter*, 1920.[27]

eye, as quick as the policemen ... the police had to dress up in plain clothes, but they could tell the walk on them. And they just used to put their finger to their mouth and whistle. A couple of whistles for a sign that the detectives were on the prowl.[28]

A further set of employees, known as 'bookie's runners', were paid by commission to collect wagers from public houses and workplaces, while a 'jockey' like Mr Pearson could expect a single payment of £5 for an appearance in court on a bookmaker's behalf.[29] As Table 6.3 suggests, nearly 90 per cent of those convicted under the Street Betting Act in Salford during 1920 were aged between 20 and 50. Most were men at the peak of their earning potential, but without work. In court, they frequently justified their actions by asserting that they were unemployed and could find no other work. Only one was a woman, and when 50-year-old Ada Grindrod was convicted in October 1920, she was reported to be the first female prosecuted under the 1906 Act in Salford.[30]

Working-class women were still able to profit from street betting. Housewives received a weekly sum, estimated by Bowen at 10*s*. 6*d*., in return for permission to use a backyard for their pitch.[31] Further substantial rewards were offered. Mrs MacLeod described a pitch held by Tommy Myers in Greengate, where, when winnings were paid out:

... they used to go in through the back door, right through the front door and out ... they used to have a basin on the table, and you used to drop a few coppers in for the woman that owned the house ... Tommy Myers, he used to send Mrs Watson away [on holiday, in return for the use of her yard].[32]

In working-class areas, where unemployment and low and irregular wages meant that economic insecurity were a feature of urban life, the bookmaker possessed considerable economic power.

In *Love on the dole*, Sam Grundy 'the gross street-corner bookmaker'

Sam Grundy paying out winnings to Harry Hardcastle, from John Baxter's
film of Walter Greenwood's *Love on the dole* (1943).

stands as the most unattractive character in Hanky Park. The character
was reputedly based on a specific Hanky Park bookmaker during the 1920s
but Greenwood chose to develop a highly unflattering portrait.[33] In the
novel, Grundy's affluence is sharply contrasted with the sufferings of the
Hardcastles, members of the district's respectable poor. Their plight is only
alleviated when their daughter agrees to become Grundy's mistress, and he
in return uses his 'influence' to secure jobs for her unemployed brother and
father at a bus company. Greenwood, himself a Labour activist in Salford,
shared the distaste for gambling expressed by many Labour leaders from
the turn of the century,[34] yet surprisingly few traces of this hostility
emerge in oral history interviews. Bookmakers rarely lived among their
clientele and thus avoided the charge of exploiting their neighbours. Moreover, because they offered no credit facilities, they had no need to enforce
payment of gambling debts.[35]

Some of the Salford bookmakers were well-established neighbourhood
philanthropists. Joe Toole described Ordsall at the turn of the century:

How people could afford to back horses always puzzled me in those
days. Money seemed so scarce, yet we had several bookmakers around
us. They served one good purpose, however, for if a baby died and

there was no insurance to bury it, one could always depend on a ready response from them. One man named Moran always obliged.[36]

Bob Moran was a well-known Ordsall bookmaker during the 1930s, which confirms Bowen's assertion that by 1932, many of the back-street pitches in Salford had been established for over 25 years.[37] In Ordsall during the inter-war decades, bookmakers were renowned for offering help to those who suffered injuries at work, and Manchester's bookmakers maintained a similar reputation for altruism, as the chief constable, John Maxwell, pointed out:

> In fact I believe they are rather good to some of the poorer people round about them. I have had several instances where they have paid rents for people in difficulties and have paid their doctors' bills. In one case, a bookmaker, I understand, presented banners to the Church, and there are quite a lot of things like that.[38]

These accounts help to explain why oral testimony concerning bookmakers is so frequently positive. Mr Wilkinson, although himself a former detective-sergeant in the local force, was adamant that Billy Byrne, 'the biggest bookmaker in Salford', should be favourably portrayed, as a benefactor of the Catholic Church rather than as a criminal, despite the illicit status of his business.[39] During the inter-war period, the Methodist Dock Mission in Ordsall organized an annual outing for 600 poor children to Blackpool. According to people who went on these trips, Jimmy Ablett, one of the leading dockland bookmakers, treated the children with coins as they departed, in front of assembled parents, in a gesture which was clearly intended to show that his business made a positive contribution to the social life of the area.[40] This argument should not be overstated. Bowen claimed that daily takings at a bookmaker's pitch could exceed £100 by 1936,[41] and despite the symbolic importance of displays of generosity, it is likely that only a small proportion of takings was invested in neighbourhood charity. It was probably their status as 'Robin Hood' figures in their struggles with the police which best explains the popularity of bookmakers in working-class districts. Police harassment was not enough to stop the bookmaker enjoying similar status to the pub landlord: each possessed a degree of wealth and a position of local influence that few manual workers could aspire to, even if, as Robert Roberts suggested, bookmakers, with 'their "morals", flash suits and bedecked wives' were never quite as respectable as publicans.[42]

Gambling schools and working-class sports

Like street betting, gambling schools were illegal, but persisted in Salford until the 1950s. They were informal groups, ranging in size from street corner gatherings of less than half a dozen participants, to more organized, regular pitches attracting several hundred gamblers and spectators. The organizers of the major schools acted as bookmakers, laying odds and arranging look-outs against the police. Dave Cowen described a pitch and toss school, held in Strangeways, Manchester:

> Within a very large circle formed by the players, the appointed 'pitcher' poised two pennies on a flat piece of wood. A great hush fell as he took his stance like a caber thrower ... The pitcher tossed the coins from their launching pad high into the air. It was the backers' ambition to predict correctly whether the coins came to rest on earth heads or tails upwards.[43]

By contrast, the smaller schools were casual affairs, often consisting of groups of friends who turned to pitch and toss, or card games such as pontoon, as a means of passing the time. In such groups, the role of banker went to anyone who had enough money to run the game.[44] Gambling schools depended entirely upon look-outs to protect themselves from arrest. There is very little evidence of collusion between the police and the schools, but police strategies had only limited impact upon this second form of working-class gambling.[45] The police raided the schools, but failed to drive them off the streets, or out of the open country around Salford and Manchester. Moreover, workplaces, canal banks, railway sidings and municipal recreation grounds were all well-known venues.

As among the street bookmakers, look-out systems were highly developed, using sign language, whistles and shouts, to warn of the approach of the police. Detectives were sufficiently well known to be given nicknames, with one Salford officer christened 'Handbag' because of his habit of talking to women in the street, but according to Mr Saunders, 'A genuine Salford lad, a local, he could *smell* the police'.[46] Oral evidence suggests that the majority of schools were successfully shielded, but even when a pitch was disrupted, arrest was a matter of chance. If detectives or constables managed to surprise a gambling clique, the crowd scattered as soon as the police arrived, and in the chases that followed, it was rare that more than four or five offenders, if any, were apprehended. As in the pursuit of street bookmakers, the police were often thwarted by the denial of public support. Sympathetic neighbours allowed the members of pitch and toss cliques to run into their homes, in order to escape detectives.[47]

The gambling schools persisted, despite periodic initiatives by the Salford force. In the early 1920s, a vigorous campaign was mounted against the larger schools. In May 1920, a police operation against a gambling school in Greengate resulted in 25 convictions. The school was a regular Saturday afternoon pitch, with a 'fairground' atmosphere according to police evidence in court. On the afternoon of the raid, an estimated 300–400 people were congregated at the pitch at the rear of Springfield Lane. Five or six disguised police officers mingled with the crowd, observing five pennies being 'manipulated in a game called chance', before arresting Robert Perry, an unemployed turner, who was later convicted of making a book on the game. A further squad of officers lay in wait on the other side of the nearby Sherbourne Street bridge, and apprehended 24 men as they attempted to escape. Twenty-two subsequently received fines ranging from 15*s*. to 40*s*. The police claimed that Perry operated in Springfield Lane on a regular basis, making 'as much money as a bookmaker'. The magistrate shared the police view of Perry as a serious nuisance to the neighbourhood, sentencing him to a £20 fine (double the usual penalty for convicted street bookmakers) with an option of 51 days imprisonment.[48]

Individual officers went to great length in their attempts to disrupt the schools. Mr Wilkinson disguised himself as a miner in an attempt to disrupt gambling among groups of colliers in the Whit Lane district of Salford, and took part in pitch and toss, and card games, in order to penetrate the schools:

> There was local crofts, where you got some of these tricky lads with cards. One used to specialise in 'Find the Lady'. Or pitching up to the mott, which I have done, being ragged up and going down Whit Lane, where the colliers were with their clogs on, my clogs on an' all, ragged up as a miner. And we'd put a piece of mott in the ground, and we'd get pennies off one another, and then we'd toss the pennies up, heads or tails. And you used to win a bob or two at that game if you were clever.
> *Was there much police action against people for something like pitch and toss?*
> Oh no. They took that in their stride really. I mean, you've got to be friendly in a way with them, I know, I've got right near the feller's back where the cards have been, and there's somebody in the crowd spotted me, and I've just done that [signalled to be quiet] and it's been enough. Instead of giving me a good hiding. Because it was all in the game ...[49]

He risked injury as members of the school might have turned against him, but police intervention was an accepted risk among street gamblers.

However, there is evidence that the adoption of certain tactics by the police did provoke physical resistance. Elsewhere in Salford, squads of police hid in the back of motor ambulances, pulling up alongside schools of gamblers in order to launch surprise raids in Ordsall and the Adelphi. One such raid led by Sergeant Lamb of the Salford force during 1920 led to convictions for 11 members of an Adelphi gang caught playing at crown and anchor on a Sunday afternoon.[50] However, when furniture vans full of plain-clothed police were used in attempts to trick look-outs guarding the Ordsall dockland pitches, fighting broke out, which indicates that only certain forms of policing were tolerated. The use of furniture vans is widely remembered in Ordsall:

> I'll tell you one time the police got wary to it, and they hired a furniture van. And about eight policemen got in, plain clothes ... and rode down Taylorson Street, [and] all at once opened the door. There was

about twenty or thirty men gambling ... they dashed out and there
was a right dust-up. Lamby, chief-detective Lamb was the instigator
of that.
Was there scuffling?
Oh aye, yes, the police raided 'em, stop the gambling.[51]

In the roughest areas, some families were notorious for their willingness to
tackle the police. Mr Lomas described an incident which took place in the
Adelphi during the 1920s:

... during one of these raids, the house a-facing the Adelphi croft was
where a very notorious family lived, and the husband was being
arrested, and he was scuffling with the policeman outside his house,
he was trying to get in. And his wife opened the bedroom window,
and she poured all of the slops out of the bucket, the policeman let go
and her husband flew away.[52]

In August 1931, a police raid on gambling schools in the Hulme district
of Manchester aroused fierce local opposition. The raid was launched on a
Sunday afternoon by a team of plain-clothed officers concealed in a furniture van complete with peep-holes for the police to see what was going on
in the streets. Eight youths, aged between 16 and 21, were arrested for
playing pitch and toss in Percy Street and Hargreaves Street. According to
the police, a crowd of 200 followed the van to Great Jackson Street police
station, where several thousand people gathered to protest against the
police action. As the police acknowledged, it was the use of the furniture
van in the raid which provoked such great resentment.

The crowd outside the station clashed with police reinforcements, who
had been called to Hulme from the city centre. In the melée, a further 11
people were arrested, on charges of disorderly behaviour and obstructing
or assaulting the police. In court the following day, the police claimed the
crowd had intended to raid the police station in order to free the youths.
One officer testified that he had been attacked with a stick, and that
manure had been hurled at the police. A number of youths were fined
between 10*s*. and £2 for disorderly behaviour. Two 28-year-old men were
sentenced to a month's imprisonment for assaulting the police, while Sarah
Hicks, of Park Place, Hulme, was fined £2 for assaulting an officer who
claimed that she had 'locked her arms round his neck from behind, put her
knee in his back and bore him to the ground'.

Two protest meetings were immediately organized by the Hulme Young
Labour Party, requesting a Home Office inquiry into police conduct during
the incident, and raising objections to the prison sentences imposed earlier
in the day. The first, held in Duke Street, Hulme, attracted a crowd of
around a 1000, while several hundred people attended a meeting held later
that evening in Hargreaves Street. Leonard Corcoran of the Young Labour
Party told the *Manchester Guardian* that it was felt that the police handling
of the incident had been badly misjudged, and that the use of batons

against the crowd should be the subject of an inquiry. The *Guardian* noted that: 'Until late there was a buzz of excitement in Hulme. Any strange taxi or car was watched with interest, and people remained out of bed, talking at the street corners until very late.'[53]

A fortnight later, a further meeting, attended by several hundred people, was held in Christchurch Square, Hulme. Among those who addressed the crowd were a local Labour councillor, and Andrew McElwee, Labour MP for Hulme. They explained that they were attempting to raise the incident in Parliament and at the next meeting of the Manchester City Council. Their efforts met with little reward. In the city council, a proposal to reduce the salaries of the chief constable and the stipendiary magistrate by £100, as a vote of censure against the two officials, was decisively rejected. The incident was raised in the House of Commons by Andrew McElwee in mid-September. He asked the Home Secretary if he was aware that:

> ... one of the men who received imprisonment arising out of the disturbance in Manchester on August 16 had gone to the place to search for one of his children when he was assaulted by the police, and if in these circumstances he would order an inquiry into the conduct of the police.

The Home Secretary replied that an inquiry had been made, and that he could find no grounds for complaints against the police.[54]

The following year, John Maxwell, Manchester's chief constable, perhaps underestimated the difficulties posed for the police by street gaming. He claimed, before the Royal Commission on Lotteries and Betting, that gambling schools were dying out: 'Gaming in the streets is not now so prevalent as formerly. The offence is generally committed by youths playing "pitch and toss" ... and, when discovered, is quickly dealt with by the police.'[55] If the level of convictions offered a reliable guide, we might assert that street gaming did decline during the inter-war period, although in Manchester the main fall did not occur until the late 1930s, as Table 6.4 shows. However, the policing of gambling was such a haphazard affair that police statistics simply cannot be taken as evidence of a decline in the incidence of this form of popular recreation.

In Manchester, the sudden shifts in the level of arrests, in 1928, 1932 and 1934 for example, appear to reflect changes in police priorities, as it is clearly unlikely that the popularity of gambling schools rose and fell as quickly as the rate of arrests. In Salford, where police campaigns against bookmakers were exceptionally vigorous, little attention was paid to street gaming by the 1930s, but it is likely that police attention was diverted away from the schools as pressure to combat street bookmaking increased after 1930. Oral evidence suggests that gambling schools were an important haunt of the unemployed during the inter-war period, and with unemployment among adult males peaking in Salford at 35.7 per cent in September 1931, the schools were far from redundant as a form of leisure.[57] In the absence of any substantial documentation, retrospective evidence provides

Table 6.4 Prosecutions for street gaming in Manchester and Salford, 1927–39

Year	Manchester	Salford
1927	505	—
1928	374	—
1929	243	—
1930	334	—
1931	361	10
1932	284	30
1933	264	22
1934	165	10
1935	217	13
1936	184	5
1937	141	6
1938	133	—
1939	102	—

Source: Chief Constable's Reports.[56]

the only means to examine Maxwell's assertion, and his claim is sharply contradicted by the weight of oral testimony. Street gaming is commonly described in accounts of Salford neighbourhoods in the 1930s. Greengate, the Adelphi, Whit Lane and Ordsall still harboured gambling schools, and there is evidence that pitch and toss still formed a Sunday afternoon sport in Hanky Park as late as the 1950s.[58] Perhaps Maxwell's claim in 1932 was prompted by a desire to maintain the reputation of the Manchester force, in the light of the admitted difficulties in policing street betting.

The street gambling schools offered a means of earning money as well as an inducement to spend. In the smaller, more informal schools, the look-out position went to one of those present who did not have the resources to take an active part in the gambling. Mr Aitken grew up in Ordsall, watching street gambling among the dock labourers. He became a keen member of the schools himself:

> That was our main enjoyment I think, gambling ... Now if you were playing a long while and you got skint, they'd put you 'on crow' ... They'd put you watching out at the corner, to see if there was any detectives ... And after you'd been there so long, they'd give you so many coppers so you could come back in the school.[59]

Clearly, in areas where participation in commercialized leisure was constrained by poverty and unemployment, forms of entertainment which provided a free spectacle to non-participants and offered a means to earn extra income possessed a strong economic appeal. Mr Oliver described a pitch in Ordsall:

Thirty shillings was a lot of money then, and I could get that on a Saturday afternoon on crow. In the wide back [alley] there, there used to be about hundred men. And there used to be darts, rings, cards, pitch and toss, and there used to be gambling going. And I used to have a bike, and I used to keep going round and round, and we had another lad helping at [the other] end and we used to split the money ... out of every shilling they put ha'penny in a hat for the crow. And I used to go round on crow, the two of us used to get about fifteen shillings each.[60]

Football was a focus for widespread gambling, even before the growth of the national pools companies in the 1920s. During the 1900s, it was common for working men and lads to organize coupon betting themselves, while throughout the inter-war period, amateur football was widely associated with side-betting.[61] Contemporary observers estimated that the volume of working-class gambling increased during the 1920s and 1930s, partly as a result of the growth of the football pools and the emergence of greyhound racing.[62] The pools were popular among women as well as men, and offered a convenient form of gambling to those women whose domestic responsibilities dictated that many evenings were spent at home. As John Hilton found, working people filled in pools coupons for much the same reasons that they placed bets with bookmakers. The pools were a source of intense interest, providing a focus for discussion among students of form, while the lingering prospect of a win brightened lives dulled by poverty. One of his correspondents, an unemployed ship's greaser, declared:

The reason why I and thousands of other unemployed have a modest 6*d*. or 1*s*. which we can ill afford on the pools each week is that one day we may have the luck to win a decent sum and so put an end to this strangling existence which we lead.[63]

The pools were legal because they were conducted on credit, with payment required the week after the coupon entry.[64]

The first greyhound track in Britain opened in Manchester in 1926, and by the 1930s, Manchester possessed two tracks with a third located in Salford. The tracks were built in densely populated areas in the cities and drew regular crowds from the surrounding districts. William Bowen feared that the sudden popularity of greyhound racing was based upon the spread of gambling among young people and women:

I have been to the Salford Albion dog races. On the last occasion when I was present there were about 3,000 people. It was an evening meeting, and there were 25 bookmakers to look after the people and take the bets. Amongst the people were young boys and girls of 14 or 15 years of age. In the case of one boy in particular, his own mother was giving him money to put on. For a time there was a part of the ground where the mothers could take the baby in and leave the carriage. At Salford Greyhound Racecourse I have seen the mothers taking the babes in the carriage on to the ground.

The greyhound tracks offered a cheap night's entertainment. Stakes as low as 1*d*. and 2*d*. were accepted by bookmakers, which helps to explain their popularity among women.[65]

Whippet racing was more informally organized. Despite occasional police raids, contests were held in open fields or along canal banks on the outskirts of the two cities throughout the inter-war period. Colliers at the Salford pits in Pendleton and Brindleheath, and in the outlying mining districts such as Swinton, Agecroft and Pendlebury were keen followers of the sport. Moreover, the miners in the Bradford district of Manchester shared their enthusiasm, as Mick Burke recalled:

> The colliers at Bradford Pit were great fellows for whippet racing and used to go on the fields up Ten Acres Lane. They would throw some kind of ball, slip the dog and time how long it took the dog to catch the quarry. A good slipper would throw a dog about twenty yards – that was the art of the game ... [the dogs] were better fed than the people![66]

Mr Aston was born in 1900, and grew up on Trafford Park estate, which borders Ordsall. He described foot races held on the fringe of Trafford Park which provided an additional focus for betting:

> That was a great thing, they used to run in the woods that was half way between the [Trafford] Park Hotel and Barton, and they used to gamble amongst themselves.
> *Running races?*
> Running, yes, 100 yards, 200 yards, and they'd gamble. People would come from Salford to run, but there again they had the same fiddle: 'Don't you win this time, don't you win now, wait till the odds come better' ... I remember one we had, he was called Ritson and he could run, he was a good one, he could win whenever he wanted, but he didn't win every time.[67]

Oral evidence also provides glimpses of the survival of cruel sports in clandestine encounters during the 1920s:

> *Mrs Rae*: I shouldn't say this, but the local bobby, he had fighting cocks ... [there] was a little entry behind where they lived, and these two cocks used to fight ... and I think there was betting went on there.
> *Mr Rae*: Well there was heavy betting on cockfighting you know.
> *Where was that? Was it in Swinton somewhere?*
> *Mrs Rae*: Yes. Everton Street, off Partington Lane ...
> *So would there be people watching then if there was betting going on?*
> *Mrs Rae*: No, it was in the back entry and I don't think the neighbours liked it, if you wanted to move about your own back it was frightening ...[68]

In this instance, a policeman promoted cruel sports to the annoyance of the local working-class community. There is no evidence that police involvement in cockfighting occurred outside Swinton, a cotton and mining district which borders Salford, yet this extract is useful because the irony noted by Mr Rae, whereby a police officer perpetrated a breach of the law, reminds us that the police were not always suitable 'domestic missionaries'.[69] By the turn of the century, cockfighting was a rare occurrence, especially when compared with the breadth of interest in other communal sports such as pigeon flying and whippet racing.[70] However, the sheer range of sports associated with side-betting confirms the centrality of gambling in working-class culture.

Gambling and working-class culture

Gambling schools were a male preserve, and membership of the schools formed part of the cult of masculinity among those who joined street corner society. Age divisions were much less rigid here than elsewhere, and in newspaper reports of prosecutions for street gaming, it is common to find youths gambling alongside men two or even three times older.[71] Around 40 per cent of those convicted for street gaming in one year in Salford were youths aged under 20, with a further 40 per cent men aged between 20 and 40, as Table 6.5 shows.

Jerry White found that in Campbell Bunk, the 'worst street in North London', gambling schools formed one of the central arenas for masculine recreation. However, oral evidence indicates that in Manchester and Salford, street gaming was not confined to the 'lumpen' poor. In Strangeways, according to Dave Cowen, the pitch and toss schools attracted a cross-section of local workers, including weavers, waterproof garment-makers, bakers, boilermen and 'tradesmen'.[73] In Salford, street gaming flourished in many areas within the central working-class districts of the city, in Greengate, the Adelphi, Hope Street and Hanky Park, while schools

Table 6.5 Convictions for street gaming in Salford during 1920: Age profile

Age	Number convicted	Percentage of those convicted
60–69	1	0.7
50–59	6	4.1
40–49	14	9.6
30–39	23	15.7
20–29	40	27.4
10–19	62	42.5
Total	146	100.0

Source: Compiled from data in the *Salford City Reporter*, 1920.[72]

were also commonly held in workshops during dinner breaks.[74] According to retrospective accounts, members of the schools ranged from casual labourers to 'penny capitalists', including barbers.[75] Dock labourers congregating in 'Little Africa' in Ordsall shared a reputation as heavy gamblers and drinkers with the Whit Lane colliers, and both areas were notorious for harbouring pitch and toss and crown and anchor cliques.

However, participation in gambling schools was less widespread than betting on horse races. Although it is impossible to provide reliable estimates for the proportion of the Salford population taking part in either activity, it is feasible in the light of oral evidence that figures may have matched a 1927 estimate that 50–75 per cent of men in a poor district in Liverpool took part in betting.[76] Again, an analysis of gambling offers little support to the labour aristocracy thesis: men placing bets with street bookmakers in Salford ranged from skilled engineers to labourers, and it is significant that skilled workers sometimes resorted to acting as 'jockeys', appearing in court on behalf of local bookmakers during spells of unemployment.[77] Men without work still placed bets of their own, but there is evidence of cooperative betting among the unemployed, some of whom paid 3*d*. each towards a communal shilling wager.[78]

The allocation of household resources in favour of the husband, which was central to the broader sexual division of leisure, helps to explain why certain forms of gambling such as street gaming and betting on whippet and pigeon races were exclusively male pastimes. None the less, some working-class women gambled on greyhound races and the football pools, while others resorted to street bookmakers, and the Liverpool survey of 1927 suggested that 50 per cent of the women in a poor district were habitual gamblers.[79] In Manchester and Salford, the 'One o'clock', the midday paper which gave starting prices, was sold and discussed among housewives and women in workplaces, as well as among men. Charles Russell claimed that the spread of the 'gambling pestilence' among housewives by the 1900s reflected:

> ... the deadly monotony, the loneliness, the drudgery, and want of beauty in the lives of the women ... in some cases, owing to her unseemly attire, hardly moving outside the area of her own back street, hardly able to contemplate a holiday, unable to purchase new clothes, her life one continual round of endeavouring to make both ends meet and keep the home together.[80]

For many housewives, Russell argued, the lure of a win on a race and the temporary alleviation of poverty were irresistible. Retrospective evidence suggests that women were likely to bet smaller amounts, and less regularly than their husbands, while women in severe poverty could seldom afford a wager, but racing did provide a focus of interest within the street networks which formed one of the principal avenues of female sociability. According to Canon Peter Green in 1924:

Selling the racing papers: 'Mid-day special', L.S. Lowry, 1926.

Within a stone's-throw of this house where I am writing there is a street where every single woman buys the 'One o'clock' ... and not half a mile away there are two poor streets of which the rent collector said to me: 'On the morning of a racing day you'd think there was a picnic on ... half the women out of doors reading the "One o'clock" and talking about their losses'.[81]

Women's attitudes towards gambling were as diverse as attitudes towards drink. Some respondents were surprised even to be asked whether their mothers gambled on horse races, but others were quick to point out that gambling was popular among women as well as men. Notions of respectability were, as ever, highly fluid: some housewives paid another woman to act as a 'runner', handing their bets over for them, yet others ventured down the back entries themselves to gamble openly. Equally, many women gambled small amounts from week to week, yet others, bound by the notion of the self-sacrificing 'good' mother, only allowed themselves a flutter once or twice a year, on a 'big' race, like the Derby.[82]

Contemporary social observers were horrified by the prospect of women gambling. It was deemed inexcusable among men by middle-class moral reformers, who often asserted that spending on recreation among the poor was immoral, and in fact constituted the objective cause of poverty. But women's betting was considered doubly offensive, for it was with the housewife that responsibility for managing the household budget finally lay. In the words of William Cobley, writing in the Manchester church magazine 'Odds and Ends' in 1933: 'Anyone who knows the industrial areas knows the grimy optimists at every factory gate, the slatternly women betting their children's living away in nearly every back street.'[83] According to this stereotype, the working-class mother had fallen victim to the turf mania which had gripped Manchester life since the mid-nineteenth century, and was now to be seen, in her most depraved moments, stripping her children at the pawnshop doorway, pledging the clothes off their backs to raise cash to wager on the day's racing. This is an example of the effective moral lobby which prevented the legalization of cash betting until 1960.

People who knew the industrial areas from the inside gave a different estimate of the scale of popular gambling. Even Canon Peter Green admitted that bets were often placed for as little as 3d. during the 1920s, a figure which matches oral testimony for the inter-war period.[84] McKibbin cited evidence provided by the chief constable of Manchester, who, when summoned before the Royal Commission on Lotteries and Betting in 1932, disappointed the commissioners by insisting that few bets exceeded 6d. or 1s.[85] Working people spent a few pence on a wager as a form of amusement, but it was usually a sober indulgence. This was reflected in the uses to which winnings were put. A major win on a horse race meant extra pocket money in many instances, but oral evidence shows that winnings also went on better food, and shoes and clothing, and for others, it was the prospect of luxuries like these which made a bet worthwhile. Joe Toole described how his father took advantage of an outstanding win on a race to buy suits and dresses for his entire family, as well as paying for a trip to Blackpool.[86]

From this survey it should be clear that people from each section of the working class took part in betting, and this provides further confirmation that the intervention of the state never succeeded in marginalizing bookmakers. As suggested in Chapter 2, however, gambling did become a problem in the minority of cases where men kept so much of their earnings for their wagers that their wives were left with little or no housekeeping. This was not the universal state of affairs that social critics claimed, and it would be misleading to stereotype working-class marriages as characterized by such extreme male selfishness. However, the domestic tensions caused by excessive gambling were severe, and provided the basis for working-class opposition to betting:

... my father used to pawn everything he could get his hands on for a bet. I had my best coat, and it had gone ... he pawned the stair-rods, everything. He took the pictures off the wall and sold them. My mother had to go round the shops and tell them not to let him have anything, because he used to get [things on] credit [and sell them]. My sister was saving to get married, and her bedding, her bottom drawer was in the wardrobe, and she used to lock it, and when she went in one day, he'd taken the back off and everything had gone ... She left home and went in service.[87]

McKibbin was justified in arguing that working-class betting generally involved only a modest outlay,[88] but it is important to recognize that addictive gambling could severely undermine a family's well-being. In homes where the father's bets drained the housekeeping resources, children could grow up with a loathing of gambling which lasted a lifetime. Recognizing the dangers of over-indulgence, many working people of both sexes therefore did not bet.[89]

In 1906, an Ordsall newsagent, surprised when asked by the journalist James Haslam why betting was so popular, declared: 'What else have they to take an interest in? ... the magistrates will never stop it – can't be stopped. It's in 'em – in the people! ... it's in t' blood ...'[90] For many Ordsall boys, gambling was simply a part of growing up. As Mr Paterson recalled, even those without a ha'penny to wager would take part in the junior gambling schools: '... every street corner as kids, we'd be about twelve, thirteen, corner of our street, used to gamble for ha'pennies, and buttons, matches, used to gamble 'cause it was in the blood ...'.[91] Betting was an integral feature of working-class culture, and as Russell and Campagnac acknowledged:

... gambling ... is held by many working people ... to be entirely legitimate if a man risks no more than he can afford to lose. It is an amusement ... a diversion, for which a man is willing to pay so much. Whether he wins or loses he gets his money's worth; and who is to prevent him doing as he wills with his own?[92]

Whereas police interference was evaded, the use of leisure was effectively constrained by poverty and low wages, and it is in this area that we should locate the real regulation of popular leisure. In Salford, small-scale gambling was an acceptable hobby, and was only immoral when someone staked more than they could reasonably afford. Ironically, it was only after their operations were legalized, in 1960, that the majority of back street bookmakers were eventually wiped out. Competition succeeded where prohibition and the police had failed for nearly a century, as individual bookmakers were driven out of business not by legal sanctions, but by the spread of the national betting chains like Ladbroke's and Coral's, and the growth of Done's, a local firm, in Salford.[93]

Conclusion

Working-class leisure has usually been viewed with suspicion by social and political commentators. Hostility to 'unruly' popular amusements was a common strand in Victorian social criticism, and according to temperance propaganda, reckless spending on drink was the principal cause of misery in slum districts. In the early twentieth century, many observers still saw expenditure on leisure as subverting the domestic economy of the working classes. Drink and gambling were readily acknowledged as 'causes' of poverty, but few commentators recognized that the equation could be easily reversed: that poverty could in fact restrict access to all the arenas of commercial leisure, including the pub. Most observers simply took the question of participation in leisure for granted, assuming that the presence of working people in beerhouses, music halls and cinemas was evidence of the behaviour of an entire class.

Social observers who sought to defend the working man against charges of intemperance usually argued that it was the poverty of working-class life which drove men into pubs. In 1914, Charles Russell stated that:

> ... no one at all familiar with the conditions existing in northern slum districts can fail to be aware of the terrible evil wrought by drunkenness. Few who have close acquaintance with the subject would be prepared to deny that the extremes of poverty, dirt and dinginess, drabness and ugliness, overcrowding and stuffiness, combined with the deadly monotony of life, are in themselves the inducement for recourse to alcohol as the only means of relief available in such wretched surroundings.[1]

The question of how the poor found the money for this 'recourse to alcohol' was still obscured. Socialists, from Engels onwards, frequently adopted this social explanation of drunkenness, and therefore shared the tendency to exaggerate the level of working-class expenditure on leisure found throughout the range of contemporary opinion.[2]

This failure to examine the role of poverty as a constraint upon working-class social life has been maintained among historians, who have generally turned instead to the analysis of leisure as a means of relief, or escapism. The pub, music hall and cinema have all been viewed as providing opportunities to escape from everyday problems. Indeed, the growth of mass leisure has sometimes been seen as one of the roots of political fatalism: viewed through a Marxist perspective, leisure appears to have diverted the interests, energies and organizational abilities of working people away from the political sphere. This perception has been used to help to explain the reformist character of working-class politics in Britain, and the consequent absence of a strong revolutionary tradition.[3] In echoes of Orwell's claim that cheap luxuries stalled any prospect of revolution during the 1930s, mass leisure is still sometimes viewed as a 'problem'.[4]

Attempts to connect the study of leisure to the study of politics have their origins in an optimistic assessment of the potential of social history widely held during the 1960s and 1970s. Historians turned to the analysis of social trends in the search for explanations of political change, in a process perhaps best demonstrated in Stedman Jones' powerful essay on working-class culture and working-class politics in late nineteenth century London, first published in 1974. In this essay, Stedman Jones made a direct link between the consolidation of a fatalistic, leisure-orientated culture and the emergence of a defensive form of Labour politics. This piece retains a strong influence upon historians of leisure.[5]

Following an observation made by Hobsbawm in *Industry and empire*, Stedman Jones identified the late nineteenth century as the period which saw the emergence of 'traditional' working-class culture in Britain.[6] An emphasis upon the 1880s, in particular, as a decade which saw key shifts in working-class leisure has been maintained in many subsequent studies in this field. However, this periodization was not based upon a detailed contrast between leisure in 1850 and 1900. Rather, the late nineteenth century was identified as a key period in the development of working-class politics, leading to the emergence of the Labour Party, and an analysis of leisure was used to provide part of a social explanation for political trends.

Significantly, a detailed study of leisure in Salford and Manchester reveals that many of the most important working-class leisure activities during the 1930s were well established by the mid-nineteenth century. Within the sphere of commercialized leisure, for example, the pub played a central role throughout this period. However, some of the most striking continuities in urban recreation are found within the realm of informal, or communal leisure, which has received scant attention in previous social histories. In working-class areas, many leisure activities drew upon the collective life of the streets and markets. Despite the growth of the capitalist mass entertainment industry, leisure was therefore largely rooted in neighbourhood life. Gambling schools, corner gangs, monkey parades and street markets were all key features in the social life of working-class districts in Salford and Manchester around 1850. They all feature equally strongly in oral testimony describing life in the two cities during the inter-war period. The notion of a 'transformation' of leisure in the late nineteenth century refers only to the pace of change in the commercial leisure industries. Moreover, the commercialization of leisure was clearly a partial process, and in the communal life of working-class areas, continuities were much stronger.[7] Indeed, the survival of a Victorian pattern of street life alongside more glamorous, modern entertainments such as the cinema, forms one of the most striking characteristics of working-class leisure during the 1930s.

The impact of policing forms a second theme in existing accounts of the 'transformation' of working-class leisure, yet a detailed local study casts some doubt upon the effectiveness of the police as an agency of control. The vigorous street life of working-class areas was maintained despite legislation intended to keep the streets clear for commercial traffic, or to suppress gambling and disorderly behaviour. By 1900, the police were an established presence in the daily life of urban districts, and considerable energies were devoted to shielding illicit gatherings, particularly gambling networks, from the forces of the law. Yet although arrests were frequently made, for bookmaking, for 'loitering' or for drunken behaviour on the streets, the patterns of behaviour which legislation was intended to suppress were widely maintained. Moreover, the relationship between the police and the people was often ambiguous. Officers were well aware of the difficulties posed by implementing class-partisan legislation, and in the classic case of street betting, relations between bookmakers and the police were strongly characterized by collusion, at least until exposure in the press threatened to bring the police into disrepute.

This study has attempted to depart from established historical perspectives on leisure and working-class culture, by drawing upon the approach usually labelled 'history from below'.[8] The use of oral history alongside more conventional documentary sources provides a basis for an analysis of the role of leisure at individual, family or neighbourhood level, and within this methodological framework, the question of participation in leisure has been examined in some depth. This attempt to construct an alternative analysis of leisure, from a working-class perspective, suggests that an examination of poverty and of gender roles should be central to our understanding of working-class culture. Hugh Cunningham's analysis of leisure at the turn of the century highlighted the role of poverty in shaping social life, but the present survey provides a distinct approach, through a detailed focus on individual spending patterns and the sexual division of leisure.[9]

Despite overall improvements in living standards, social surveys revealed that urban poverty was widespread throughout the period from 1900 to 1939. Oral history is particularly useful in attempts to examine poverty and living standards, as interviews provide a means of establishing which groups within the working class most benefited from improvements in real wages. Young, single workers in particular, appear to have prospered during the early decades of the twentieth century, taking full advantage of new forms of mass entertainment such as the cinema, and new, Hollywood-led styles of dress. In terms of both leisure and fashion, it is possible to trace clear elements of a distinct 'youth culture' in Salford and Manchester prior to 1939. This was not a new phenomenon during the inter-war decades. Young workers had used leisure and dress to distance themselves from their elders during the nineteenth century, but the relative affluence of youth appears to have accelerated from the turn of the century, prior to the emergence of the 'teenager' during the 1950s.[10]

Participation in leisure was also structured by profound inequalities of gender. Women's experience of leisure was subject to a series of financial, domestic and moral constraints, and throughout the early decades of the twentieth century, women continued to bear the brunt of poverty because they took responsibility for 'making ends meet'. Although married women clearly benefited from the development of the cinema as a new form of cheap and accessible entertainment, they still tended to enjoy significantly fewer opportunities for leisure than their husbands. Surveys conducted during the 1930s showed that for many working-class women, everyday life still centred around the unrelenting struggle against poverty, and for women to manage a visit to the cinema or pub often required great resourcefulness. Women were largely still excluded from some of the most important arenas of mass leisure, such as spectator sport. Moreover, many women suffered directly as a result of the leisure patterns adopted by their husbands. Men who retained high proportions of their wages for their personal spending created untold difficulties for their wives and children, and in this sense, it is hard to avoid the conclusion that at least in terms of leisure and money management, the sufferings of many working-class women were as much a result of their sex as of their class.[11]

These findings therefore also provide a new way of looking at the standard of living debate. When examining the inter-war decades, historians tend to place considerable emphasis upon the contrasting fortunes of different regions: the 'depressed areas' of the North, and South Wales, are contrasted with the prosperous Midlands and South East. The present study, however, suggests that although poverty was widespread in the major towns and cities, experience differed sharply at local level. As Rowntree recognized at the turn of the century, there were profound inequalities in living standards even within the family, structured by the poverty cycle and gender roles, and these differences appear to have been accentuated during the 1920s and 1930s.

Established historical approaches to working-class culture in Britain have been dominated by an emphasis upon the distinctiveness of a proletarian 'way of life', with Hobsbawm, for example, highlighting the development of a uniform pattern of working-class culture, based on mass leisure, from the 1880s.[12] However, this approach obscures both the diversity of working-class experience and the impact of urban poverty in the late nineteenth and early twentieth centuries. In contrast, surveys based in part upon oral testimony continually point to the diversity of working-class behaviour. This study has attempted to examine the impact of income differentials and gender divisions in some depth, yet even within these boundaries, there is considerable evidence of further diversity in styles of behaviour. The poverty cycle, for example, impinged upon the lives of all working people. Some men moderated their personal spending in the face of poverty or unemployment, even if this meant that they were excluded from the male spheres of the pub vault and the football terraces. Others, however, put their own desires first, maintaining patterns of spending which plunged their families into destitution. Competing notions of masculinity, from the breadwinner to the hard-drinking 'real' man, were of profound importance, and oral evidence continually testifies to the importance of the division between 'good' and 'bad' husbands.

Within the broad sexual division of leisure, there is evidence of contrasting styles of behaviour among working-class women. Some women had very little experience of commercial leisure, and depended upon street and family networks for most of their social life. Others socialized regularly, in cinemas and pubs, and the striking divergence in women's attitudes towards drink highlights the subjective nature of conceptions of respectability. The notion of the 'good' mother demanded great sacrifices on the part of working-class women, yet perceptions of respectable female behaviour still varied from household to household. In the light of oral testimony, the traditional division between the 'respectable' and the 'rough' breaks down. Respectability emerges as a complex and multi-layered category, which was constantly redefined to match individual and local perspectives.

In Salford and Manchester, the way of life described in *Love on the dole* and *The classic slum* was severely undermined by slum clearance programmes from the 1930s. By the 1970s, 'Hanky Park' and 'Hope Street, Salford' no longer existed, and the disruption of 'traditional' working-class communities in the post-war period, an established concern among sociologists, poses a new challenge to social historians, who have for the most part confined their studies to the period up to 1939. Prior to the implementation of rehousing schemes, working-class culture in Salford and Manchester drew enormous strength from the pervasiveness of the street networks and the vigour of the collective life found in the central working-class districts, and despite the emphasis upon poverty throughout the present study, it should be stressed that almost all the respondents spoke highly of the districts where they grew up. Neighbourhood relationships, of course, were double-edged: both tensions and solidarities were heightened among families living in close proximity, and deeply rooted in districts where some terraced streets had stood for a century.

In August 1938, the *Salford City Reporter* described the scenes in a clearance area in Greengate. The impending demolition of this 'classic slum' was marked by a series of street parties, starting around eleven o'clock on Saturday night (as the pubs closed), and lasting until the early hours of Sunday morning. Even now, the competitive edge of respectability lent an air of rivalry to the proceedings, as 'neighbouring streets ... vie one with the other for the distinction of having the jolliest party'. In Davies Street:

> To the strains of an accordion and a drum an impromptu dance was held with the street lamps and the reflected light from the houses giving the illumination. The sound of music and laughter soon attracted others in the district and a crowd of several hundreds assembled to watch the jollifications. Community dances proved to be the most popular items of the evening with the 'Lambeth Walk', speedily rechristened the 'Greengate Walk', holding pride of place. During the festivities the musicians, followed by a large procession, marched through Paradise and other streets in the vicinity.[13]

In Greengate, demolition appeared to mark the end of a community. The impact of slum clearance schemes in Salford and Manchester, and the emergence of new patterns of social life on the post-war estates, have still to be traced in historical research on the two cities.

Appendix 1: Occupational structure of Manchester and Salford, 1923–37

Estimated number of insured workers, aged 16–64, July 1923 and July 1937

Industry	Estimated no.		Increase or decrease from July 1923 (%)	No. in industry as % insured July 1937	
	1923	1937		M & S	GB
Transport and distribution	71 240	91 510	+28	19.9	16.7
Engineering and metals (including electrical engineering)	69 850	80 060	+15	17.5	13.1
Clothing	34 000	45 230	+33	9.8	3.0
Cotton and textiles	41 660	36 530	−12	7.9	3.8
Building	19 080	24 090	+27	5.3	9.9
Printing and publishing	11 150	15 960	+43	3.5	2.1
Food and drink	10 370	14 690	+42	3.1	3.2
Chemicals	8 650	10 670	+23	2.3	1.7
Rubber	11 970	9 570	−20	2.1	0.5
Hotels, etc.	7 310	8 880	+21	1.9	3.3
Coal	7 610	5 650	−26	1.2	6.6
Docks	7 040	4 740	−33	1.0	1.2
Laundries	2 300	4 140	+80	0.9	1.3
All other industries and services	84 140	108 500	+29	23.6	33.6
Total, all industries and Services	386 370	460 220	+19	100.0	100.0

Source: Based upon figures provided by M. Fogarty, *The prospects of the industrial areas of Great Britain* (1945), p. 231.

Appendix 2: Respondents' biographical details

I have used a series of initials to identify the interviewees cited in the footnotes. A total of 60 people were interviewed: asterisks are used to denote a further six people who contributed to interviews being held with someone else. Districts in Manchester are marked (M/c). All other districts are either in Salford, or on the outskirts of the city. Where possible, I have provided details of the jobs held by the parents of the respondents. The geographical and occupational spread of the sample is shown at the end of this appendix.

Initials	Pseudonym, if used	Year of birth	Place of birth: and other areas described	Parental occupations
Mr L.A.	Aitken	1907	Grimsby; Ordsall (1914)	Not available
Mrs A.A.	Aitken	1914	Ordsall	Father a dock labourer (died 1920); mother took in sewing
Mr H.A.*	Anderson	n/a	Weaste	Not available
Mrs L.A.	Anderson	1918	Hope Street	Father a carter, foundry labourer
Mr S.B.	Brookman	1919	Lower Broughton	Father a boilerman; mother a cleaner

Initials	Pseudonym, if used	Year of birth	Place of birth: and other areas described	Parental occupations
Mr B.B.	Byrne	1910	Greengate	Father killed in 1916
Mr J.B.		(?)1918	Chapel Street	Not available
Mrs E.C.	Cooper	1916	Pendleton	Father unemployed; mother a cleaner
Mrs L.C.	Cunliffe	1903	Ordsall	Father a boatman, worked on barges on canal in Hulme; mother took in washing
Mr T.C.*		1915	Ordsall	Father a dock labourer
Mrs B.D.	Daly	1925	Greengate	Father a timber carrier; mother a factory cleaner
Mr H.D.	Deighton	(?)1914	West Liverpool Street	Father a tradesman glass-blower
Mr J.D.*	Donaghy	1910	Pendleton	Father a tube tester at copper works
Mr M.D.		1914	Cheetham Hill (M/c)	Not available
Mrs M.D.		1901	Hope Street	Father a labourer at gasworks
Mrs K.E.	Easton	1923	Ardwick (M/c); Ordsall (1934)	Mother and father kept an off-licence
Mrs E.G.		1917	Seedley	Father a colour grinder at paint works; mother a book-keeper
Ms G.G.	Garton	1901	Ordsall	Father a head lamp-lighter on Salford docks
Mr W.G.	Gilmour	1913	Adelphi	Father a printer/compositor
Mrs B.G.*	Gilmour	1916	Adelphi	Father died 1920
Mrs M.G.	Grady	1902	Ordsall	Father an engine driver on Salford dock railway

Initials	Pseudonym, if used	Year of birth	Place of birth: and other areas described	Parental occupations
Ms S.G.		1908	Greengate	Father worked at copper works (tradesman); mother a mill worker
Mr F.H.	Hatton	1908	Pendleton	Father a blacksmith, worked in ebonite works; mother a mill worker
Mrs M.H.	Henderson	1895	Hanky Park	Father a dock labourer
Mrs A.H.	Hill	1901	Hanky Park	Father a colour mixer at dyeworks
Ms C.H.		1889	Brindleheath	Father a joiner, unemployed; mother took in washing
Mrs E.H.	Holden	1904	Bolton	Father a domestic servant (gardener)
Mrs M.J.	Jackman	1895	Ordsall	Father a dyer and finisher
Mr A.J.	James	1930	Whit Lane; Hanky Park	Not available
Mr E.J	Jepson	1922	Ordsall	Father a moulder (until 1926 general strike), labourer at gasworks, clerk
Mrs C.J.	Jepson	1922	Weaste	Father a foreman dyer (until 1928), then warehouse labourer
Mr G.J.		1905	Pendlebury	Father a miner
Mr P.J.	Johnstone	1909	Harpurhey (M/c)	Father a tram guard, clerk at tram depot after wounded in First World War

Initials	Pseudonym, if used	Year of birth	Place of birth: and other areas described	Parental occupations
Ms W.J.	Johnson	1899	Adelphi	Father a railway carter (died 1910); mother a cleaner
Mr J.L.*		1911	Ordsall	Father a dock labourer
Mr L.L.	Lomas	1914	Adelphi	Father a foreman bricklayer
Mrs A.M.	MacLeod	1909	Greengate	Father died 1911; mother a corner shopkeeper
Mrs L.M.	Mullen	1917	Hanky Park; Ordsall; Adelphi	Father unemployed; mother died 1928
Mrs S.M.		1900	Hanky Park	Father a dock labourer
Mr K.N.	Nolan	1931	Adelphi	Father a vulcanizer at tyre dealers, insurance agent
Mr G.O.	Oliver	1907	Ordsall	Father a wheelwright
Mrs E.O.	Ormond	1904	Ordsall; Weaste (1911)	Father a seaman; mother died 1911, brought up by aunt (cleaner)
Ms A.O.	Osgood	1918	Weaste	Father a seaman, stoker in flour mill, unemployed; mother took in washing, cleaner, worked on market stall
Mr A.P.	Paterson	1904	Ordsall	Father a dock labourer
Mr C.P.	Pearson	1914	Salford; Knott Mill (M/c); Hulme (M/c)	Father a labourer, unemployed; mother a cleaner, barmaid
Mr J.P.	Peters	1910	Lower Broughton	Mother kept boarding house

Initials	Pseudonym, if used	Year of birth	Place of birth: and other areas described	Parental occupations
Mr R.P.*	Phelan	1922	Seedley	Not available
Mrs E.P.	Phelan	1921	Seedley	Father unemployed
Mr D.P.		1931	Pendlebury	Father a miner
Mrs H.P.		1923	Pendleton	Father a domestic servant (gardener), labourer at engineering works; mother a machinist
Mr L.P.	Prescott	1918	Hope Street	Father a park-keeper, unemployed; mother a mill worker
Mr D.R.	Rae	1915	Patricroft	Father a shopkeeper
Mrs E.R.	Rae	1917	Swinton; Worsley	Father a clerk
Mrs J.R.	Rankine	1925	Hope Street	Father worked for market police
Mr J.R.	Riordan	1901	Adelphi	Father a tradesman spreader at rubber works; mother a mill worker
Mr B.R.	Rowlings	1913	Ordsall	Father a dock labourer (died 1920); mother took in washing
Mrs G.R.	Rowlings	1918	Ordsall	Father a checker on the railway
Mrs M.R.	Ryan	1905	Pendleton	Father a tube tester at copper works
Mr H.S.	Saunders	1910	Ordsall	Father a professional footballer, dock labourer

Initials	Pseudonym, if used	Year of birth	Place of birth: and other areas described	Parental occupations
Mrs C.S.	Statham	1911	Ordsall; Moss Side (M/c)	Father killed in First World War; step-father a factory manager
Mrs A.S.	Sugden	1915	Ordsall	Father a moulder; mother a cleaner
Mr W.S.		1899	Chorlton-on-Medlock (M/c); Moss Side (M/c)	Father a plumber
Mrs F.T.	Tanner	1918	Ordsall	Father a dock labourer; mother worked at dyeworks, cleaner/usherette
Ms M.T.		(?)1910	Greengate	Father a seaman; mother a cleaner
Mr F.W.	Walters	1911	Hanky Park	Father a publican
Mr C.W.	Wilkinson	1900	Ordsall	Father killed in First World War, brought up by relatives

Geographical spread of the sample

Central Salford	Outer Salford	Surrounding area	Manchester
21 Ordsall	4 Weaste	2 Pendlebury	2 Moss Side
6 Adelphi	3 Seedley	1 Patricroft	1 Ardwick
5 Greengate	1 Lower Broughton	1 Swinton	1 Cheetham Hill
5 Hanky Park	1 Whit Lane	1 Worsley	1 Chorlton-on-Medlock
5 Pendleton	1 Brindleheath		1 Harpurhey
3 Hope Street			1 Hulme
1 Chapel Street			1 Knott Mill
1 West Liverpool Street			
Total 47	10	5	8

Ordsall, the district bounded by Trafford Road, Regent Road and the Irwell, covers a much bigger area than the other central Salford districts such as the Adelphi, Greengate and Hanky Park, so the strong bias towards Ordsall in the sample is not entirely misplaced.

Occupational spread of the sample: Cases where information regarding the main occupation(s) of the head of the household could be obtained

Managerial	1
Shopkeepers/publicans/boarding house keepers	5
Clerical	4
Skilled working class	18
Semi and unskilled	34
Unemployed	6
Total	68

Some households counted twice, where the main wage-earner fitted different categories at different times (due to periodic unemployment), and some not included at all (information unavailable).

Notes

Series editor's introduction

1 A. Reid, 'World War I and the working class in Britain', in A. Marwick (ed.), *Total war and social change* (Macmillan, London, 1988), pp. 16–24.

2 M. Pugh, *Electoral reform in war and peace, 1906–1918* (Routledge, London, 1978); S.S. Holton, *Feminism and democracy: Women's suffrage and reform politics in Britain, 1900–1918* (Cambridge University Press, Cambridge, 1986).

3 H.L. Smith (ed.), *British feminism in the twentieth century* (Edward Elgar, Aldershot, 1990).

4 J. Stevenson and C. Cook, *The Slump: Society and politics during the Depression* (Quartet, London, 1979).

5 P. Summerfield, 'Women, war and social change: Women in Britain in World War II', in A. Marwick (ed.), op. cit., note 1, pp. 95–118; P. Thane, 'Towards equal opportunities? Women in Britain since 1945', in A. O'Day and T. Gourvish (eds), *Britain since 1945* (Macmillan, London, 1991).

6 R. Hoggart, *The uses of literacy* (Harmondsworth, Penguin, 1957).

7 E.J. Hobsbawm, 'The making of the working class, 1870–1914', in *Worlds of labour: Further studies in the history of labour* (Weidenfeld, London, 1984), pp. 194–213; G. Stedman Jones, *Languages of class* (Cambridge University Press, Cambridge, 1983), pp. 179–238.

8 For example, E. Roberts, *A woman's place* (Blackwell, Oxford, 1984).

9 A. Reid, 'Intelligent artisans and aristocrats of labour', in J. Winter (ed.), *The working class in modern British history* (Cambridge University Press, Cambridge, 1983), pp. 171–86.

Introduction

1 For example, E. Hobsbawm, *Worlds of labour: Further studies in the history of labour* (London, 1984), Chs 10 and 11.

2 Ibid., see also G. Stedman Jones, *Languages of class: Studies in English working class history, 1832–1982* (Cambridge, 1983), Ch. 4.

3 For a useful critique of the labour aristocracy thesis, see A. Reid, 'Intelligent artisans and aristocrats of labour: The essays of Thomas Wright', in J. Winter (ed.), *The working class in modern British history* (Cambridge, 1983).

4 The major exception, of course, being Robert Roberts' book, *The classic slum: Salford life in the first quarter of the century* (Harmondsworth, 1973). Roberts' analysis provided one of the starting points for my own research, but his depiction of a rigid gulf between the skilled and unskilled is not universally shared in Salford.

5 See Chapter 2. Oral historians working in other areas have made similar observations. See, for example, E. Roberts, *A woman's place: An oral history of working-class women 1890–1940* (Oxford, 1984), p. 6.

6 H. Meller, *Leisure and the changing city, 1870–1914* (London, 1976); P. Bailey, *Leisure and class in Victorian England: Rational recreation and the contest for control, 1830–1885* (London, 1978); H. Cunningham, *Leisure in the industrial revolution, c.1780–c.1880* (London, 1980); S.G. Jones, *Workers at play: A social and economic history of leisure 1918–1939* (London, 1986).

7 E. Ross, 'Survival networks: Women's neighbourhood sharing in London before world war one', *History Workshop*, **15** (1983); E. Roberts, op. cit., note 5; P. Ayers and J. Lambertz, 'Marriage relations, money and domestic violence in working-class Liverpool, 1919–39', in J. Lewis (ed.), *Labour and love: Women's experience of home and family, 1850–1940* (Oxford, 1986).

8 H. Cunningham, 'Leisure', in J. Benson (ed.), *The working class in England, 1875–1914* (London, 1985), pp. 144–50.

9 E. Roberts, op. cit., note 5, pp. 3–4. For attempts to define 'working class' by historians, see also J. Benson, *The working class in Britain, 1850–1939* (London, 1989), p. 3, and S. Meacham, *A life apart: The English working class 1890–1914* (London, 1977), Ch. 1.

10 See R. Roberts, op. cit., note 4, for a striking account of this.

11 See D. Fowler, 'The age of luxury: Young wage-earners and leisure', in A. Davies and S. Fielding (eds), *Workers' worlds: Cultures and communities in Manchester and Salford, 1880–1939* (Manchester, in press).

12 J. White, *The worst street in North London: Campbell Bunk, Islington, between the wars* (London, 1986).

13 Obvious exceptions containing material relevant to the present study include R. Samuel, *East End underworld: Chapters in the life of Arthur Harding* (London, 1981), and J. White, 'Police and people in London in the 1930s', *Oral History*, **11**, 2 (1983).

14 See S.G. Jones, op. cit., note 6.

15 See S. Meacham, op. cit., note 9, p.16; E. Roberts, op. cit., note 5, pp. 4–5.

16 Manchester University Settlement, *Ancoats: A study of a clearance area. Report of a survey made in 1937–1938* (Manchester, 1945), p. 47.

17 A. Briggs, *Victorian cities* (Harmondsworth, 1968), p. 116.

18 A. Kidd and K. Roberts (eds), *City, class and culture: Studies of cultural production and social policy in Victorian Manchester* (Manchester, 1985).

19 *Census of population*, 1931. M. Fogarty estimated that the Manchester conurbation had a population of 2 400 000 in 1931, *The prospects of the industrial areas of Great Britain* (London, 1945), p. 230.
20 F. Engels, *The condition of the working class in England* (London, 1969 edn), pp. 95–6, 252–3. On Engels in Salford, see E. Frow and R. Frow, *Radical Salford: Episodes in labour history* (Swinton, 1984).
21 His second account of the Salford of his childhood, *A ragged schooling: Growing up in the classic slum* (Manchester, 1976), has also been widely used by historians.
22 For an example of an impressively researched study which still leans heavily upon Roberts' analysis, see S. Meacham, op. cit., note 9.
23 W. Greenwood, *Love on the dole* (Harmondsworth, 1969 edn). See J. Stevenson, *British society 1914–45* (Harmondsworth, 1984), pp. 321–2, 480.
24 M. Leber, 'The remarkable legacy of L.S. Lowry', *Manchester Region History Review*, **1**, 2 (1987).
25 Salford Women Citizens' Association, *Housing conditions in the St Matthias' ward, Salford* (Salford, 1931), pp. 6–7.
26 B. Stancliffe and M. Muray, 'Till we build again', *Social Welfare*, **VII**, 4 (1948), p. 90.
27 A. Kidd, 'Outcast Manchester: Voluntary charity, poor relief and the casual poor 1860–1905', in A. Kidd and K. Roberts (eds), op. cit., note 18, pp. 50–2.
28 Figure taken from J. Sullivan, *The ancient and royal borough of Salford: History, commerce and industries* (Salford, 1924), p. 32. The saying was recalled during an interview by Mr H.A.
29 J. Sullivan, op. cit., note 28, pp. 4, 33–7.
30 For example, E. Roberts, op. cit., note 5; J. White, op. cit., note 12.

Chapter 1: Poverty

1 C. Bundy and D. Healy, 'Aspects of urban poverty', *Oral History*, **6**, 1 (1978), p. 79.
2 R. Roberts, *The Classic slum: Salford life in the first quarter of the century* (Harmondsworth, 1973), p. 228.
3 For example, interview with Mrs B.D. and interview with Mr K.N., both of whom described Salford in the 1930s.
4 E. Rathbone, *How the casual labourer lives: Report of the Liverpool Joint Committee on the domestic condition and expenditure of the families of certain Liverpool labourers* (Liverpool, 1909), pp. x, xxiv.
5 B.S. Rowntree, *Poverty: A study of town life* (London, 1902 edn), pp. 115–16.
6 Ministry of Labour and National Service, *Weekly expenditure of working-class households in the United Kingdom in 1937–38* (London, 1949), p. 16.
7 J. Stevenson, *British society 1914–45* (Harmondsworth, 1984), p. 41.
8 F. Scott, 'The condition and occupations of the people of Manchester and Salford', *Transactions of the Manchester Statistical Society* (1888–89).
9 The figures given are corrected percentages, based upon those households in each occupational group where information regarding level of income was obtained. Scott used a different method to calculate the percentage of households which could be classified as very poor. See A. Davies, 'Leisure and poverty in Salford and Manchester, 1900–1939', unpublished Ph.D. thesis, University of Cambridge (1989).
10 Ibid., p. 4.
11 Ibid., pp. 11, 22.

12 F. Scott, op. cit., note 8, p. 10.

13 Ibid., p. 22.

14 Ibid., p. 11. These figures were calculated by the method adopted in Table 1.1, rather than by the method suggested by Scott.

15 Ibid., p. 4; A. Kidd, 'Outcast Manchester: Voluntary charity, poor relief and the casual poor 1860–1905', in A. Kidd and K. Roberts (eds), *City, class and culture: Studies of cultural production and social policy in Victorian Manchester* (Manchester, 1985), p. 51.

16 See A. Symonds, 'Unfashionable Manchester', *East Lancashire Review*, **18**, III (1899), p. 223.

17 E.P. Hennock, 'The measurement of urban poverty: From the metropolis to the nation, 1880–1920', *Economic History Review*, **XL**, 2 (1987), p. 209.

18 B.S. Rowntree, op. cit., note 5, p. 117. Rowntree's methodology is also discussed by J. Veit-Wilson, 'Paradigms of poverty: A rehabilitation of B.S. Rowntree', *Journal of Social Policy*, **15**, 1 (1986).

19 B.S. Rowntree, op. cit., note 5, pp. 87, 133–4.

20 Ibid., pp. 136–7.

21 J. Veit-Wilson, op. cit., note 18, p. 70.

22 B.S. Rowntree, op. cit., note 5, pp. 86–7, 141–2.

23 T.R. Marr, *Housing conditions in Manchester and Salford* (Manchester, 1904); C.E.B. Russell, *Manchester boys: Sketches of Manchester lads at work and play* (Swinton, 1984 reprint).

24 Manchester and Salford Trades and Labour Council, *Annual Report* (1903), cited in E. Frow and R. Frow, *To make that future – now! A history of the Manchester and Salford Trades and Labour Council* (Manchester, 1976), p. 59. On cyclical unemployment, see A. Kidd, op. cit., note 15, p. 68.

25 S. Chapman and H. Hallsworth, *Unemployment* (Manchester, 1909), p. 71.

26 C. Wyatt, 'The Lord Mayor's Fund for the Relief of Distress in Manchester – winter of 1908–9', *Transactions of the Manchester Statistical Society*, (1909–1910), pp. 152, 155.

27 Ibid., pp. 133, 150.

28 Figure calculated from data provided by C. Wyatt, ibid., pp. 144–9. See also p. 132.

29 J. Stevenson, op. cit., note 7, p. 116; J. Benson, *The working class in Britain, 1850–1939* (London, 1989), pp. 55–6.

30 See R. McKibbin, *The ideologies of class: Social relations in Britain, 1880–1950* (Oxford, 1990), Ch. 8.

31 J. Stevenson, op. cit., note 7, pp. 103, 266.

32 A. Bowley and M. Hogg, *Has poverty diminished?* (London, 1925), p. 16.

33 R.F. George, 'A new calculation of the poverty line', *Journal of the Royal Statistical Society*, **C** (1937).

34 H. Tout, *The standard of living in Bristol* (Bristol, 1938), pp. 19–20.

35 H. Llewellyn Smith (ed.), *The new survey of London life and labour* (London, 1932), Vol. III, pp. 78–9, 81.

36 The term 'insufficiency' was used by H. Tout in his survey, op. cit., note 34, p. 28. A Manchester University Settlement study of Ancoats used the same category without adopting the label 'insufficiency', – Manchester University Settlement, *Ancoats: A study of a clearance area. Report of a survey made in 1937–1938* (Manchester, 1945), p. 20.

37 Manchester University Settlement, op. cit., note 36, p. 20.

38 The Merseyside survey revealed that 16.0 per cent of the population were living in primary poverty, with a further 14.0 per cent living in 'insufficiency', on incomes between 0 and 50 per cent above the poverty line. These figures were based upon a survey of the population as a whole. The Bristol study, based on a survey of the working- and lower middle-class population, revealed a primary poverty level of 10.7 per cent, and an insufficiency level of 19.3 per cent. D. Caradog Jones (ed.), *The social survey of Merseyside* (Liverpool, 1934), Vol. 1, p. 154; H. Tout, op. cit., note 34, pp. 25–6.

39 E. Roberts, 'Women's strategies', in J. Lewis (ed.), *Labour and love: Women's experience of home and family, 1850–1940* (Oxford, 1986), p. 224; J. Stevenson, op. cit., note 7, pp. 136–7.

40 J. Benson, op. cit., note 29, pp. 40–3.

41 J. Andrew, 'Unemployment in Manchester (October 1922)', in J. Astor *et al.* (eds), *The third winter of unemployment* (London, 1923), p. 233.

42 *Salford City Reporter*, 10 January 1936.

43 For example, interview with Mrs M.G.

44 Interview with Mr B.R.

45 These figures obscure considerable variations between districts across the two cities.

46 M. Fogarty, *The prospects of the industrial areas of Great Britain* (London, 1945), p. 230; Figure for Jarrow in S.G. Jones, *Workers at play: A social and economic history of leisure 1918–1939* (London, 1986), p. 109.

47 J. Andrew, op. cit., note 41, p. 232.

48 A. Purcell, *The slow murder of the unemployed* (1932), cited in E. Frow and R. Frow, op. cit., note 24, p. 138.

49 Manchester University Settlement, op. cit., note 36, pp. 24, 45. The Ministry of Labour survey, also conducted in 1937–38, gave a figure of around 40 per cent from a national sample of 9000 families; op. cit., note 6, p. 12.

50 R.F. George, op. cit., note 33, p. 74.

51 B.S. Rowntree, *Poverty and progress: A second social survey of York* (London, 1941), *The human needs of labour* (London, 1937).

52 B.S. Rowntree, *Poverty and progress*, op. cit., note 51, pp. 28–9; R.F. George, op. cit., note 33, pp. 74–6.

53 B.S. Rowntree, *Poverty and progress*, op. cit., note 51, pp. 32, 108–9.

54 C.E.B. Russell and E.T. Campagnac, 'Poor people's music halls in Lancashire', *Economic Review*, **X** (1900), pp. 290–1.

55 For example, interview with Mrs L.C. See also E. Roberts, *A woman's place: An oral history of working-class women 1890–1940* (Oxford, 1984) and 'Women's Strategies', op. cit., note 39.

56 N. Richardson, T. Flynn and A. Gall, *Salford's pubs* (Swinton, 1979), Vol. 3, p. 4.

57 Manchester Social Service Group of the Auxiliary Movement, *Report on a survey of housing conditions in a Salford area* (Manchester, 1930), p. 5.

58 Manchester University Settlement, op. cit., note 36, p. 21; H. Tout, op. cit., note 34, pp. 25–6.

59 A third of the families in the Ancoats sample and half of those in Bristol were living on incomes above the poverty and 'insufficiency' lines, but below the level deemed 'comfortable'.

60 For an alternative and slightly less pessimistic assessment of the scale of poverty, see J. Benson, op.cit., note 29, p. 65.

Chapter 2: Men: Poverty, unemployment and the family

1 See V. Hey, *Patriarchy and pub culture* (London, 1986).
2 Leisure patterns do not appear to have been inherited. Some men followed their fathers, as gamblers, drinkers or followers of sport. Others, however, were put off by their fathers' behaviour, especially in cases where the father drank or gambled heavily.
3 J. Lanigan, 'Thy kingdom did come' (n.d.). Manuscript autobiography held at Brunel University Library, p. 9.
4 Interview with Mrs M.G.
5 Interview with Ms G.G.
6 M.S.T.C. 517.
7 Mass Observation, *The pub and the people* (London, 1987 edn), pp. 55–6, 114.
8 Ibid., p. 39.
9 Ibid., pp. 59–60; interview with Mrs E.O.
10 Interview with Mr L.P.
11 Mass Observation, op. cit., note 7, p. 41.
12 R Roberts, *The classic slum: Salford life in the first quarter of the century* (Harmondsworth, 1973), pp. 49–50.
13 *Manchester City News*, 15 July 1911.
14 R. Heaton, *Salford my home town* (Swinton 1982), p. 7.
15 E. Oman, *Salford stepping stones* (Swinton, 1983), p. 3.
16 This was confirmed in a number of interviews, e.g. by Mr B.R.
17 Interview with Mr H.D.
18 M.S.T.C. 780.
19 Interview with Mr H.S. See E. Rathbone, *How the casual labourer lives: Report of the Liverpool Joint Committee on the domestic condition and expenditure of the families of certain Liverpool labourers* (Liverpool), 1909, pp. xxv–vi.
20 R. Roberts, op. cit., note 12, p. 19.
21 M.S.T.C. 780.
22 Interview with Mr H.D.
23 M.S.T.C. 491/2. The 'Manchester' racecourse was situated in Ordsall until 1905, when the races moved to Kersal, an outlying Salford district.
24 Interview with Mr P.J.
25 J. Hilton (ed.), *Why I go in for the pools* (London, 1936); see also T. Mason, *Association football and English society 1863–1915* (Brighton, 1980), pp. 148, 154–8.
26 The higher cost of living on municipal estates was discussed by F. Thompson, 'A survey of the development of facilities for recreation and leisure occupation on new housing estates, with special reference to Manchester', unpublished thesis for the Diploma in Social Study, University of Manchester, 1937, p. 65.
27 See E. Hobsbawm, *Worlds of labour: Further studies in the history of Labour* (London, 1984), Chs 10 and 11.
28 Interview with Mr L.L.
29 Interview with Mr E.J.
30 *New York Post*, 25 April 1936.
31 D. Caradog Jones (ed.), *The social survey of Merseyside* (Liverpool, 1934), Vol. 3, pp. 274–6.
32 Interview with Mr C.P.

33 Interview with Mr H.A.
34 J. Walton, 'The demand for working-class seaside holidays in Victorian England', *Economic History Review*, **XXXIV**, 2 (1981), pp. 257–8.
35 S.G. Jones, 'The Lancashire cotton industry and the development of paid holidays in the nineteen-thirties', *Transactions of the Historic Society of Lancashire and Cheshire for the year 1985*, **135** (1986), p. 101.
36 *Daily Worker*, 22 February 1938. Cited by S.G. Jones, op. cit., note 35, p. 103.
37 Manchester University Settlement, *Ancoats: A study of a clearance area. Report of a survey made in 1937–1938* (Manchester, 1945), p. 47.
38 See, for example, E. Oman, op. cit., note 15, p. 77.
39 Interview with Mr C.P.
40 Interview with Mrs B.D.
41 Interview with Mrs A.H.
42 Interview with Mr L.P.
43 See E. Roberts, *A woman's place: An oral history of working-class women 1890–1940* (Oxford, 1984), pp. 198–9.
44 S.G. Jones, *Workers at play: A social and economic history of leisure 1918–1939* (London, 1986), pp. 118–20.
45 R. McKibbin, *The ideologies of class: Social relations in Britain, 1880–1950* (Oxford, 1990), pp. 243, 257–8.
46 Manchester University Settlement, op. cit., note 37, p. 25.
47 B.S. Rowntree and B. Lasker, *Unemployment: A social study* (London, 1911), p. 230.
48 H. Llewellyn Smith (ed.), *The new survey of London life and labour* (London, 1932), Vol. IX, p. 254.
49 Interviews with Mr C.P. and Mr R.P.
50 Cited in T. Mason, op. cit., note 25, p. 148.
51 Mass Observation, op. cit., note 7, pp. 284–91.
52 C. Cameron, A. Lush and G. Meara, *Disinherited youth* (Edinburgh, 1943), p. 104. See also S.G. Jones, op. cit., note 44, p. 119.
53 T. Middleton, 'An enquiry into the use of leisure amongst the working classes of Liverpool', unpublished M.A. thesis, University of Liverpool, 1931, p. 195.
54 See Chapter 3.
55 Compare E. Oman, op. cit., note 15, p. 55, with W. Greenwood, *Love on the dole* (Harmondsworth, 1969 edn), p. 65.
56 Interview with Mrs E.P.
57 Interview with Mr B.R.
58 W. Greenwood, *There was a time* (London, 1967), p. 190.
59 W. Greenwood, op. cit., note 55, pp. 172–3.
60 W. Greenwood, op. cit., note 58, p. 240.
61 *Manchester Guardian*, 29 October 1925.
62 W. Greenwood, op. cit., note 55, p. 77; interview with Mrs F.T., M.S.T.C. 780.
63 C. Bundy and D. Healy, 'Aspects of urban poverty', *Oral History*, **6**, 1 (1978), p. 81.
64 Lounging and other mundane activities such as 'sitting out' in the streets are discussed in Chapters 4 and 5.
65 Interview with Mr L.P.
66 Letter from Mr L.P. to the author.
67 See A. Davies, 'Leisure and poverty in Salford and Manchester, 1900–1939', unpublished Ph.D. thesis, University of Cambridge (1989), p. 60.
68 W. Greenwood, op. cit., note 58, p. 223.
69 W. Greenwood, op. cit., note 55, pp. 170–1.

70 This was perhaps more the case in Salford, where men in different jobs lived in close proximity, than in Liverpool, where the predominance of casual dock labour meant that less stigma was attached to unemployment.

71 B.S. Rowntree, *Poverty: A study of town life* (London, 1902 edn), p. 142.

72 *Manchester City News*, 4 August 1906.

73 Interview with Mrs A.H.

74 Manchester University Settlement, op.cit., note 37, p. 23.

75 Interview with Mr C.P.

76 Interview with Mrs A.S.

77 Interview with Mr S.B.

78 *Manchester City News*, 4 August 1906.

79 C.E.B. Russell and E.T. Campagnac, 'Poor people's music halls in Lancashire', *Economic Review*, **X** (1900), pp. 290–1.

80 Interview with Mrs E.P.

81 *Salford City Reporter*, 23 September 1938.

82 *Salford City Reporter*, 6 January 1939. Surnames given in extracts from the local press have been altered in the text.

83 *Salford City Reporter*, 6 May 1938.

84 Interview with Mrs A.M.

85 Interview with Mrs E.P.

86 Interview with Mrs L.M.

87 Interview with Mrs A.M.

88 H. Watkin, *From Hulme all blessings flow* (Swinton, 1985), p. 57.

89 S.G. Jones, op. cit., note 44; J. Walvin, *Leisure and society 1830–1950* (London, 1978).

Chapter 3: Women: Housekeeping, leisure and independence

1 For suggestive but very brief comments concerning women's leisure, see P. Bailey, *Leisure and class in Victorian England: Rational recreation and the contest for control, 1830–1885* (London, 1978), p. 181; S.G. Jones, *Workers at play: A social and economic history of leisure 1918–1939* (London, 1986), pp. 58–61. On women as household managers, see E. Roberts, *A woman's place: An oral history of working-class women 1890–1940* (Oxford, 1984).

2 R. Hoggart, *The uses of literacy: Aspects of working-class life with special reference to publications and entertainments* (Harmondsworth, 1958 edn), p. 56.

3 This is one of the principal conclusions of E. Roberts, op. cit., note 1, p. 203.

4 Interview with Mrs A.M.

5 Further discussions of women's leisure are contained in Chapters 5 and 6.

6 Salford Mothers' Guild and Ladies Public Health Society, *Report – for the year 1932–33* (Salford, 1933), pp. 3–4.

7 Interview with Mrs M.R. and Mr J.D.

8 C.E.B. Russell and L. Rigby, *Working lads clubs* (London, 1908), p. 272.

9 B. Stancliffe and M. Muray, 'Till we build again', *Social Welfare*, **VII**, 4 (1948), p. 96.

10 M.S.T.C. 517.

11 Interview with Mrs L.M; W. Greenwood, *There was a time* (London, 1967), p. 26.

12 W. Greenwood, *Love on the dole* (Harmondsworth, 1969 edn), pp. 11–12.

13 Interview with Mr G.O.

14 H. Mitchell, *The hard way up* (London, 1977 edn), pp. 112, 203.
15 A. Foley, *A Bolton childhood* (Manchester, 1973), p. 64.
16 Interview with Mrs A.M. by Alison Dickens.
17 For other examples, see A. Davies, 'Leisure and poverty in Salford and Manchester, 1900–1939', unpublished Ph.D. thesis, University of Cambridge (1989), p. 18.
18 Interview with Ms M.T; B. Stancliffe and M. Muray, op. cit., note 9, p. 93.
19 M. Spring Rice (ed.), *Working-class wives: Their health and conditions* (London, 1981 edn), pp. 109–10.
20 Interview with Mrs L.M.
21 M.S.T.C. 494.
22 Interview with Mrs J.R.
23 M. Spring Rice (ed.), op. cit., note 19, p. 94, 99, 114.
24 Interview with Mrs E.H.
25 Mass Observation, *The pub and the people* (London, 1987 edn), p. 38.
26 B.S. Rowntree, *Poverty and progress: A second social survey of York* (London, 1941), pp. 351–3.
27 B.S. Rowntree, *Poverty: A study of town life* (London, 1902 edn), pp. 315–26.
28 B.S. Rowntree, op. cit., note 26, p. 353.
29 T. Simpson, *The underworld of Manchester in war time* (Manchester, 1915), p. 21; M.S.T.C. 491/2.
30 Interview with Mr C.P.
31 M.S.T.C. 491/2.
32 M. Burke, *Ancoats lad: The recollections of Mick Burke* (Swinton, 1985), p. 54.
33 R. Roberts, *A ragged schooling: Growing up in the classic slum* (Manchester, 1976), p. 23.
34 Interview with Mrs A.M. by Alison Dickens.
35 Interview with Mrs E.O.
36 T. Simpson, op. cit., note 29, p. 13.
37 Interview with Mrs E.H.
38 Interview with Mrs F.T.
39 M.S.T.C. 516.
40 M.S.T.C. 780.
41 Mass Observation, op. cit., note 25, pp. 144–6.
42 Interview with Mrs L.C.
43 Interview with Mrs A.A.
44 C. Chinn, *They worked all their lives: Women of the urban poor in England, 1880–1939* (Manchester, 1988), p. 119.
45 Interview with Mrs M.D.
46 M. Burke, op. cit., note 32, p. 5.
47 Interview with Mr P.J.
48 Interview with Mrs L.A.
49 Interview with Mrs B.D.
50 B. Harrison, *Drink and the Victorians: The temperance question in England 1815–1872* (London, 1971), p. 171.
51 T. Simpson, op. cit., note 29, p. 24.
52 M.S.T.C. 516.
53 M.S.T.C. 816.
54 A. Burgess, *Little Wilson and big God: Being the first part of the confessions of Anthony Burgess* (London, 1987), p. 23.

55 A. Davies, 'A modern miracle? Nancy Dickybird and representations of North Manchester, 1900–1931', unpublished paper.
56 M. Bertenshaw, *Sunrise to sunset: A vivid personal account of life in early Manchester* (Manchester, 1980), pp. 22–4.
57 A. Davies, op. cit., note 55.
58 F. Doran, 'Down memory lane', manuscript autobiography held in the Local History Department, Manchester Central Reference Library (1973), p. 12.
59 E. Rathbone, *How the casual labourer lives* (Liverpool, 1909), p. xxiv.
60 C.E.B. Russell, *Social problems of the North* (London, 1914), pp. 112–13.
61 Interview with Mr C.P.
62 E. Roberts, op. cit., note 1, p. 110.
63 C.E.B. Russell, op. cit., note 60, p. 97.
64 J. Richards, *The age of the dream palace: Cinema and society in Britain 1930–1939* (London, 1984), p. 11; B.S. Rowntree, op. cit., note 26, p. 413.
65 J. Hobbins, 'From the threepenny gallery: Some impressions of the cheap theatre', 'Odds and Ends', **XLIX** (1903), pp 378–80; W. Tomlinson, *Bye ways of Manchester life* (Manchester, 1887), p. 70.
66 R. Low, *The history of the British film 1906–1914* (London, 1949).
67 Conference on Christian Politics, Economics and Citizenship, *Commission report on leisure* (London, 1924), pp. 26–7.
68 C.E.B. Russell, op. cit., note 60, p. 98.
69 R. Roberts, op. cit., note 33, p. 209.
70 M. Spring Rice (ed.), op. cit., note 19, pp. 103, 110, 112.
71 W. Greenwood, op. cit., note 12, p. 42; interviews with Ms A.O. and Mrs B.D.
72 Manchester University Settlement, *Ancoats: A study of a clearance area. Report of a survey made in 1937–1938* (Manchester, 1945), p. 49.
73 Interview with Mrs A.M. and Mrs L.M.
74 Interview with Mrs L.A.
75 R. Roberts, op. cit., note 33, p. 209.
76 Interview with Mrs E.H.
77 For example, interview with Mrs M.G.
78 Interview with Mrs F.T.
79 This contradicts the view put forward by R. Roberts, *The classic slum: Salford life in the first quarter of the century* (Harmondsworth, 1973), p. 176.
80 M.S.T.C. 491.
81 R. Roberts, op. cit., note 33, pp. 52, 208; op. cit., note 79, p. 175.
82 Interview with Mrs A.M.
83 Interviews with Mrs E.P, Mrs L.M and Ms W.J.
84 Interview with Mrs E.P.
85 R. Heaton, *Salford my home town* (Swinton, 1982), p. 23.
86 R. Roberts, op. cit., note 33, p. 151.
87 Interview with Mrs L.M.
88 Interview with Mrs A.M.
89 Interview with Mrs A.M and Mrs L.M.
90 Interview with Mrs E.C.
91 Interview with Mrs A.M and Mrs L.M.
92 Interview with Mrs E.P.
93 W. Greenwood, op. cit., note 12, pp. 95–102; *Manchester City News*, 15 September 1906.
94 Interview with Mrs L.M.

Chapter 4: Young workers: Parents, police and freedom

1 See D. Fowler, 'The age of luxury: Young wage-earners and leisure', in A. Davies and S. Fielding (eds), *Workers' worlds: Culture and communities in Manchester and Salford, 1880–1939* (Manchester, in press); see also the critical discussion in S. Hall and T. Jefferson (eds), *Resistance through rituals: Youth subcultures in post-war Britain* (London, 1976), pp. 17–25.

2 See S. Humphries, *Hooligans or rebels? An oral history of working-class childhood and youth 1889–1939* (Oxford, 1981), and *A secret world of sex. Forbidden fruit: the British experience, 1900–1950* (London, 1988); J. Springhall, *Coming of age: Adolescence in Britain, 1860–1960* (Dublin, 1986); S. Alexander, 'Becoming a woman in London in the 1920s and 1930s', in D. Feldman and G. Stedman Jones (eds), *Metropolis. London: Histories and representations since 1800* (London, 1989).

3 C.E.B. Russell, *Manchester boys: Sketches of Manchester lads at work and play* (Swinton, 1984 reprint); A. Fielder, 'Adolescents and the cinema: Report of an enquiry', unpublished dissertation submitted for the Diploma in Social Studies, University of Manchester (1932); J. Harley, 'Report of an enquiry into the occupations, further education and leisure interests of a number of girl wage-earners from elementary and central schools in the Manchester district, with special reference to the influence of school training on their use of leisure', unpublished M.Ed. dissertation, University of Manchester (1937); H. James and F. Moore, 'Adolescent leisure in a working-class district', *Occupational Psychology*, **XIV**, 3 (1940).

4 J. Toole, *Fighting through life* (London, 1935), p. 61; W. Greenwood, *There was a time* (London, 1967), p. 114.

5 For example, A. Bowley and M. Hogg only asserted that household incomes were not necessarily pooled: *Has poverty diminished?* (London, 1925), p. 16.

6 Manchester University Settlement, *Ancoats: A study of a clearance area. Report of a survey made in 1937–1938* (Manchester, 1945), p. 21; J. Harley, op. cit., note 3, pp. 56–7.

7 See B.S. Rowntree, *Poverty and Progress: A second social survey of York* (London, 1941), Ch. III.

8 Manchester University Settlement, op. cit., note 6, p. 23.

9 Interview with Mr L.P.

10 Interviews with Mrs M.J. and Mrs M.H.

11 W. Greenwood, op. cit., note 4, p. 114.

12 Interview with Mr H.S.

13 E. Hadden, 'Women's recreation in Ancoats', 'Odds and Ends', **L** (1904), p. 316.

14 See A. Davies, 'Leisure and poverty in Salford and Manchester, 1900–1939', unpublished Ph.D. thesis, University of Cambridge (1989), p. 118.

15 Interview with Mrs B.G.

16 Lanigan, 'Thy kingdom did come', manuscript autobiography (n.d.), pp. 10, 11, 14, 18.

17 Interview with Ms W.J.

18 See Chapter 2.

19 Interview with Mrs A.S.

20 Interview with Mr S.B.

21 Interview with Mrs E.C.

22 C.E.B. Russell, op. cit., note 3, p. 3. See G. Pearson, *Hooligan: A history of respectable fears* (London, 1983).

23 Interview with Mrs A.S.
24 Interview with Mrs E.C.
25 For example, R. Roberts, *The classic slum: Salford life in the first quarter of the century* (Harmondsworth, 1973), pp. 232–6.
26 Interview with Mrs A.S.
27 Interview with Mrs E.C.
28 M.S.T.C. 556/7.
29 Interview with Mr B.R.
30 Interview with Ms A.O.
31 Interview with Mr H.S.
32 Interview with Mrs C.S.
33 Interview with Mr B.R.
34 Interview with Mrs L.M.
35 Interview with Mrs W.G.
36 Interview with Mr C.W.
37 Interview with Mr L.L.
38 E. MacColl, 'Theatre of action, Manchester', in R. Samuel, E. MacColl and S. Cosgrove (eds), *Theatres of the left 1880–1935: Workers' theatre movements in Britain and America* (London, 1985), p. 233.
39 Interview with Mr G.O; S. Humphries, *A secret world of sex*, op. cit., note 2, pp. 156–8.
40 Interview with Mr L.P.
41 On scuttling, see G. Pearson, op. cit., note 22, pp. 94–6.
42 J. Harley, op. cit., note 3, p 108.
43 H. James and F. Moore, op. cit., note 3, p. 139.
44 Ibid., p. 137; J. Harley, op. cit., note 3, p. 112; W. Greenwood, *Love on the dole* (Harmondsworth, 1969), p. 65.
45 S. Alexander, op. cit., note 2, p. 265; M. Bertenshaw, *Sunrise to sunset: A vivid personal account of life in early Manchester* (Manchester, 1980), pp. 98–101
46 A. Fielder, op. cit., note 3, pp. 4, 19, 22, 36.
47 Ibid., p. 28.
48 T. Aldgate, 'Comedy, class and containment: The domestic British cinema of the 1930s', in J. Curran and V. Porter (eds), *British cinema history* (London, 1983), p. 270.
49 J. Harley, op. cit., note 3, p. 110.
50 Ibid., p. 107; A. Fielder, op. cit., note 3, p. 35.
51 H. James and F. Moore, op. cit., note 3, p. 139. See also J. Springhall, op. cit., note 2, p. 139.
52 J. Harley, op. cit., note 3, p. 102.
53 Interview with Mrs G.R. On the role of girls in street gangs, see S. Humphries, *A secret world of sex*, op. cit., note 2, Ch. 6.
54 Interview with Mr B.R.
55 Interview with Mr B.R.
56 Interview with Mrs E.H. See J. Harley, op. cit., note 3, pp. 114–16, on conversations between girls at work.
57 Interview with Mr A.P.
58 R. Roberts, op. cit., note 25, pp. 156–7.
59 Interview with Mrs C.J.
60 *Manchester Guardian*, 6, 11, 12 January 1906.
61 *Manchester Guardian*, 27 March 1906.
62 *Salford City Reporter*, 28 August 1920.

63 M.S.T.C. 530.
64 Interview with Mrs E.P. and Mr R.P.
65 *Salford City Reporter*, 28 August 1920.
66 Interview with Mr L.L.
67 For example, interview with Mr L.P., describing Hanky Park. See A. Davies, op. cit., note 14, p. 140.
68 *The Shadow*, 27 February, 20 March and 19 June 1869.
69 *Salford City Reporter*, 29 March 1924.
70 C.E.B. Russell, op. cit., note 3, p. 30.
71 Interview with Mr H.S.
72 M.S.T.C. 556/7.
73 Interview with Mrs L.C.
74 Interview with Mrs M.G.
75 C.E.B. Russell and L. Rigby, *Working lads' clubs* (London, 1908), p. 267.
76 Interview with Mrs L.A.
77 Interview with Mr W.G. and Mrs B.G.
78 C.E.B. Russell, op. cit., note 3, p. 30; Lanigan, op. cit., note 16, p. 11.
79 Interview with Mr L.L.
80 Interview with Mr F.H.
81 Interview with Mr A.P.
82 A. Cox and P. Duffin (eds), *Day in, day out: Memories of North Manchester from women in Monsall Hospital* (Manchester, 1985), pp. 34–5.
83 *Salford City Reporter*, 1 March 1924.
84 *Salford City Reporter*, 29 March 1924.
85 Interview with Mr L.L.
86 M.S.T.C. 556/7.
87 My own assessment differs from David Fowler's at this point.
88 J. Richards, 'The cinema and cinema-going in Birmingham in the 1930s', in J. Walton and J. Walvin (eds), *Leisure in Britain 1780–1939* (Manchester, 1983), p. 45.
89 M.S.T.C. 556/7.
90 This was shown in their survey of the weekend leisure patterns of youths in Hulme: H. James and F. Moore, 'Adolescent leisure in a working-class district, part II', *Occupational Psychology*, **XVIII**, 1 (1944), pp. 28, 33.
91 Information provided by Mike Stott.
92 Interview with Mrs B.D.

Chapter 5: Streets, markets and parks

1 R. Roberts, *The classic slum: Salford life in the first quarter of the century* (Harmondsworth, 1973), p. 124.
2 See E. Hobsbawm, *Worlds of labour: Further studies in the history of labour* (London, 1984) and G. Stedman Jones, *Language of class: Studies in English working-class history, 1832–1982* (Cambridge, 1983) for an emphasis on the late nineteenth century as a turning point.
3 R. Roberts, op. cit., note 1, pp. 47–9; and *A ragged schooling: Growing up in the classic slum* (Manchester, 1976), p. 119.
4 R. Roberts, op. cit., note 1, pp. 47–9, 124; and *A ragged schooling*, op. cit., note 3, pp. 117–19, 140.

5 A. Reach, *Manchester and the textile districts in 1849* (Helmshore, 1972 edn), p. 8.
6 H. James and F. Moore, 'Adolescent leisure in a working class district', *Occupational Psychology*, **XIV**, 3 (1940) p. 133.
7 Interview with Mrs B.D.
8 I am grateful to Pat Ayers for this point.
9 R. Roberts, op. cit., note 1, p. 13; and *A ragged schooling*, op. cit., note 3, p. 14, 140–1.
10 Interview with Mr C.P.
11 Interview with Mrs B.D.
12 R. Heaton, *Salford my home town* (Swinton, 1982), p. 3.
13 Salford Mothers' Guild and Ladies Public Health Society, *Annual report for 1932–1933*, pp. 6–7.
14 H. Philips, *Open spaces for recreation in Manchester* (Manchester, 1896), pp. 52–3.
15 B.S. Rowntree, *Poverty: A study of town life* (London, 1902 edn), p. 318.
16 Interview with Mrs C.S.
17 See the account of Whit Walks below.
18 J. White, *The worst street in North London: Campbell Bunk, Islington, between the wars* (London, 1986), pp. 86–8.
19 M.S.T.C. 517.
20 M.S.T.C. 506.
21 See A. Davies, 'Leisure and poverty in Salford and Manchester, 1900–1939', unpublished Ph.D. thesis, University of Cambridge (1989), pp. 158–9.
22 J. Benson discussed street entertainment in some depth in *The penny capitalists: A study of nineteenth-century working-class entrepreneurs* (Dublin, 1983).
23 J. White, op. cit., note 18, p. 61.
24 J. Page (F. Folio, pseud.), *The hawkers and street dealers of the North of England manufacturing districts* (Manchester, 1858), p. 117.
25 For example, J. Lockhart, 'Some reflections on street singing', 'Odds and Ends', **XXX**, (1884), pp. 386–9.
26 F. Roberts, *Memories of a Victorian childhood and working life in Miles Platting, Manchester* (Swinton, 1983), p. 5.
27 W. Jordan, 'Itinerant musicians', 'Odds and Ends', **XLVIII** (1901), p. 361; *Manchester Examiner and Times*, 17 November 1893.
28 See A. Davies, op. cit., note 21, p. 161–2.
29 H. Cunningham, 'Leisure', in J. Benson (ed.), *The working class in England, 1875–1914* (London, 1985), p. 145.
30 W. Jordan, op. cit., note 27, p. 361.
31 M.S.T.C. 775/2; M.S.T.C. 766/1.
32 C.E.B. Russell and E.T. Campagnac, 'Poor people's music halls in Lancashire', *Economic Review*, **X** (1900), p. 305.
33 C. Barstow, 'A dance in the city', *Faces and Places*, **XIV**, 5 (1903).
34 Interview with Mrs L.C; M. Bertenshaw, *Sunrise to sunset: A vivid personal account of life in early Manchester* (Manchester, 1980), p. 11.
35 Interview with Mrs A.S.
36 J. Toole, *Fighting through life* (London, 1935), p. 53.
37 Interview with Mr J.R.
38 C.E.B. Russell, *Manchester boys: Sketches of Manchester lads at work and play* (Swinton, 1984 reprint), p. 13.
39 J. White, op. cit., note 18, p. 57.
40 Interview with Mrs B.D.

41 *Salford City Reporter*, 7 July 1939.
42 M. Bertenshaw, op. cit., note 34, pp. 50–2, 66–7.
43 T.R. Marr, *Housing conditions in Manchester and Salford* (Manchester, 1904), p. 63.
44 Interview with Mrs E.O.
45 Interview with Mrs M.G.
46 Interview with Mrs B.D.
47 See the account by Ewan MacColl cited below.
48 Interview with Mrs E.H.
49 R. Roberts, op. cit., note 1, p. 150; F. Doran, 'Down memory lane', manuscript autobiography (1973), p. 18.
50 Interview with Mrs B.D.
51 Interview with Mr C.W.
52 City of Manchester, *Police Instruction Book* (Manchester, 1908, 1923), p. 413.
53 E. MacColl, 'Theatre of action, Manchester', in R. Samuel, E. MacColl and S. Cosgrove (eds), *Theatres of the left 1880–1935: Workers' theatre movements in Britain and America* (London, 1985), pp. 211–13.
54 Interview with Mrs M.R.
55 S. Fielding, 'The Catholic Whit-walk in Manchester and Salford 1890–1939', *Manchester Region History Review*, **1**, 1 (1987), p. 3.
56 Interview with Mrs K.E.
57 S. Fielding, op. cit., note 55, p. 3.
58 Interview with Mr B.B.
59 Interview with Mr C.P.
60 Manuscript essay by Mr C. Slater, held as part of the series 'Life in Manchester' deposited in the archives department of Manchester Central Library.
61 Interview with Mrs E.P.
62 Interview with Mrs M.R.
63 Interview with Mrs L.C.
64 May queens and 'nigger' troupes were described in many interviews.
65 *Faces and Places*, **XIV** (1903), p. 181.
66 *Manchester Guardian*, 11 May 1923; interview with Mrs L.C.
67 Interview with Mrs E.O.
68 Interview with Mrs L.C.
69 Interview with Mrs A.S.
70 M.S.T.C. 512. Strangeways gaol is in Manchester, and 'peaky lads' refers to the 'peaky blinders', a name given to Birmingham youth gangs, the equivalent of Manchester's 'scuttlers' at the turn of the century. See G. Pearson, *Hooligan: A history of respectable fears* (London, 1983), p. 96. The second rhyme refers to Pendlebury, one of the pit villages on the outskirts of Salford. A 'brew' is a slope or hill.
71 *Manchester Guardian*, 11 May 1923.
72 See A. Davies, op. cit., note 21, p. 182.
73 Interview with Mrs E.H.
74 See J. Walton and R. Poole, 'The Lancashire Wakes in the nineteenth century', in R. Storch (ed.), *Popular culture and custom in nineteenth century England* (London, 1982), p. 100
75 Interview with Mrs A.A.
76 The uniformity of working-class culture was emphasized by Hobsbawm in 'The formation of British working class culture', in his *Worlds of labour*, op. cit., note 2.

77 F. Jordan, 'A night in the city', in 'Odds and Ends', **L** (1904), pp. 323–4. For a fuller account of the use of markets and working-class leisure patterns, see A. Davies, 'Saturday night markets in Manchester and Salford, 1840–1939', *Manchester Region History Review*, **1**, 2 (1987).

78 J. Page, op. cit., note 24, pp. 72–4.

79 *Free Lance*, **2**, 53 (1867); *Shadow*, 16 April 1870.

80 *Free Lance*, **2**, 53 (1867).

81 *City Lantern*, 17 May 1878.

82 See A. Davies, op. cit., note 77, p. 5.

83 *City Jackdaw*, 17 October 1879.

84 R. Roberts, op. cit., note 1, p. 39.

85 *Manchester Guardian*, 26 May 1906.

86 A. Foley, *A Bolton childhood* (Manchester, 1973), p. 26.

87 Interview with Mrs E.H.

88 For example, F. Osman, *For the love of Ada ... and Salford* (Swinton, 1984), pp. 16–17.

89 Interview with Mrs G.R.

90 Interview with Mrs E.C. and Mrs L.M.

91 Interview with Mrs A.M. and Mrs L.M.

92 *Salford City Reporter*, 26 August 1938.

93 Interview with Ms A.O.

94 M.S.T.C. 816.

95 C.E.B. Russell, op. cit., note 38, p. 29.

96 J. Toole, op. cit., note 36, p. 37.

97 Interviews with Mrs A.M. and Miss W.J.; see J. White, op. cit., note 18, p. 201.

98 Interview with Mr J.P.

99 F. Jordan, op. cit., note 77, pp. 328–30.

100 J. Toole, op. cit., note 36, pp. 87–8, 110.

101 Annual Report cited in J. Liddington and J. Norris, *One hand tied behind us: The rise of the women's suffrage movement* (London, 1978), p. 20.

102 T. Swindells, *Manchester streets and Manchester men*, Vol. 2 (Manchester, 1907).

103 *Manchester Guardian*, 31 August 1931; M. Burke, *Ancoats lad: The recollections of Mick Burke* (Swinton, 1985), p. 56.

104 J. Toole, op. cit., note 36, pp. 74–6.

105 *Manchester Guardian*, 10 August 1844.

106 Manchester Parks and Cemeteries Committee, *Illustrated handbook of the Manchester city parks and recreation grounds* (Manchester, 1915), p. 4.

107 Ibid., p. 4.

108 H. James and F. Moore, op. cit., note 6, p. 134.

109 County Borough of Salford, Museum, Libraries and Parks Committee, *Annual report* (1903).

110 Interview with Mrs M.D.

111 Mrs E.H., letter to the author.

112 Interview with Mrs M.D.

113 County Borough of Salford, Museum, Libraries and Parks Committee, *Annual report* (1927).

114 Interview with Mr W.G.

115 County Borough of Salford, Museum, Libraries and Parks Committee, *Annual report* (1921, 1923).

116 M.S.T.C. 512.

117 R. Heaton, op. cit., note 12, p. 12.
118 County Borough of Salford, Museum, Libraries and Parks Committee, *Annual report* (1926, 1929).
119 M. Burke, op. cit., note 103, p. 56; M.S.T.C. 512.
120 Interview with Mr L.P.
121 B. Stancliffe and M. Muray, 'Till we build again', *Social Welfare*, **VII**, 4 (1948), p. 90.

Chapter 6: Gambling

1 See R. McKibbin, 'Working class gambling in Britain 1880–1939', *Past and Present*, **82** (1979); D. Dixon, ' "Class law": The Street Betting Act of 1906', *International Journal of the Sociology of Law*, **8** (1980). For an example of the moral lobby against working-class gambling at the turn of the century, see B.S. Rowntree (ed.), *Betting and gambling: A national evil* (London, 1905).
2 'Introduction: persistence and change in nineteenth-century popular culture', in R. Storch (ed.), *Popular culture and custom in nineteenth-century England* (London, 1982), pp. 10, 13.
3 R. McKibbin, op. cit., note 1.
4 R. Samuel, *East End underworld: Chapters in the life of Arthur Harding* (London, 1981); J. White, *The worst street in North London: Campbell Bunk, Islington, between the wars* (London, 1986) and 'Police and people in London in the 1930s', *Oral History*, **11**, 2 (1983).
5 *Police Review and Parade Gossip*, 15 July 1910. Article reprinted from an edition of 1900.
6 A description of bookmakers' pitches in Salford was provided by William Bowen, *Royal Commission on Lotteries and Betting, 1932–3, Minutes of Evidence*, p. 310.
7 Interview with Mr C.W.
8 *Royal Commission on Lotteries and Betting, 1932–3, Minutes of Evidence*, Q. 4447.
9 Interview with Mr C.P. On Salford, see R. Heaton, *Salford my home town* (Swinton, 1982), p. 10.
10 *Salford City Reporter*, 20 November 1920.
11 *Royal Commission on Lotteries and Betting, 1932–3, Minutes of Evidence*, Q. 4384–93.
12 See A. Davies, 'The police and the people: Gambling in Salford, 1900–1939', *Historical Journal*, **34**, 1 (1991), p. 94, f. 28.
13 J. Hilton (ed.), *Why I go in for the pools* (London, 1936), pp. 70–1.
14 R. Roberts, *The classic slum: Salford life in the first quarter of the century* (Harmondsworth, 1973), p. 164.
15 *Manchester Guardian*, 8 October 1885.
16 Extracts from Salford Watch Committee Minutes, 20 October 1885. Typescript held at Salford Local History Library.
17 *The People*, 20 November 1932. Green's speech reiterated claims made in his book *Betting and gambling* (London, 1924), pp. 43–5; and in the *Manchester Guardian*, 9 May 1928.
18 *Daily Express*, 21 November 1932; *Manchester Guardian*, 22 and 23 November 1932; *Daily Dispatch*, 24 November 1932.
19 *Manchester Guardian*, 24 November 1932; *Daily Dispatch*, 24 November 1932.
20 *Manchester Guardian*, 22, 23, 24, 26, 29 November 1932.
21 *Manchester Guardian*, 29 November 1932.

22 W. Greenwood, *Love on the dole* (Harmondsworth, 1969), p. 110.
23 *The Woman Citizen*, 20 November 1933.
24 Extracts from Salford Watch Committee Minutes, 25 November 1935; *Manchester Guardian*, 8 January 1936.
25 The report was published in the *Salford City Reporter*, 10 January 1936. In contrast, the chief constable of Oldham refused to accept that the police were incapable of dealing with street bookmakers. See A. Davies, op. cit., note 12, p. 99.
26 *Royal Commission on Lotteries and Betting, 1932–3, Minutes of Evidence*, p. 310.
27 The police columns in the paper reported 244 of the 512 convictions under the 1906 Act made in Salford during 1920. The age of the offender was given in 233 cases, or 45.5 per cent of the total convictions.
28 Interviews with Mrs B.D. and Mrs A.S.
29 Interview with Mr C.P.
30 *Salford City Reporter*, 1 May, 16 October 1920.
31 *Royal Commission on Lotteries and Betting, 1932–3, Minutes of Evidence*, p. 310.
32 Interview with Mrs A.M.
33 W. Greenwood, op. cit., note 22, p. 24; letter to the author from Mrs A. Edwards.
34 See Ramsay MacDonald's contribution to B.S. Rowntree (ed.), *Betting and gambling*, op. cit., note 1.
35 This was confirmed by William Bowen, *Royal Commission on Lotteries and Betting, 1932–3, Minutes of Evidence*, p. 312.
36 J. Toole, *Fighting through life* (London, 1935), p. 55.
37 M.S.T.C. 488; *Royal Commission on Lotteries and Betting, 1932–3, Minutes of Evidence*, p. 311.
38 *Royal Commission on Lotteries and Betting, 1932–3, Minutes of Evidence*, Q. 736.
39 Interview with Mr C.W. (Byrne is a pseudonym).
40 Interviews with Mr B.R. and Mrs G.R.
41 *Manchester Guardian*, 8 January 1936.
42 R. Roberts, op. cit., note 14, p. 37.
43 *Manchester Evening News*, 7 January 1964.
44 Interview with Mr C.P.
45 None of my own respondents mentioned attempts to bribe the police by the members of gambling schools, but see R. Samuel, op. cit., note 4, p. 176.
46 Interviews with Mr H.S. and Mr L.P.
47 Interview with Mrs A.M.
48 *Salford City Reporter*, 15 May 1920.
49 Interview with Mr C.W. 'Ragging up' in miner's dress was necessary to penetrate the schools. 'Pitching up to the mott' refers to pitch and toss.
50 *Salford City Reporter*, 24 July 1920.
51 Interview with Mr A.P. Similar accounts were given by Mr H.S and Mr B.R; and in the *Salford City Reporter*, 14 April 1938.
52 Interview with Mr L.L.
53 *Manchester Guardian*, 17, 18 August 1931.
54 *Manchester Guardian*, 31 August, and 3, 18 September 1931.
55 *Royal Commission on Lotteries and Betting, 1932–3, Minutes of Evidence*, p. 54.
56 The tables are incomplete because there are only partial sets of Chief Constable's Reports for this period available in Manchester Central Reference Library and Salford Local History Library.

57 Interview with Mr L.P.
58 Interviews with Mrs B.D., Mr A.A., Mr A.J. and Mrs K.E.
59 Interview with Mr L.A.
60 Interview with Mr G.O. 'Rings' refers to a game involving throwing rings at hooks on a wall.
61 C.E.B. Russell and E.T. Campagnac, 'Gambling and aids to gambling', *Economic Review*, **X** (1900), p. 485; on amateur football, see Chapter 2.
62 R. McKibbin, op. cit., note 1, p. 150.
63 J. Hilton (ed.), op. cit., note 13, p. 23.
64 R. McKibbin, op. cit., note 1, p. 148.
65 *Royal Commission on Lotteries and Betting, 1932–3, Minutes of Evidence*, Q. 4441, 732.
66 M. Burke, *Ancoats lad: The recollections of Mick Burke* (Swinton, 1985), p. 23.
67 M.S.T.C. 780.
68 Interview with Mr D.R. and Mrs E.R.
69 This phrase was used by Robert Storch: 'The policeman as domestic missionary: Urban discipline and popular culture in Northern England, 1850–1880', *Journal of Social History*, **9** (1976).
70 Only one other respondent referred to cockfighting in Salford, claiming that miners took fighting cocks to the Brindleheath railway sidings: interview with Mr J.P.
71 A report in the *Salford City Reporter* of 15 May 1920 listed 25 men convicted for taking part in a street gambling school. The offenders' ages ranged from 16 to 48.
72 Based on reports of convictions for street gaming in Salford during 1920. Cases which occurred at the Salford racecourse have been excluded.
73 *Manchester Evening News*, 7 January 1964.
74 R. Heaton, op. cit., note 9, pp. 11–12.
75 Interview with Mr C.P.
76 Liverpool Council of Voluntary Aid, *Report on betting in Liverpool* (Liverpool, 1927), p. 7.
77 Interview with Mrs A.S.
78 Evidence of the Chief Constable of Manchester, *Royal Commission on Lotteries and Betting, 1932–3, Minutes of Evidence*, Q. 715.
79 Liverpool Council of Voluntary Aid, op. cit., note 76, p. 7.
80 C.E.B. Russell, *Social problems of the North* (London, 1914), pp. 109–16.
81 P. Green, op. cit., note 17, p. 37.
82 Interviews with Mrs M.G, Ms A.O, Mrs B.D. and Mrs M.R.
83 W. Cobley, 'The ethics of sport', 'Odds and Ends', **LXXIII** (1933), p. 291.
84 *Report from the Select Committee on Betting Duty, 1923, Minutes of Evidence*, Q. 6860.
85 R. McKibbin, op. cit., note 1, p. 156.
86 J. Toole, op. cit., note 36, p. 56; interview with Mrs E.H.
87 Interview with Mrs E.C.
88 R. McKibbin, op. cit., note 1, pp. 155–7.
89 R. Heaton, op. cit., note 9, p. 12; interview with Mrs E.C.
90 *Manchester City News*, 30 June 1906.
91 Interview with Mr A.P.
92 C.E.B. Russell and E.T. Campagnac, op. cit., note 61, p. 482.
93 Many of the newly opened licensed betting shops in the city changed hands during the 1960s, as individual businesses were bought out by chains. Interview with Mr B.B.

Conclusion

1 C.E.B. Russell, *Social problems of the North* (London, 1914), p. 5.
2 See F. Engels, *The condition of the working class in England* (London, 1969 edn), pp. 133–4; and A. Clarke, *The effects on the factory system* (London, 1899), pp. 137–9.
3 See G. Stedman Jones, *Languages of class: Studies in English working-class history 1832–1982* (Cambridge, 1983), Ch. 4 and R. McKibbin, 'Why was there no Marxism in Great Britain?', *English Historical Review*, **XCIX**, 391 (1984), for the most sophisticated statements of this position.
4 G. Orwell, *The road to Wigan Pier* (London, 1937).
5 Stedman Jones, however, had largely abandoned attempts to find social explanations for shifts in political history by the early 1980s. See the Introduction to his *Languages of class*, op. cit., note 3.
6 E. Hobsbawm, *Industry and empire* (London, 1968), pp. 164–5.
7 This periodization has been re-examined elsewhere. For example, in H. Cunningham, *Leisure and the industrial revolution c.1780–c.1880* (London, 1980) and S.G. Jones, *Workers at play: A social and economic history of leisure 1918–1939* (London, 1986).
8 The distinctiveness of this approach was discussed by R. Samuel in the Editor's introduction to *Village life and labour* (London, 1975).
9 H. Cunningham, 'Leisure', in J. Benson (ed.), *The working class in England 1875–1914* (London, 1985).
10 See G. Pearson, *Hooligan: A history of respectable fears* (London, 1983) and J. Springhall, *Coming of age: Adolescence in Britain, 1860–1960* (Dublin, 1986).
11 This contradicts the view put forward by Elizabeth Roberts in *A woman's place: An oral history of working-class women 1890–1940* (Oxford, 1984), p. 5. Although most of my findings correspond with her analysis of North West Lancashire, on these points, my observations tend to echo the findings of Pat Ayers in her work on dockland Liverpool. See P. Ayers and J. Lambertz, 'Marriage relations, money and domestic violence in working-class Liverpool, 1919–39', in J. Lewis (ed.), *Labour and love: Women's experience of home and family, 1850–1940* (Oxford, 1986). More work is needed to explain regional differences.
12 See E. Hobsbawm, *Worlds of labour: Further studies in the history of labour* (London, 1984), Chs 10 and 11.
13 *Salford City Reporter*, 19 August 1938.

Select bibliography

Manuscript sources

Manchester Central Library, Archives Department

(a) Articles in 'Odds and Ends', the annual manuscript magazine of the St Paul's Literary and Educational Society, Manchester:
E. Hadden, 'Women's recreation in Ancoats', **L** (1904).
J. Hobbins, 'From the threepenny gallery: Some impressions of the cheap theatre', **XLIX** (1903).
F. Jordan, 'A night in the city', **L** (1904).
W. Jordan, 'Itinerant musicians', **XLVII** (1901).
(b) 'Life in Manchester'. Forty manuscript essays, submitted for a competition organized by Age Concern in 1983.

Manchester Central Library, Local History Department

F. Doran, 'Down memory lane', manuscript autobiography (1973).

Brunel University Library

J. Lanigan, 'Thy kingdom did come', manuscript autobiography (n.d.).

Salford Local History Library

Salford Watch Committee Minutes, 1861–1935 (extracts), typescript.

Printed works

Contemporary surveys: Manchester, Salford and surrounding districts

Astor, J. *et al.* (eds), *The third winter of unemployment: The report of an enquiry undertaken in the autumn of 1922* (London, 1923).

Chapman, S. and Hallsworth, H., *Unemployment* (Manchester, 1909).

City of Manchester, *Police Instruction Book* (Manchester, 1908, 1923).

Engels, F., *The condition of the working class in England* (London, 1969 edn).

Fogarty, M., *Prospects of the industrial areas of Great Britain* (London, 1945).

Green, P., *Betting and gambling* (London, 1924).

Inman, J., *Poverty and housing conditions in a Manchester ward: Miles Platting* (Manchester, 1934).

James, H. and Moore, F., 'Adolescent leisure in a working class district', *Occupational Psychology*, **XIV**, 3 (1940).

James, H. and Moore, F., 'Adolescent leisure in a working class district, part II', *Occupational Psychology*, **XVIII**, 1 (1944).

Leech, H., *Salford past and present* (Manchester, 1910).

Manchester City Parks and Cemeteries Committee, *Illustrated handbook of the Manchester city parks and recreation grounds* (Manchester, 1915).

Manchester University Settlement, *A survey of housing and social amenities on Belle Vue, Gorton, new housing estate, 1942–1943* (Manchester, 1944).

Manchester University Settlement, *Ancoats: A study of a clearance area. Report of a survey made in 1937–1938* (Manchester, 1945).

Manchester and Salford District Branch of the NSPCC, *Annual report* for the years 1899–1902, 1907, 1929, 1938–9 (Manchester, 1899–1939).

Marr, T.R., *Housing conditions in Manchester and Salford* (Manchester, 1904).

Page, J. (Felix Folio – pseud.), *The hawkers and street dealers of the North of England manufacturing districts* (Manchester, 2nd edn, 1858).

Philips, H., *Open spaces for recreation in Manchester* (Manchester, 1896).

Reach, A., *Manchester and the textile districts in 1849* (Helmshore, 1972).

Russell, C.E.B., *Manchester boys: Sketches of Manchester lads at work and play* (Swinton, 1984 reprint).

Russell, C.E.B., *Social problems of the North* (London, 1914).

Russell, C.E.B. and Campagnac, E.T., 'Gambling and aids to gambling', *Economic Review*, **X** (1900).

Russell, C.E.B. and Campagnac, E.T., 'Poor people's music-halls in Lancashire', *Economic Review*, **X** (1900).

Russell, C.E.B. and Rigby, L., *Working lads' clubs* (London, 1978).

Salford Dock Mission, *Annual report* for 1901 and 1905 (Salford, 1901, 1905).

Salford Mothers' Guild and Ladies Public Health Society, *Report – for the year 1932–33* (Salford, 1933).

Salford Women's Citizens Association, *Housing conditions in the St Matthias' ward, Salford* (Manchester, 1931).

Scott, F., 'The conditions and occupation of the people of Manchester and Salford', *Transactions of the Manchester Statistical Society* (session 1888–89).

Simpson, T., *The underworld of Manchester in war time* (Manchester, 1915).

Stancliffe, B. and Muray, M., 'Till we build again', *Social Welfare*, **VII**, 4 (1948).

Sullivan, J., *The ancient and royal Borough of Salford: History, commerce and industries* (Salford, 1924).

Symonds, A., 'Unfashionable Manchester', *East Lancashire Review*, **18**, III (1899).

Tomlinson, W., *Bye-ways of Manchester life* (Manchester, 1887).

Wyatt, C., 'The Lord Mayor's Fund for the Relief of Distress in Manchester. Winter of 1908–9', *Transactions of the Manchester Statistical Society* (session 1909–1910).

Contemporary surveys: General

Beales, H. and Lambert, R. (eds), *Memoirs of the unemployed* (London, 1934).

Booth, C., *Life and labour of the people of London*, Vol. VIII (London, 1896).

Bowley, A. and Hogg, M., *Has poverty diminished?* (London, 1925).

Caradog Jones, D. (ed.), *The social survey of Merseyside*, 3 vols (Liverpool, 1934).

Clarke, A., *The effects on the factory system* (London, 1899).

George, R., 'A new calculation of the poverty line', *Journal of the Royal Statistical Society*, new series, **C** (1937).

Hilton, J. (ed.), *Why I go in for the pools* (London, 1936).

Llewellyn Davies, M. (ed.), *Maternity: Letters from working women* (London, 1978).

Llewellyn Smith, H. (ed.), *The new survey of London life and labour*, 9 vols (London, 1930–35).

Mass Observation, *The pub and the people* (London, 1987).

Ministry of Labour and National Service, *Weekly expenditure of working-class households in the United Kingdom in 1937–38* (London, 1949).

Orwell, G., *The road to Wigan pier* (Harmondsworth, 1962).

Rathbone, E., *How the casual labourer lives* (Liverpool, 1909).

Rowntree, B.S. (ed.), *Betting and gambling: A national evil* (London, 1905).

Rowntree, B.S., *Poverty: A study of town life* (London, 1902 edn).

Rowntree, B.S., *Poverty and progress: A second social survey of York* (London, 1941).

Rowntree, B.S. and Lasker, B., *Unemployment: A social study* (London, 1911).

Spring Rice, M. (ed.), *Working class wives: Their health and conditions* (London, 1981).

Tout, H., *The standard of living in Bristol* (Bristol, 1938).

Autobiographies

Bertenshaw, M., *Sunrise to sunset: A vivid personal account of life in early Manchester* (Manchester, 1980).

Burgess, A., *Little Wilson and big God: Being the first part of the confessions of Anthony Burgess* (London, 1987).

Burke, M., *Ancoats lad: The recollections of Mick Burke* (Swinton, 1985).

Foley, A., *A Bolton childhood* (Manchester, 1973).

Greenwood, W., *There was a time* (London, 1967).

Heaton, R., *Salford my home town* (Swinton, 1982).

MacColl, E., *Journeyman* (London, 1990).

Mitchell, H., *The hard way up* (London, 1968).

Oman, E., *Salford stepping stones* (Swinton, 1983).

Osman, E., *For the love of Ada ... and Salford* (Swinton, 1984).

Roberts, F., *Memories of a Victorian childhood and working life in Miles Platting, Manchester* (Swinton, 1983).

Roberts, R., *The classic slum: Salford life in the first quarter of the century* (Harmondsworth, 1973).

Roberts, R., *A ragged schooling: Growing up in the classic slum* (Manchester, 1976).

Toole, J., *Fighting through life* (London, 1935).

Watkin, H., *From Hulme all blessings flow* (Swinton, 1985).

Novels

Greenwood, W., *Love on the dole* (Harmondsworth, 1969).
Kennedy, B., *Slavery: Pictures from the depths* (London, 1905).

Parliamentary papers

Report from the Select Committee of the House of Lords on Betting: P.P. 1901 and 1902.
Report from the Select Committee on Betting Duty: P.P. 1923.
Royal Commission on Lotteries and Betting. Minutes of Evidence: P.P. 1932–3.

Secondary works

Alexander, S., 'Becoming a woman in London in the 1920s and 1930s', in D. Feldman and G. Stedman Jones (eds), *Metropolis, London: Histories and representations since 1800* (London, 1989).

Ayers, P. and Lambertz, J., 'Marriage relations, money and domestic violence in working-class Liverpool, 1919–39' in J. Lewis (ed.), *Labour and love: Women's experience of home and family, 1850–1940* (Oxford, 1986).

Bailey, P., *Leisure and class in Victorian England: Rational recreation and the contest for control, 1830–1885* (London, 1978)

Benson, J., *The penny capitalists: A study of nineteenth-century working-class entrepreneurs* (Dublin, 1983).

Benson, J., *The working class in Britain, 1850–1939* (London, 1989).

Briggs, A., *Victorian cities* (Harmondsworth, 1968).

Bundy, C. and Healy, D., 'Aspects of urban poverty', *Oral History*, **6**, 1 (1978).

Chinn, C., *They worked all their lives: Women of the urban poor in England, 1880–1939* (Manchester, 1988).

Clarke, J., Critcher, C. and Johnson, R. (eds), *Working class culture: Studies in history and theory* (London, 1979).

Constantine, S., 'Amateur gardening and popular recreation in the 19th and 20th centuries', *Journal of Social History*, **14**, 3 (1981).

Constantine, S., '"Love on the Dole" and its reception in the 1930s', *Literature and History*, **8**, 2 (1982).

Corrigan, P., 'Doing nothing', in S. Hall and T. Jefferson (eds), *Resistance through rituals: Youth subcultures in post-war Britain* (London, 1976).

Cunningham, H., *Leisure in the industrial revolution c.1780–c.1880* (London, 1980).

Cunningham, H., 'Leisure', in J. Benson (ed.), *The working class in England 1875–1914* (London, 1985).

Davies, A., 'Saturday night markets in Manchester and Salford, 1840–1939', *Manchester Region History Review*, **1**, 2 (1987).

Davies, A., 'The police and the people: Gambling in Salford, 1900–1939', *Historical Journal*, **34**, 1 (1991).

Davies, A. and Fielding, S. (eds), *Workers' worlds: Cultures and communities in Manchester and Salford, 1880–1939* (Manchester, in press).

Dixon, D. '"Class law": the Street Betting Act of 1906', *International Journal of the Sociology of Law*, **8** (1980).

Fielding, S., 'The Catholic Whit walk in Manchester and Salford, 1890–1939', *Manchester Region History Review*, **1**, 1 (1987).

Gittins, D., *Fair sex: Family size and structure, 1900–39* (London, 1982).

Hennock, E.P., 'The measurement of urban poverty: From the metropolis to the nation, 1880–1920', *Economic History Review*, **XL**, 2 (1987).

Hey, V., *Patriarchy and pub culture* (London, 1986).

Hobsbawm, E., *Worlds of labour: Further studies in the history of labour* (London, 1984).

Hoggart, R., *The uses of literacy: Aspects of working-class life with special reference to publications and entertainments* (Harmondsworth, 1958 edn).

Humphries, S., *Hooligans or rebels? An oral history of working-class childhood and youth 1889–1939* (Oxford, 1983).

Humphries, S., *A secret world of sex. Forbidden fruit: The British experience, 1900–1950* (London, 1988).

Jones, S.G., 'The Lancashire cotton industry and the development of paid holidays in the nineteen-thirties', *Transactions of the Historical Society of Lancashire and Cheshire*, **135** (1986).

Jones, S.G., *Workers at play: A social and economic history of leisure 1918–1939* (London, 1986).

Kidd, A. and Roberts, K. (eds), *City, class and culture: Studies of social policy and cultural production in Victorian Manchester* (Manchester, 1985).

Leber, M., 'The remarkable legacy of L.S. Lowry', *Manchester Region History Review*, **1**, 2 (1987).

MacColl, E., 'Theatre of action, Manchester', in R. Samuel, E. MacColl and S. Cosgrove (eds), *Theatres of the left 1880–1935: Workers' theatre movements in Britain and America* (London, 1985).

Manchester Women's History Group, 'Ideology in bricks and mortar: Women's housing in Manchester between the wars', *North West Labour History*, **12** (1987).

Mason, T., *Association football and English society, 1863–1915* (Brighton, 1980).

McKibbin, R., 'Working class gambling in Britain 1880–1939', *Past and Present*, **82** (1979).

McKibbin, R., 'Why was there no Marxism in Great Britain?' *English Historical Review*, **XCIX**, 391 (1984).

McKibbin, R., *The ideologies of class: Social relations in Britain, 1880–1950* (Oxford, 1990).

Meacham, S., *A life apart: The English working class 1890–1914* (London, 1977).

Pearson, G., *Hooligan: A history of respectable fears* (London, 1983).

Reid, A., 'Intelligent artisans and aristocrats of labour: The essays of Thomas Wright', in J. Winter (ed.), *The working class in modern British history* (Cambridge, 1983).

Richards, J., 'The cinema and cinema-going in Birmingham in the 1930s', in J. Walton and J. Walvin (eds), *Leisure in Britain 1780–1939* (Manchester, 1983).

Richards, J., *The age of the dream palace: Cinema and society in Britain 1930–1939* (London, 1984).

Richards, J. and Sheridan, D. (eds), *Mass Observation at the movies* (London, 1987).

Roberts, E., *A woman's place: An oral history of working-class women 1890–1940* (Oxford, 1984).

Ross, E., 'Survival networks: Women's neighbourhood sharing in London before World War One', *History Workshop Journal*, **15** (1983).

Samuel, R., *East End underworld: Chapters in the life of Arthur Harding* (London, 1981).

Springhall, J., *Coming of age: Adolescence in Britain, 1860–1960* (Dublin, 1986).

Stedman Jones, G., *Languages of class: Studies in English working-class history 1832–1982* (Cambridge, 1983).

Stevenson, J., *British society, 1914–1945* (Harmondsworth, 1984).

Storch, R. (ed.), *Popular culture and custom in nineteenth-century England* (London, 1982).

Tebbutt, M., *Making ends meet: Pawnbroking and working class credit* (London, 1984).

Thompson, P., *The voice of the past: Oral history* (Oxford, 1978).

Thompson, P., *The Edwardians: The remaking of British society* (London, 1984).

Treble, J., *Urban poverty in Britain 1830–1914* (London, 1979).

Vamplew, W., *The turf: A social and economic history of horse racing* (London, 1976).

Veit-Wilson, J., 'Paradigms of poverty: A rehabilitation of B.S. Rowntree', *Journal of Social Policy*, **15**, 1 (1986).

Vincent, D., *Bread, knowledge and freedom: A study of nineteenth-century working-class autobiography* (London, 1981).

Walton, J., 'The demand for working-class seaside holidays in Victorian England', *Economic History Review*, **XXXIV**, 2 (1981).

Walvin, J., *Leisure and society 1830–1950* (London, 1978).

White, J., 'Police and people in London in the 1930s', *Oral History*, **11**, 2 (1983).

White, J., *The worst street in North London: Campbell Bunk, Islington, between the wars* (London, 1986).

Unpublished theses

Davies, A., 'Leisure and poverty in Salford and Manchester, 1900–1939', Ph.D., University of Cambridge (1989).

Fielder, A., 'Adolescents and the cinema: Report of an enquiry', Diploma in Social Studies, University of Manchester (1932).

Harley, J., 'Report of an enquiry into the occupations, further education and leisure interests of a number of girl wage-earners from elementary and central schools in the Manchester district, with special reference to the influence of school training on the use of leisure', M.Ed., University of Manchester (1937).

Middleton, T., 'An enquiry into the use of leisure amongst the working classes of Liverpool', M.A., University of Liverpool (1931).

Thompson, F., 'A study of the development of facilities for recreation and leisure occupation on new housing estates, with special reference to Manchester', Diploma in Social Studies, University of Manchester (1937).

Index

Aldgate, Tony, 96
Alexander, Sally, 94
Andrew, J., 25
Ayers, Pat, 3

Bailey, Peter, 2
begging, 116, 120–1
Benson, John, 24
betting, *see* gambling
Blackpool, 41–2, 89, 90–1, 155
Bolton, 32–4, 44, 61–2, 129–30, 133, 139
bookmakers, 142–55
Booth, Charles, 15, 17
Bowley, A., 22
bowls, 141
Briggs, Asa, 7
Bristol, 22–4, 26, 29
Bundy, Colin, 14
Burgess, Anthony, 70

Campagnac, E.T., 27, 51, 117, 167
Chaplin, Charlie, 121
Chinn, Carl, 66
cinemas, 45, 54, 73–9, 83, 94–6, 98, 106–7, 121

Cobley, William, 166
cockfighting, 142, 162–3
commercialization, 2–3, 59, 109–10, 136, 169–70
Cunningham, Hugh, 2, 3, 117, 170

dancing
    in dance halls, 57, 89–94, 107
    in parks, 140, 141
    in streets, 117–18, 173
Delaney, Shelagh, 9
domestic violence, 48–9, 50, 69, 87–9
drinking
    among men, 30, 32–7, 43, 48–53, 115–16
    among women, 58, 59, 61–73

Engels, Friedrich, 7, 8, 169
escapism, 78–9, 81, 96

fashion, 94–5, 104–5
Fielder, A., 83, 95–6
Fielding, Steven, 124
football, 32, 38–9, 44, 101, 141, 161
football pools, 142, 161
fortune tellers, 79–81
Fowler, David, 4, 82

gambling, 1, 2, 5, 37–8, 46–7, 48–9, 51–3, 72–3, 98, 141, Chapter 6 *passim*, 168
gambling schools, 98, 142, 143, 155–61, 163–4
gang violence, 92–4
George, R.F., 22, 26–7
gossip, 112
gramophones, 39–40, 111
Green, Peter, 148–9, 150, 164, 166
Greenwood, Walter, 9, 40, 46, 47–8, 57, 76, 81, 83, 85, 94, 149, 154
greyhound racing, 142, 161–2

Harley, Joan, 83, 84, 94, 96–7
Harrison, Brian, 69
Haslam, James, 81, 167
Healy, Dermot, 14
Hennock, E.P., 17
Hilton, John, 147, 161
Hobsbawm, Eric, 2, 38, 169
holidays, 40–2, 155
housing conditions, 11, 113–14
Humphries, Steve, 93–4

Inman, John, 24
Italian street musicians, 116, 117, 120, 121

James, H.E.O., 83, 94, 96, 107, 111, 139
Jones, Stephen, 3, 40, 43
Jordan, Frank, 130, 136
Jordan, William, 117

Kidd, Alan, 11, 17

labour aristocracy, 2, 31, 37, 164; *see also* skilled workers
Lambertz, Jan, 3
Liverpool, 15, 23, 26, 40, 44, 45, 164
London, 15, 17, 22, 44, 47, 60–1, 62, 94, 119, 143, 163
Lowry, L.S., 9

MacColl, Ewan, 93, 97, 123–4
McKibbin Ross, 43, 143, 166, 167
Manchester City Football Club, 38
Manchester United Football Club, 32, 38, 44
markets, 130–8

Marr, T.R., 19
Marx, Karl, 7
Mass Observation, 32–4, 44, 61–3, 66
May queens, 126–8
means test, 40, 120
Meller, Helen, 2
men, leisure patterns, 1–2, 4, Chapter 2 *passim*, 55–6, 61–3, 68–9, 77, 111, 131–3, 139–40, 155–64, 171–2
monkey parades, 102–8
Moore, F.T., 83, 94, 96, 107, 111, 139
Muray, M., 57
music, 63, 111, 116–24, 139–40
music halls, 73, 82, 121

neighbourliness, 110–13, 114–15

Oldham, H.J., 48–9, 51
oral history, 5–7, 143–4
Orwell, George, 169

pace-egging, 129–30
Page, John, 116, 131
parental discipline, 88–9, 103
parks, 88, 104, 138–41
penny capitalism, 79–80
Philips, Herbert, 114
Philips, Mark, 138
pianos, 40
pigeon fancying, 44, 142
police
    corruption, 146–50
    and gambling, 5, Chapter 6 *passim*, 170
    and street entertainers, 117, 122–3
    and street fights, 70–1, 115–16, 151–2
    and youths, 92–3, 99–102, 106
politics, 2, 6–7, 58, 136–8, 169
poverty cycle, 3, 18, 20, 33–4, 41, 56, 76, 82
poverty line, 17–19, 22–3, 26–7
public houses, *see* drinking
Purcell, Alf, 25

racial stereotypes, 129
Rathbone, Eleanor, 15, 71
Reach, Angus, 110
relative deprivation, 42–3
religion, 7, 115, 124–5

respectability, 35, 52, 61, 67, 71, 77–8, 141, 163, 172
Richards, Jeffrey, 107
Roberts, Elizabeth, 3, 24, 55, 73
Roberts, Robert, 8–9, 14, 34, 37, 63, 77–9, 89, 98, 109–10, 112, 131, 148, 155
Ross, Ellen, 3
Rowntree, B.S., 15, 17–19, 26–7, 33, 43, 48–9, 61–3, 82, 84, 115
rugby league, 44, 141
Russell, C.E.B., 19, 27, 51, 72–4, 83, 102, 104, 117, 119, 136, 164, 167, 168

Salvation Army, 71
Samuel, Raphael, 143
Scott, Fred, 15–17
scuttling, 94
Simpson, Theo, 64, 69
sitting out, 110–11, 115
skilled workers, 2, 16–17, 19–20, 24, 28, 31, 32, 37, 50, 51, 89–90, 163–4
spiritualism, 79–81
Spring Rice, Margery, 59, 60–1, 75–6
Stancliffe, B., 57
Stedman Jones, Gareth, 2, 169
Stevenson, John, 20, 24
Storch, Robert, 143
street corner gangs, 96–102
street entertainers, 116–24

street fights, 70–1, 115–16, 124–5, 151–2

Toole, Joe, 119, 136–7, 154, 166
Tout, H., 22, 23, 24, 29

unemployment
    extent of, 19, 20, 24–5
    and male leisure patterns, 43–8, 159, 160, 164
    and poverty, 22, 25–6, 43–4
    and street entertaining, 117, 123

Veit-Wilson, J., 18

Walton, John, 40
Warren, Tony, 9
whippet racing, 142, 162
Whit walks, 7, 124–6
White, Jerry, 5, 115, 116, 119, 143, 163
wirelesses, 39–40, 111, 119–20
women, leisure patterns, 4, Chapter 3
    passim, 111–14, 118–19, 131–5, 139–41, 161–2, 164–6, 171–2
Wyatt, Charles, 19–20

York, 15, 17–19, 26–7, 43, 48, 61–2, 84
young workers, leisure patterns, 4, 41, 45, 47–8, 54, Chapter 4 *passim*, 111, 117–18, 127–8, 136, 139–41, 163, 171
youth culture, 4, 171; *see also* young workers